THE SIEGE OF
KUT-AL-AMARA

TWENTIETH-CENTURY BATTLES

Edited by Spencer C. Tucker

The SIEGE of
Kut-al-Amara

AT WAR IN
MESOPOTAMIA
1915-1916

NIKOLAS GARDNER

INDIANA UNIVERSITY PRESS   *Bloomington & Indianapolis*

This book is a publication of

INDIANA UNIVERSITY PRESS
Office of Scholarly Publishing
Herman B Wells Library 350
1320 East 10th Street
Bloomington, Indiana 47405 USA

iupress.indiana.edu

Telephone orders 800-842-6796
Fax orders 812-855-7931

Manufactured in the
United States of America

Cataloging information is available
from the Library of Congress

ISBN 978-0-253-01384-2 (cloth)
ISBN 978-0-253-01389-7 (ebook)

1 2 3 4 5   19 18 17 16 15 14

CONTENTS

PREFACE

IN COMPARISON TO THE WESTERN FRONT, THE MESOPOTAMIA campaign has long remained on the periphery of scholarship and public interest in the First World War. Nonetheless, in a conflict in which industrial technology played an unprecedented role, the premodern aspects of the war in Mesopotamia hold a grim fascination. The campaign opened in November 1914 immediately following Britain's declaration of war against the Ottoman Empire, as Indian Expeditionary Force "D" (IEFD) landed at the port of Basra with the intent of evicting Ottoman forces from the vicinity and securing the nearby oil fields of the Anglo-Persian Oil Company. Enticed by easy victories against a disorganized enemy, British leaders grew more ambitious, and in the fall of 1915 6 Indian Division, under Major-General Charles Townshend, advanced up the Tigris River with the intent of capturing Baghdad. After encountering superior Ottoman forces at the Battle of Ctesiphon in late November, however, the division retreated to the town of Kut-al-Amara, where it was besieged from December 1915 until its surrender in late April 1916. Of approximately 15,000 soldiers and camp followers in Townshend's force, nearly 4,000 became casualties during the siege, and thousands more would die in Ottoman captivity. In addition, more than 23,000 soldiers were killed or wounded in a series of unsuccessful attempts to relieve 6 Indian Division.

No episode of the conflict in Mesopotamia exhibits its premodern character more clearly than the siege of Kut-al-Amara. While soldiers on the Western Front suffered casualties on a much greater scale than those in Mesopotamia, they benefited from logistical support and medical care that surpassed that provided to their predecessors in earlier conflicts by a significant margin. The British and Indian soldiers besieged inside Kut, however, faced starvation as well as deficiency diseases such as scurvy and beriberi due to a lack of adequate rations. The forces sent to relieve 6 Indian Division endured similar diseases as well as an absence of adequate medical care, with wounded soldiers left on the battlefield for days without receiving treatment. Inside and outside of Kut, soldiers also suffered from conditions associated with poor sanitation such as dysentery and even cholera.

In explaining the circumstances that led to the siege, the suffering endured by the soldiers involved, and its ultimate outcome, historians have followed the Mesopotamia Commission of 1917, which focused primarily on strategic-level decisions made in Basra, India, and London regarding the objectives of the campaign and the resources delegated to achieving them. Beginning in the late 1960s, following the fiftieth anniversary of the siege, authors such as A. J. Barker, Russell Braddon, and Ronald Millar published vivid accounts demonstrating how the parsimony and ineptitude of senior military and political leaders left soldiers to fight with inadequate resources, resulting in one of Britain's most notorious military defeats of the twentieth century.[1] Similar to studies of command on the Western Front written in the same period, these accounts also heap opprobrium on field commanders such as Townshend and his counterparts in the relief force. They contain little analysis, however, of the choices made by these commanders during active operations, assuming implicitly that the decisions of senior figures far from the front made defeat on the battlefield virtually inevitable.

The past decade has seen a revival of interest in the Mesopotamia campaign, sparked at least in part by the U.S.-led invasion of Iraq. Patrick Crowley has provided a new account of the siege of Kut-al-Amara that focuses in depth on the fate of Townshend's force after its surrender.[2] The historian Charles Townshend, not to be confused with the commander of 6 Indian Division, has written a well-researched overview of the campaign and the subsequent formation of the modern state of Iraq.[3] Most recently Kaushik Roy and Ross Anderson have examined the role of logistics, while Andrew Syk has assessed the conduct of operations in the Mesopotamia campaign.[4] Edward Erickson's study of Ottoman military effectiveness in the First World War has shed new light on the campaign from a different angle, demonstrating the strength and sophistication of Ottoman defenses in Mesopotamia in 1915 and 1916.[5] All of these studies provide new insights into the war in Mesopotamia. With the exception of Syk's work, however, they do not analyze in detail how British commanders involved in the campaign conducted operations with the limited resources at their disposal.

Just as significantly, existing accounts tell us little about how the composition of 6 Indian Division and the forces directed to relieve it influenced the outcome of the siege. While studies of the Mesopotamia campaign are replete with anecdotes from the diaries and memoirs of British soldiers that convey their often colorful reactions to the conditions they faced, they largely overlook the Indian sepoys, sowars, and followers who comprised more than two-thirds of IEFD. To a certain extent this is understandable, given that most Indians who fought in the war were illiterate and therefore generated no written records of their service. Nevertheless, it is difficult to assess the morale and discipline of 6 Indian Division and the relief force in the face of extreme privations without considering the response of the majority of their personnel to these conditions. Fortunately, the past three decades have seen the emergence of a significant body of scholarship on Britain's Indian Army in the First World War.[6] It is possible to combine the insights of this scholarship with evidence from British observers involved in the siege, as well as the few surviving samples of correspondence produced by Indians in Mesopotamia. Together these sources shed significant new light on the experiences of sepoys involved in the siege of Kut-al-Amara and the concurrent relief operations.

Accordingly, this study approaches the siege of Kut-al-Amara with two principal questions in mind. First, how did Charles Townshend and the commanders of the relief force conduct operations against Ottoman forces from the beginning of Townshend's advance on Baghdad in September 1915 until the suspension of relief efforts in late April 1916? Secondly, how did the response of Indian personnel to the conditions they faced in Mesopotamia influence the outcome of the siege? This is not to suggest an exclusive focus on these themes. Indeed, it is impossible to understand the origins, conduct, and outcome of the siege without recognizing the resource constraints that plagued IEFD throughout this period. Nor is it possible to ignore the contribution of the enemy. While this study does not offer a detailed analysis of Ottoman operations in this period, it draws upon recent scholarship as well as accounts by Ottoman officers involved in the campaign to provide an outline of Ottoman actions and their rationale. It will focus in particular, however, on the conduct of operations by the commander of 6 Indian Division and his counterparts in the relief force, as well as the response of IEFD's Indian personnel to the conditions they faced in Mesopotamia. As it will demonstrate, it is impossible to understand the siege of Kut-al-Amara without considering these factors.

These two principal themes dictate the organization of this study. In comparison to existing accounts, it focuses to a greater extent on the origins of the siege than the events that followed it. The first chapter introduces the soldiers, sepoys, and followers who comprised 6 Indian Division as well as their commander, Sir Charles Townshend. It considers the Indian response to the conditions of the Mesopotamia campaign, the progression of Townshend's career prior to 1915, and his relationship with Indians under his command. The second and third chapters focus on the Battle of Ctesiphon and 6 Indian Division's subsequent retreat to Kut. Both of these events, and particularly the retreat, are summarized briefly in most studies of this period, which assume the siege to have been almost inevitable following the decision to advance on Baghdad. In order to understand why and where the siege occurred, however, it is essential to examine the events that preceded it. The fourth chapter discusses the opening weeks of the siege inside Kut, considering the morale of 6 Indian Division and its commander in this period. The fifth chapter turns to the initial operations to relieve Townshend's force in January 1916. Drawing on official unit war diaries that all but the most recent studies have neglected, it explains the conduct of operations as well as key reasons for their failure. The sixth chapter examines conditions inside Kut in February and March 1916 as well as the relief force's resumption of operations in early March. The final chapter explains the measures enacted by Townshend to prolong his resistance in April as well the innovative but ultimately unsuccessful attempts to relieve the Kut garrison before its surrender. Overall, by focusing on the experiences of those who actually fought in Mesopotamia in 1915 and 1916, this study will offer significant new insights into the origins, conduct, and outcome of the siege of Kut-al-Amara. In the process it will shed new light on the role of the Indian Army in the First World War and the response of its soldiers to the trying conditions they faced in Mesopotamia.

ACKNOWLEDGMENTS

PORTIONS OF THIS WORK APPEARED PREVIOUSLY IN THE following publications: "Sepoys and the Siege of Kut-al-Amara, December 1915–April 1916," *War in History* 11, no. 3 (July 2004): 307–326; "Charles Townshend's Advance on Baghdad, September–November 1915," *War in History* 20, no. 2 (April 2013): 182–200; "Morale and Discipline in a Multiethnic Army: The Indian Army in Mesopotamia, 1914–1917," *Journal of the Middle East and Africa* 4, no. 1 (April 2013): 1–20; and "Morale and Discipline in the Indian Army in Mesopotamia, 1914–1917" in Kaushik Roy, ed., *The Indian Army in the Two World Wars* (Leiden: Brill Academic, 2011), 393–417. I wish to thank the Trustees of the Liddell Hart Centre for Military Archives and the Imperial War Museum for allowing me to quote from collections in their possession. The USAF Air War College and the Class of '65 Chair in Leadership at the Royal Military College of Canada provided support for much of my archival research in the United Kingdom.

Numerous individuals made essential contributions in the inception, development, and completion stages of this project. Longer ago than I care to admit, Spencer Tucker invited me to propose a monograph for inclusion in the Twentieth Century Battles series with Indiana University Press. He and Bob Sloan displayed remarkable patience as the book slowly took form. Jenna Whittaker and Darja Malcolm-Clarke guided the manuscript through the publication process. Carol Kennedy provided thorough and insightful copyediting, improving the clarity of my arguments. These arguments also benefited significantly from the insights of friends and colleagues who offered helpful comments at conferences, in correspondence, in print, and in conversation. In particular I would like to thank Dennis Showalter, Matthew Hughes, Michael Neiberg, Michael Ramsay, and Kaushik Roy. I am also grateful to several anonymous reviewers for their suggestions and criticisms regarding my research in its earlier stages. Any errors of fact or interpretation that remain are my own.

Most of all I wish to express my gratitude to my family. My father, Jim Gardner, long ago introduced me to what the British called the North West Frontier, sparking my ongoing interest in the Indian Army. My wife, Carina, read the entire manuscript and improved it significantly. She and my children, Holly and Joey, tolerated my periodic absences on research and provided valuable moral support as the project drew to a close. For that in particular I am grateful.

THE SIEGE OF
KUT-AL-AMARA

ONE

CHARLES TOWNSHEND
AND HIS ARMY

6 INDIAN DIVISION IN THE FALL OF 1915

IN ORDER TO UNDERSTAND THE OUTCOME OF CHARLES Townshend's unsuccessful advance on Baghdad and the siege of Kut-al-Amara that followed, it is essential to understand the soldiers who participated. Like the other formations of the Indian Army in the initial stages of the First World War, 6 Indian Division consisted primarily of Indian personnel. Each of its three infantry brigades had three Indian battalions and a single battalion of British soldiers. Attached to the division in November 1915 was an additional infantry brigade of similar composition. Townshend's force also included a cavalry brigade comprising three regiments of Indian cavalry, a battalion of Indian Pioneers, three companies of Indian Sappers and Miners, six British artillery batteries as well as a "Volunteer" battery composed of mixed-race Eurasian personnel, and an assortment of divisional troops including a signal company and an ammunition column. In the fall of 1915 Indian personnel made up approximately 78 percent of the strength of Townshend's force.[1] The division was also accompanied by approximately 3,500 Indian followers.[2] These included "higher" followers such as stretcher bearers and animal drivers, who formed distinct units, and "lower" followers such as cooks, *bhistis* (water carriers), and sweepers, who were attached to combat units.[3]

Existing accounts of the Mesopotamia campaign acknowledge the composition of 6 Indian Division, and include a variety of anecdotes that offer glimpses of the war primarily through the eyes of the British personnel who comprised the bulk of its strength. There has been no systematic assessment, however, of the response of its soldiers to service in

1

Mesopotamia. Nor have historians evaluated the relationship between Charles Townshend and his subordinates. Accordingly, this chapter will provide an overview of the soldiers of 6 Indian Division, focusing in particular on the Indians who comprised the majority of its strength. It will discuss their motivations for service and their response to the conditions they encountered in Mesopotamia up to the fall of 1915. It will also consider Townshend's ambitions, his previous experiences with Indian soldiers, and the way that these factors shaped his interaction with his subordinates, and ultimately his command decisions, in 1915 and 1916.

PERSONNEL OF 6 INDIAN DIVISION

Discerning the motivations of Indian sepoys and followers and their responses to the Mesopotamia campaign poses significant challenges. The vast majority of Indian soldiers and followers in this period were illiterate, and consequently generated no written records of their experiences during the campaign. While some sepoys employed scribes to write letters on their behalf during the First World War, the bulk of the letters that survive refer to conditions on the Western Front. Thus, in order to understand the experiences of Indians serving in 6 Indian Division in 1915–1916, it is necessary to examine the correspondence of their counterparts serving in Europe as well as the few existing letters written by Indians in Mesopotamia. This material must be treated with caution. Dictated to scribes who seem to have relied on stock phrases and coded language intended to escape scrutiny by censors, the letters were also intended to be read to public gatherings in India. It is therefore highly unlikely that they reveal the innermost thoughts of most Indian soldiers. Moreover, this correspondence is available to the historian only in the form of excerpts of letters translated and included in the reports of British censors.[4] These factors filter and possibly distort our understanding of the way Indians responded to overseas service during the First World War.

Given these limitations to the evidence produced by Indians themselves, it is also necessary to draw upon the diaries, correspondence, and memoirs of British officers and soldiers who served with them. This evidence is also problematic, as it provides the perspective of individuals with an imperfect understanding of the motivations and priorities of Indian soldiers. British regimental officers serving in Indian battalions often had extensive knowledge of the language, habits, and religious practices of their subordinates, and their observations can provide useful insights into the state of Indian morale. Their accounts, however, can also paint a distorted picture of Indian soldiers' experiences. Based on a careful examination of sepoys' letters, David Omissi has argued that these officers overestimated their own role in maintaining Indian morale and discipline. According to Omissi, "The cult of the British officer partly reflected the tendency of the ruling elite to explain other processes in terms of themselves. It also suited the British to believe themselves essential. It gave them a sense of purpose, and inflated their self-esteem."[5]

Thus, while the observations of British officers can help shed light on the experiences of Indians in Mesopotamia, we should not simply accept these officers' characterization of their subordinates as dependent on their leadership. Certainly, regimental officers played a vital role as intermediaries between Indian soldiers and the higher command structure of the Indian and British Armies in the midst of a conflict of unprecedented scale and intensity.[6] As a result, the loss of familiar British officers had a detrimental effect on the morale of their Indian subordinates. Nonetheless, soldiers' letters make clear that this was certainly not the only, nor even the predominant, factor that influenced their behavior. Therefore, rather than conceiving of Indian soldiers as dependent on their British officers, this chapter will follow recent scholarship in interpreting the relationship between sepoys and the command structure above them in contractual terms.[7] Rather than simply serving their "sahibs" with steadfast devotion, Indian soldiers agreed to perform a defined set of tasks over a specified duration, in return for which they received a range of tangible and intangible rewards and benefits. These included regular pay and rations, adequate medical care, and the prospect of a pension for themselves or their families if they were wounded or killed on active service. In addition, Indian soldiers expected their superiors to support their traditional beliefs and practices, including religious ceremonies and dietary requirements. Their morale suffered when they believed the command structure to be in breach of its contractual obligations. Under the conditions they faced in Mesopotamia they could and did reconsider their commitment to service.

The response of Indian soldiers to these conditions was shaped by a variety of factors, including their ethnic and religious identities. The composition of the Indian Army at the outset of the First World War was the product of recruitment and retention strategies developed in response to the Mutiny of 1857. In the decades after the uprising, and particularly from the 1880s, the focus of the army's recruiting efforts shifted steadily northward. By 1914, soldiers from Nepal, Punjab, and the North-West Frontier Province of India comprised 80 percent of the strength of the Indian Army.[8] Colonial authorities defined the inhabitants of the areas from which they recruited as "martial classes," assigning recruits from specific ethnic, religious, and linguistic groups such as Gurkhas, Sikhs, and Rajputs to homogenous regiments or companies. The British extolled supposedly inherent characteristics that made specific groups particularly suitable to military service. At least as important as any of these alleged martial traits, however, was their perceived amenability to British rule. These groups usually inhabited remote and overwhelmingly rural areas with low rates of literacy, authoritarian social structures, and little exposure to Western notions of self-government. Not surprisingly, they had also abstained from the uprising in 1857.[9] In addition to recruiting from ostensibly compliant sections of Indian society, British military authorities emphasized distinctions between different groups to reduce the likelihood of their Indian subordinates uniting against them. By supporting specific religious practices, dietary restrictions, and religious ceremonies, the British facilitated the construction of unique identities for the groups they recruited.[10] They sought to reinforce and perpetuate these identities by recruiting sepoys and followers from particular communities and even families. Gordon Corrigan has observed, "In some areas pre-war recruitment had become more and more incestuous, with specific small villages, sub clans and families providing most of their menfolk to one or two regiments."[11]

Thus, at the outset of the First World War, 6 Indian Division was an intricate mosaic of "martial" classes grouped into distinct battalions and companies drawn from specific areas. For example, the 2nd battalion of the 7th Gurkhas consisted entirely of Gurkha sepoys from Nepal.

The 20th Infantry Regiment contained companies of Sikhs, Muslim Pathans, and Hindu Dogras.[12] The 120th Infantry included a company of high-caste Rajputs and two companies of lower-caste Hindus, all from the state of Rajputana, as well as a company of Muslims from the area around Delhi. The regimental followers emanated from the same locales as the soldiers. According to H. H. Rich, a lieutenant in the 120th, "The cooks and bhistis were of the same class as the sepoys; often their relatives who could not make the physical grade; sometimes young men for whom there was no vacancy, and who were waiting until one cropped up." Given their line of work, sweepers were "untouchables," of a lower caste than the sepoys, but in the 120th they were interrelated. Thus, even followers of the lowest class were recruited from highly specific sources.[13]

While these practices reinforced distinctions between ethnic and religious groups in the army and Indian society more generally, the regimental system also provided a means for individual soldiers to gain status within their own communities. In particular, loyal service to the king-emperor of India was a means of acquiring *izzat*, a concept similar to honor or prestige. Omissi has observed, "Judging from their letters, Indian soldiers fought, above all, to gain or preserve *izzat* – their honour, standing, reputation or prestige."[14] Izzat did not derive solely from military service. Indeed, its acquisition on campaign had to be balanced against the maintenance of izzat associated with the ability to maintain one's family and property at home. The wife of a Pathan illustrated this reality in a letter to her husband in the army, admonishing him: "If you want to keep your *izzat* then come back here at once."[15] Thus, it seems that most Indians who enlisted neither anticipated nor desired an extended deployment overseas. On the contrary, most expected to participate in small-scale operations in the Subcontinent, operating against "Afghan tribesmen or urban crowds."[16] In 1914, however, the scale and duration of the First World War was largely unknown to most senior British military and political leaders, let alone sepoys from remote villages in India. Therefore, most Indians do not appear to have anticipated that the conflict would entail unprecedented sacrifices on their part. For some, the prospect of travel overseas may have been an enticement.[17] Thus, most Indian soldiers appear to have welcomed the outbreak of war in 1914 as an opportunity to accrue izzat in a campaign of limited duration while serving alongside familiar comrades and even relatives from their own communities.

During the first two years of the campaign in Mesopotamia, however, a combination of factors progressively corroded Indian morale. Foremost among these was the inadequacy of the logistical system supporting IEFD. Port facilities at Basra, the principal point of entry for supplies arriving in Mesopotamia, were woefully inadequate from 1914–1916.[18] Moreover, there was not enough river transport available to supply the force as it advanced up the Tigris from Basra. In the fall of 1915, British ships operating on the Tigris were able to provide only 150 of the 208 tons of supplies required by Townshend's force on a daily basis.[19] Consequently, British and Indian units faced a growing shortage of essential supplies such as blankets, tents, clothes, and boots. They also lacked adequate rations. The only fruits or vegetables shipped from India in this period were onions and potatoes, which often spoiled due to a lack of cold-storage facilities in Mesopotamia. This dearth of fresh produce had a particularly detrimental effect on the Indians, who received much smaller rations than their British counterparts. To supplement these rations, British military authorities provided the Indians with an allowance so that they could purchase food in accordance with their "custom, caste and religion."[20] In the relatively austere environment of Mesopotamia, however, they were unable to secure sufficient quantities of meat, fruits, or vegetables on a regular basis. As a result, medical authorities noticed the appearance of scurvy among Indian soldiers as early as March 1915. The disease grew more prevalent as the campaign progressed and the nutritional deficiencies of Indian soldiers worsened. According to Mark Harrison, "over 11,000 Indian troops succumbed to scurvy in the last six months of 1916."[21]

In addition to scurvy, soldiers suffered from dysentery due to a lack of clean drinking water. The incidence of malaria also increased significantly during the summer of 1915.[22] Shortages of medical supplies and personnel inhibited the treatment of these diseases, as well as wounds suffered in battle. Throughout 1914 and 1915, IEFD lacked sufficient numbers of field ambulance beds, stretcher bearers, and medical officers. This not only prolonged the suffering of the sick, it also meant that soldiers wounded in combat were left lying on the battlefield, where they risked being robbed or killed by Arabs allied with the Ottomans.[23] Nor could sick and wounded personnel expect a prompt return to India. According to Kaushik Roy, until June 1915 there was only one hospital ship available to evacuate casualties from East Africa and Mesopotamia to Bombay.[24] While the dearth of adequate rations, supplies, and medical care did nothing to increase the enthusiasm of Indian soldiers for the campaign in Mesopotamia, the uncertainty of a prompt return home for those who became casualties was likely even more vexing. An Indian soldier who sustained a wound while on active service generally believed that he had faithfully fulfilled his commitment to the army, and he expected to be discharged and allowed to return to India. Sir Walter Lawrence, commissioner for Indian hospitals in England and France, explained in a letter to Lord Kitchener in 1915, "His simple idea is that he has done his duty, and that having been wounded it is his right to go home."[25] For wounded sepoys, the inability of the command structure to honor its perceived obligation and promptly extract them from an inhospitable environment and return them to their homes was particularly discouraging.

For those soldiers who remained with their units, the loss of leaders and comrades also strained morale. As discussed above, it is possible to overestimate the extent of sepoys' devotion to their sahibs. Nonetheless, experienced British officers were essential to the cohesion and effective performance of Indian units in combat. At the beginning of the First World War an Indian battalion at full strength contained seventeen Indian Viceroy's Commissioned Officers (vcos) and thirteen British King's Commissioned Officers (kcos), including a medical officer. Given that most Indian officers were illiterate, kcos played a vital role in interpreting and disseminating operation orders to their Indian subordinates. In addition, they led these subordinates personally in battle. According to Corrigan, "British officers led from the front. They had to, even when it was patent tactical nonsense so to do. If you want to lead men who do not share your culture, background or cause, you have to demonstrate your own belief in that which you have ordered them to do."[26]

Given the intensity of the campaigns in East Africa, Europe, and Mesopotamia during the first year of the war, however, this leadership style took a heavy toll on the Indian Army's cadre of officers. By the autumn of 1915, the shortage of British officers had become so acute in Mesopotamia that units in Townshend's 6 Indian Division were reduced to a cadre of only seven KCOs in each unit, a level that Townshend called "criminally foolish."[27] Moreover, the British officers who arrived as reinforcements were seldom as effective as their predecessors. In the first months of the war, hundreds of British civilians in India took commissions in the Indian Army Reserve of Officers. While these volunteers helped replenish the army's rapidly dwindling officer corps, most had little combat experience and lacked sufficient knowledge of Indian languages to communicate effectively with their troops. The willingness to follow one's superiors into battle depended in no small part on trust in their leadership capabilities. It is therefore not surprising that Indian soldiers preferred to serve under British officers with whom they were familiar.[28] The progressive disappearance of such officers, and the difficulty of forming bonds with their replacements given linguistic barriers and the stress of active operations, left Indian soldiers increasingly without the leadership to which they had grown accustomed before the war.

Given that Indian officers who became casualties could be replaced by sepoys promoted from the ranks of the same battalion, Indian units did not face the same shortage of VCOs. Nonetheless, the loss of experienced Indian officers also had detrimental effects. At the outset of the war, senior VCOs in Indian units were held in high esteem accrued over decades of service. This was particularly true of the *subedar major,* the highest-ranking VCO in any battalion. H. H. Rich described the subedar major of the 120th Rajputana Infantry as "a man of great authority, character and prestige. He was the C.O.'s right-hand man and confidential adviser on all matters pertaining to the troops. He was also the personal friend of every officer and the mentor of the young subalterns. Ours, a Pathan called Khitab Gul, was well known throughout India. He held the Indian officers and men of the Regiment in the hollow of his hand."[29] During the First World War, this status allowed senior VCOs to serve as intermediaries between the Indian rank and file and British officers seeking to explain the new environments and technologies they encountered during expeditionary operations. An illuminating example can be found in the war diary of the 27th Punjabis, which describes the difficulty of convincing soldiers to accept inoculations for cholera in Mesopotamia the spring of 1916. According to the diary, "On May 9th half the Regiment received its first inoculation against Cholera. The Khattacks except the Indian officers and NCOs refused to be done as they still believed the stories they had heard in Egypt about all inoculation rendering men impotent. Even when told in turn that this inoculation was not voluntary but by order they still refused and had to be marched back to camp under arrest. Subedar Major Mir Akbar found out who was at the bottom of this refusal and persuaded them to agree to be inoculated the following day."[30] This case may seem trivial in comparison to some of the challenges faced by the Indian Army in the First World War, but it demonstrates the vital liaison role played by senior VCOs. While fallen VCOs could be replaced by sepoys from the ranks, the loss of experienced and highly respected figures undoubtedly weakened morale and discipline in Indian units.

The loss of comrades also affected the morale of Indian soldiers in several ways. The Indian Army was not prepared for the level of casualties it suffered in the initial stages of the First World War. Its prewar recruitment practices left class companies and regiments reliant on reinforcements from specific communities that were not large enough to replace casualties over an extended period. Communities that did not contain preferred classes remained untapped regardless of the enthusiasm of their inhabitants for military service. Thus, the army's pool of willing and able reinforcements was quickly depleted. According to Phillip Stigger, "As early as 1 January 1915, it was estimated that 72% of the potential pool of Dogras had been recruited, together with 37% of the Jat Sikhs and 31% of the Punjabi Musulmans."[31] By the spring of 1915 the situation had become sufficiently dire that the army was recalling reservists with eighteen to twenty-five years of previous service. Lieutenant-Colonel H. S. Vernon of the 27th Punjabis described the reservists he encountered while serving in the Indian Corps in France. According to Vernon, "The Reservists were the most disappointing. Many too old, many consistently half-starved since their last training two years before. I was surprised at the number with very bad teeth. There were some Sikhs who were perfectly useless unless they had doped themselves with opium."[32] The fact that these men were often in poor health undermined the fighting efficiency of Indian units. Moreover, many had little enthusiasm for an extended deployment overseas.[33] Their demeanor likely did little to lift the spirits of the soldiers in the units they joined. The summer and autumn of 1915 also saw the arrival of new recruits, many of whom had enlisted since the outbreak of the war. These soldiers, however, had little military experience. According to A. J. Barker: "The best drafts – those of trained soldiers – were sent to units serving in France, and Mesopotamia had to be content with recruits who had no more than eight months service."[34]

In addition to being of uneven quality, reinforcements progressively undermined the cultural homogeneity of Indian units as the Mesopotamia campaign progressed. This was particularly true of drafts sent from battalions in India to reinforce units overseas. Edwin Latter has observed that "recruiting was too localized, and specialized, to permit the replacement of wastage without changing the social, and even ethnic, make up of company level units. Drafts, even from battalions of the same martial race, might not speak the same tongue or eat the same food."[35] Sir Walter Lawrence explained the impact of repeated reinforcement on the esprit de corps of Indian units. "The Sepoys," he maintained, "have been accustomed to look upon their regiment as a family: they have lost the officers whom they knew, and the regiment, which formerly was made up of well-defined and exclusive castes and tribes, is now composed of miscellaneous and dissimilar elements. . . . This is no longer a regiment. It has no cohesion."[36]

In addition to diluting the esprit de corps of Indian units, the arrival of reinforcement drafts created tensions among soldiers vying for promotion. Under normal circumstances, sepoys gained promotion on the basis of seniority. Thus, it was not uncommon for a soldier to serve for decades before being even reaching the rank of *naik,* roughly equivalent to a corporal in the British army.[37] War brought the opportunity for relatively rapid advancement as VCO casualties frequently created vacancies to be filled in Indian units. Soldiers from these units naturally expected first consideration for these positions, but so too did members of reinforcement drafts, who were often older men, handpicked by the commander of their own regiment on the basis of their courage and competence. The war diary of the 27th Punjabis describes the resulting dilemma:

> A Regiment suffers heavy casualties in action. The class which has the heaviest
> losses not unnaturally regards this as one of those opportunities for quick
> advancement in war time which is held out as an inducement to the soldier. A
> draft of the same class arrives from another Unit as reinforcement. This draft
> has been induced to volunteer, partly by hopes of rapid promotion. Because it
> has come from a Regiment which is not on service and therefore has not suffered
> casualties it probably contains a number of senior men – the Commanding
> Officer of the battalion from which it comes is likely to have tried to pick the best
> men possible and will have written saying so. The Commanding Officer of the
> reinforced regiment knows nothing of the new arrivals, wants to do the best he
> can for the men who have been in the thick of heavy fighting, wants to promote
> men who have actual experience of the conditions of the campaign, [and] wants
> to be fair to the new arrivals.[38]

Perhaps not surprisingly, commanders appear to have favored soldiers of their own units over the members of reinforcement drafts, often despite the seniority or other attributes of the reinforcements. This
frustrated soldiers who had volunteered for service overseas in the hope
of gaining an accelerated promotion but then found themselves overlooked in both their original units and those that they joined. As one
sepoy complained in a letter to a newspaper for Indian soldiers serving
in Europe, "the rank and file of these drafts do not get promotion either
in the regiment into which they are incorporated or in their own regiment, whilst their juniors are given promotion and thus become their
seniors."[39]

In addition to this range of hardships and disappointments, news
from India also increased soldiers' desire to return home. As 1915 progressed, reports of drought, disease, and price inflation increased their
concern for the welfare of their families. They also worried about the
prospect of their children entering into unsuitable marriages, or the
failure of their own marriages in their absence.[40] Sir Walter Lawrence
explained the anxieties of Indian soldiers in a letter to Lord Kitchener
in June 1915, "Their enemies in the village are trying to seize their land;
they have trouble about their debts; and they are anxious to look after
marriages and other domestic details which form an important part in
the life of an Indian."[41] These concerns were especially prevalent among
Pathans, the third-largest martial class in the Indian Army in 1914.[42]
The British distinguished between "cis-frontier" Pathans, who lived in
the British-administered North-West Frontier Province of India, and

"trans-frontier" Pathans, whose homes were in the tribal areas beyond the control of British colonial authorities. The latter group had particular reason for concern. Edwin Latter has explained that "the security of their wives, children, cattle and land depended on their occasional appearance in their village. Their interests could not be protected by the magistrates and police of the Raj."[43]

Such domestic concerns appear to have fueled religious objections to the war, particularly among Indians serving in Mesopotamia. Muslims comprised approximately 40 percent of the strength of the Indian Army in 1914.[44] Many had reservations about fighting the Ottomans, who not only were fellow Muslims, but served the Ottoman sultan, recognized by Sunnis as the khalifa. In addition, Shia Muslims expressed concern about fighting near holy cities and sites in Mesopotamia, such as Karbala and Salman Pak.[45] The Ottomans attempted to capitalize on Muslim ambivalence by portraying the war against Britain as a jihad. The British countered by emphasizing that the Ottomans had initiated hostilities against the king-emperor. Moreover, they pledged not to attack Islamic holy cities and shrines in the Middle East, and secured statements of support from Indian Muslim leaders such as the nizam of Hyderabad.[46] These efforts were apparently sufficient to dispel the concerns of most Muslim soldiers. Members of Pathan tribes, however, voiced strong objections to the war on religious grounds. Abstentions and desertions among Pathans in the initial stages of the campaign exceeded those among all other martial classes.[47] In early 1915, two Pathan units refused even to embark for service in Mesopotamia, with members of one unit opening fire on their officers.[48]

The intransigence of Pathans in comparison to other Muslim soldiers stemmed from a combination of factors. First, they were apparently influenced to a greater extent than other Indian Muslims by extreme, anti-Western variants of Islam emanating from Afghanistan. Of particular concern to colonial authorities was a Wahabi community in Afghanistan, which for decades had preached jihad against the British. While these exhortations clearly had little resonance with Pathan sepoys, it would not be surprising if the circulation of such sentiments in relatively close proximity to their home communities diminished their enthusiasm for a war against a Muslim power.[49] Second, while the majority of trans-frontier Pathans initially proved willing to fight the Ottomans, the length of the campaign left them increasingly anxious about the security of their interests at home. At the same time, they could not abandon their military commitment without losing izzat. In this context, the British author and war correspondent Edmund Candler argued that an appeal to Islam "offered the one decent retreat from an intolerable position," as it justified refusal to serve without a loss of face.[50] Finally, the fact that their homes lay beyond the control of British authorities meant that Pathans could consider desertion without the same fear of punishment that probably deterred other Muslim soldiers.[51]

All of these factors combined to place increasing strain on the morale of Indian soldiers during the first year of the campaign in Mesopotamia. Pathans proved particularly vulnerable. As Omissi has observed, "From early 1915, letters written by Pathan sepoys show that they were willing to consider absconding."[52] By March, Major-General Arthur Barrett, the original commander of 6 Indian Division in Mesopotamia, had twice requested the replacement of four companies of Pathans that he did not trust. The authorities in India refused on the grounds that they could not depend on Muslim troops to fight on the North-West Frontier either, and therefore could not spare any non-Muslim units for service overseas.[53] Thus, as the campaign intensified in the spring of 1915, 6 Indian Division retained several units that displayed little enthusiasm for active operations against the enemy. Casualties sustained in the spring and summer further undermined morale and unit cohesion, as soldiers lost familiar leaders and comrades, who were replaced by inexperienced reservists. In addition, the harsh climate of Mesopotamia, combined with the dearth of rations, medical care, and other necessities, discouraged many soldiers, particularly those familiar with the relative abundance of amenities enjoyed by Indians in France. One cavalryman complained in a letter to a friend in Europe, "The country in which we are encamped is an extremely bad place. There are continual storms and the cold is very great, and in the wet season it is intensely hot. . . . If I had only gone to France, I could have been with you and seen men of all kinds. We have all got to die someday, but at any rate we would have had a good time there."[54]

In comparison to their Indian counterparts, the British members of Charles Townshend's force were a relatively homogenous group. Like the soldiers who embarked for France in August 1914, the British infantry battalions and artillery batteries that advanced up the Tigris in 1915 were part of the regular army. Unlike the units of the original British Expeditionary Force, however, the British elements of 6 Indian Division did not require the addition of large numbers of reservists to fill their ranks at the outset of the war.[55] Stationed in India in 1914, they were at full strength, their ranks made up almost entirely of long-service professional soldiers. As a result, these units may well have begun the war with higher standards of cohesion and tactical proficiency than even the vaunted "Old Contemptibles." Casualties suffered during the first year of the Mesopotamia campaign necessitated the dispatch of reinforcements to replenish their ranks. These consisted of volunteers from battalions of the Territorial Army, which had been deployed to India in late 1914 to replace regular British units sent to fight in Europe, East Africa, or Mesopotamia. G. L. Heawood, for example, was a member of the Officer Training Corps at Oxford University when war broke out in August 1914. This qualified him for a commission in the 4th Wiltshire Territorial Battalion, which went to India in the fall of 1914. In the summer of 1915 he responded to a call for one officer and sixty other ranks from each territorial battalion in India to reinforce British units in Mesopotamia, and in August 1915 he found himself in command of a platoon of the 1st Oxford and Buckinghamshire Light Infantry, part of the 17th Brigade of 6 Indian Division.[56]

Reinforcements such as Heawood certainly lacked the experience of the soldiers they replaced. Moreover, territorials who had only left England in late 1914 had difficulty adjusting to the heat of the Mesopotamian summer.[57] More generally, British soldiers in Mesopotamia served with the knowledge that they were fighting in a secondary theater of the war, against an enemy that did not pose an immediate threat to Britain, and that their exploits received little media coverage as a result.[58] Recognition of these realities undoubtedly dampened morale. None of these factors, however, seem to have diminished significantly the performance of Townshend's British units. Whatever difficulties territorials encountered adjusting to conditions in Mesopotamia, they shared a common language and cultural background with the soldiers they joined. While the motivations of regulars and territorials may have differed slightly, in the context of the First World War they were united by the imperative of defeating Britain's enemies, with whom they shared few linguistic, cultural, or religious affinities, especially in Mesopotamia. In addition, the fact that British units in Mesopotamia still retained a large majority of their original members in the fall of 1915 eased the transition of new arrivals. According to Heawood, most of his new subordinates were veterans of at least twelve years' active service. In his words: "they were very efficient and I was aware at once I was in definitely a regular Regiment which was a quite different atmosphere from our Territorial Battalion."[59]

Thus, the British battalions of Townshend's force retained a large measure of their effectiveness even after a year of operations in Mesopotamia. In his memoir of the war, E. O. Mousley, a lieutenant who joined one of the division's artillery batteries in November 1915, described the composure of its members in the trying circumstances that prevailed during the retirement from Ctesiphon. According to Mousley, "Every man of the fatigued army worked as happens on manoeuvres. It was only the battered condition of the gun carriages, the gaping wounds in the diminished teams of horses and that quiet 'balanced up' look in the eyes of every Tommy that told of a reality more grim."[60] The relative stability of British units in the fall of 1915 helps explain why Charles Townshend referred to them as "my sheet anchor" in his memoir of the war.[61]

COMMANDER OF 6 INDIAN DIVISION

Significantly, Townshend's own experiences and ambitions also influenced his attitudes toward his British and Indian subordinates. Fifty-four years of age in 1915, Charles Townshend had achieved distinction relatively early in his military career. After graduating from Sandhurst in 1881, he was commissioned into the Royal Marines. He subsequently transferred to the Indian Army, and in 1891 he participated in the campaign that extended British control over the princely states of Hunza and Nagar. In 1895 Townshend gained widespread celebrity for his successful defense of the British fort at Chitral. He distinguished himself further in Sudan in 1898, leading the 12th Sudanese Regiment in battle at Atbara and Khartoum. Townshend's early combat experiences convinced him of the importance of personal leadership in battle. As he explained on his departure from Africa in 1898, "When things are warm, you must be prepared to lead the way, be your men Europeans or natives of India or the Sudan."[62]

The trajectory of Townshend's career leveled off around the turn of the twentieth century, due in part to his unconventional interests and personality. Townshend was a skilled banjo-player, a talented mimic, an avid theater-goer, an admirer of French culture, and an enthusiastic student of military history, especially that of the Napoleonic period. Nor was he particularly modest about his varied fields of expertise. As a captain he treated George Curzon to an extended banjo recital of French songs when the future viceroy of India visited Fort Gupis on the North-West Frontier of India in 1894.[63] Townshend was particularly fond of demonstrating his command of military history to his subordinates. Sir John Mellor, who served in 6 Indian Division in 1915, recalled after the war that Townshend "was always quoting from what Napoleon had done on some occasion or something like what Wellington had done in order to illustrate his purpose." [64]

While Townshend's interests marked him as an outlier in an officer corps that generally favored hunting and sports over intellectual and cultural pursuits, they were not sufficient in themselves to hinder his career progression. Indeed, his traits seem to have endeared him to many subordinates. According to Mellor, "he used to sometimes come round to the Officer's Mess for a drink and he was a very amusing character, full of good stories and really a bit of a card in some ways."[65] Townshend had achieved significant renown at a relatively early age, however, becoming a Companion of the Order of the Bath in 1895, the same year he was promoted to the rank of major. To more senior officers jealous of this early success, Townshend's idiosyncratic interests were likely a cause of irritation. Ronald Millar has remarked, "These traits, which could possibly be viewed with amused tolerance if detected in a junior officer, were somewhat out of place in a soldier of standing and distinction."[66] Even more exasperating was his unrelenting ambition, which led him continually to solicit the assistance of senior figures in the army and government in hopes of securing new and ostensibly advantageous postings. His most sympathetic biographer, his cousin Erroll Sherston, acknowledged that Townshend was "one of the most restless individuals in the whole of the Army. As soon as he had obtained one appointment by the incessant wire-pulling among his influential friends, he thirsted for a change."[67]

When war broke out in South Africa in 1899, Townshend lobbied Lord Curzon, now the viceroy, for permission to proceed there on "special service" in early 1900. Dissatisfied with the position that he was assigned on the staff of the military governor of Bloemfontein, he enlisted the aid of Lord Lansdowne, then secretary of state for war, to secure a post in the Royal Fusiliers Regiment. By October 1900 Townshend was back in England with the Royal Fusiliers. He quickly became so disenchanted with the peacetime duties of a regimental officer, however, that he took an unpaid leave to Canada with the intent of mapping roads of strategic significance in the event of war with the United States. Upon his return he secured a transfer to the Royal Fusiliers battalion stationed in Burma. Even before joining his new unit, however, Townshend began petitioning for another staff position.[68]

Despite their admiration for his earlier exploits at Chitral, Atbara, and elsewhere, Townshend's superiors grew weary of his incessant maneuvering. As Lord Kitchener's protégé, Lieutenant-General Sir Archibald Hunter, informed him in 1904, "Lord Kitchener said to me that you need not write any more, that he will not forget you and that your interests were more likely to be furthered than forgotten by silence on your part."[69] Townshend's efforts at self-promotion abated temporarily, but this likely stemmed as much from the revitalization of his career as from increased circumspection on his part. In 1908 he was promoted to the rank of colonel, and in March 1909 he took command of the Orange River Colony district in South Africa, a position that carried the rank of brigadier-general. Two years later he was promoted again to major-general. This series of successes did little to satiate Townshend's ambitions. While he actively pursued promotion throughout his career, he also coveted the accolades that he earned through his exploits on active operations. Thus, when offered command of a territorial division in 1911, he very nearly refused in hopes of obtaining a regular division instead. Strong advice from senior patrons led him reluctantly to accept the offer, but in 1913 Townshend requested yet another transfer to India, where he took command of an Indian brigade "to get away from the Territorials."[70]

Thus, in August 1914 Townshend found himself in command of the Rawal Pindi Brigade in India. For an ambitious commander who had spent his career studying the campaigns of Napoleon and Wellington, the outbreak of war in Europe was the professional opportunity of a lifetime. It was also almost certainly the last such opportunity that would present itself to a senior commander in his mid-fifties. The opening months of the First World War were therefore a period of mounting frustration for Townshend, as officers his own age such as Douglas Haig, Edmund Allenby, and Julian Byng commanded divisions and even corps in active operations against the German Army. To make matters worse, several Indian formations departed the continent for operations in Europe, East Africa, and Mesopotamia in 1914, commanded by officers who proved unprepared for the strains of active campaigning. Townshend commented in a 1915 letter to Curzon, "I saw some go from India whom it was a scandal to send."[71] Meanwhile Townshend's brigade remained in India to guard against a large-scale native uprising that did not materialize. Townshend grew increasingly despondent as his efforts to secure an appointment in Europe failed to bear fruit. In March 1915, however, he received a stroke of luck when Sir John Nixon was appointed to command IEFD in Mesopotamia. The original commander of 6 Indian Division, Lieutenant-General Sir Arthur Barrett, saw Nixon's appointment as a slight and refused to continue in his post. Impressed with Townshend's performance on maneuvers in India in 1913, Nixon requested his appointment to replace Barrett. Townshend leapt at the opportunity, embarking for Mesopotamia in April 1915.[72]

The new commander of 6 Indian Division wasted no time distinguishing himself. Leading an advance party of less than 100 soldiers and sailors, Townshend captured the town of Amara on 2 June, bluffing nearly 1,000 Ottoman troops into surrendering and holding them overnight until reinforcements arrived the next morning in the form of "Townshend's Regatta," an improvised fleet of river boats carrying the 17th Brigade of 6 Indian Division.[73] In the immediate aftermath of his victory at Amara, however, Townshend became violently ill with "relaps-

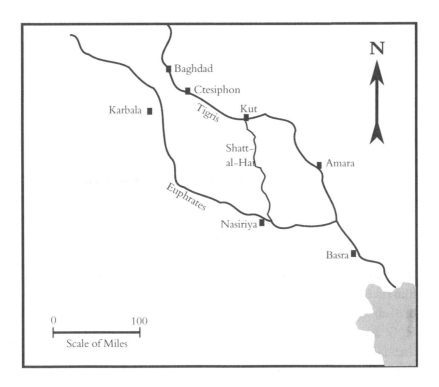

Baghdad
Ctesiphon
Karbala
Tigris
Kut
Shatt-al-Hai
Amara
Euphrates
Nasiriya
Basra
N
0   100
Scale of Miles

1.1. *Lower Mesopotamia*

ing fever," a condition he had apparently first contracted in East Africa.[74] Vomiting and suffering from severe diarrhea, he was sent back to India to recuperate. Describing this period of convalescence in his memoir, Townshend emphasized his growing disquiet over the prospect of advancing beyond Amara when he rejoined his division in Mesopotamia. He recounted his 10 August meeting with the commander-in-chief of the Indian Army, Sir Beauchamp Duff, in which Townshend explained the "grave risks" of an advance on Baghdad in insufficient strength, opining that a full corps, or at least two infantry divisions, would be necessary to capture and hold the city. Whatever reservations Townshend may have had about an advance on Baghdad, however, he was eager to resume the offensive. He later admitted to Curzon that he "lied to the doctors" about the extent of his recovery in order to return to Mesopotamia.[75] Townshend's victory at Amara had heightened his stature in the eyes of his troops, and he clearly reveled in their adulation. He boasted in a letter to his wife, "You should have seen the British and Indian soldiers cheering me as I stood on the *Comet.* I must have the gift of making men (I mean the soldier men) love me and follow me. I have only known the 6th Division for six months, and they'd storm the gates of hell if I told them to."[76] Thus, at his meeting with Duff he in fact "guaranteed" the commander in chief that he would evict the Ottoman army from formidable defensive positions below the town of Kut-al-Amara, driving it "into the Tigris."[77]

Townshend's future objectives and past experiences had significant implications for his leadership of 6 Indian Division upon his return to Mesopotamia in late August 1915. In taking the offensive without adequate medical infrastructure or logistical support, Townshend was making considerable demands upon his subordinates. He hoped to sustain their morale through the charismatic leadership that had brought him success in the past. There is ample evidence that the British soldiers of 6 Indian Division held their commander in high esteem. According to H. G. Thomson, commander of the howitzer battery attached to 6 Indian Division, Townshend was "almost a hero" among his men. A. G. Kingsmill, a corporal in the 2/Queen's Own Royal West Kent Regiment, recalled that in the autumn of 1915 the soldiers "would go and do anything he commanded."[78]

Significantly, Townshend was never able to elicit the same affection from the Indians who comprised the majority of his force. Given the linguistic and cultural barriers between them, there were probably limits to the loyalty that any senior British commander could muster in Indian soldiers, particularly under the trying circumstances of the campaign in Mesopotamia. Townshend's limited contact with sepoys throughout his career, however, left him particularly ill-prepared to establish a bond with his subordinates in 1915. Townshend had commanded sepoys periodically since the early 1890s, when he had been charged with improving the training and discipline of the 1st Kashmir Regiment, a unit of Imperial Service Troops in Gilgit. Yet he had never served as a regimental officer in an Indian Army battalion over an extended period, an experience that imparted the linguistic skills, cultural sensitivities, and general familiarity with sepoys and followers that enabled the formation of personal ties. Given the frenetic pace at which Townshend moved from position to position, his contact with Indians was always temporary, usually distant, and occasionally marred by bad experiences, such as during his defense of Chitral, when he characterized the Imperial Service Troops under his command as "pretty well useless."[79] Townshend was undoubtedly aware of the considerable religious, ethnic, and cultural diversity of the Indian units under his command in 1915. Nonetheless, he seems to have lacked a detailed knowledge of his subordinates, much less the affection with which many KCOs regarded them. This limited his ability to gain their allegiance. According to H. H. Rich, while Townshend's British subordinates liked and respected him, "[in] the Indian Army he was certainly not popular."[80]

Townshend's distant relationship with Indian personnel did nothing to assuage his apprehension regarding their reliability. Events in India during late 1914 and early 1915 had already raised concerns among senior British officers regarding the possibility of a native uprising. In addition to unrest among the Pathan tribes on the North-West Frontier, there had been turmoil within Sikh regiments inspired by the Ghadrite movement. Moreover, Muslim sepoys in Rangoon and Singapore had mutinied in early 1915 following the news of their deployment to Mesopotamia.[81] Having negotiated with disaffected Sikh officers in February 1915, Townshend was well aware of the potential for disciplinary problems before he even arrived in Mesopotamia. Without an intimate knowledge of his Indian subordinates and the distinctions between them, he was inclined to view them with suspicion throughout the campaign.

CONCLUSION

In the summer of 1916, J. A. Lovat-Fraser wrote to Lord Curzon articulating his views on the type of leader needed to revive British fortunes in Mesopotamia after Townshend's surrender of Kut. As Lovat-Fraser explained, "You certainly do *not* want a 'brisk young General' who will be damning the Indian troops all the time, and fancying he is about to conquer half Asia." In order to succeed, the commander "must thoroughly understand Indian troops, and what they can do and cannot do. He must be able to talk to them, and he must be *known* to them."[82] In writing to Curzon, Lovat-Fraser undoubtedly had the experiences of

6 Indian Division in mind. As Charles Townshend's force embarked on its offensive up the Tigris, the morale of the Indians who composed the majority of its strength was fragile for a variety of reasons. Morale and the factors affecting it, however, varied widely among battalions and companies of different ethnic and religious background. The concerns of trans-frontier Pathans, for example, were quite different from those of Gurkhas or Rajputs. Significantly, the ambitious commander of 6 Indian Division was not inclined to differentiate between the groups under his command. As a result, he tended to magnify the fragility of his force, assuming that disaffection among one group was symptomatic of a broader malaise. Townshend certainly had faith in his British battalions, but their apparent steadfastness simply underlined the apparent unreliability of the bulk of his force. This tendency would have a significant impact on Townshend's decisions from the outset of his advance on Baghdad in September 1915 until his surrender of Kut-al-Amara at the end of April 1916.

TWO

TOWNSHEND'S
ADVANCE ON BAGHDAD

SEPTEMBER–NOVEMBER 1915

IN LATE SEPTEMBER 1915, CHARLES TOWNSHEND'S 6 INDIAN
Division defeated Ottoman forces under the command of Nurettin at
Kut-al-Amara. Townshend subsequently continued his advance up the
Tigris toward Baghdad, but did not engage substantial enemy forces
again until nearly two months later. From 22 to 25 November, 6 Indian
Division, with a fighting strength of approximately 14,000, attempted to
dislodge Ottoman forces at least 18,000 strong from prepared positions
around Ctesiphon, just below Baghdad. After failing to achieve this objective during three days of costly fighting, Townshend initiated a hasty
retreat that ended in his ill-fated decision to stand at Kut and await relief.

These engagements had pivotal consequences. The inability of 6 Indian Division to defeat the enemy decisively left Baghdad under Ottoman control. In addition, the heavy losses it suffered at Ctesiphon
contributed to Townshend's decision to seek refuge at Kut. Nonetheless,
Charles Townshend's conduct of operations during this period remains
poorly understood. Accounts published in the 1960s treat the outcome
of the advance on Baghdad as almost a foregone conclusion. For example, A. J. Barker suggests that the numerical superiority of Ottoman
forces at Ctesiphon made victory prohibitively difficult for 6 Indian Division.[1] Russell Braddon has suggested that once the British government sanctioned the advance to Baghdad, "the fate of thirteen thousand
of Townshend's troops was sealed; and the deaths of thousands more in
the Relief Force became inevitable."[2] Ronald Millar concurs. Given the
superiority of Ottoman forces in the region, Millar has called Ctesiphon
"a totally unnecessary battle."[3]

More recent scholarship has shed light on the decision-making process that led to the advance on Baghdad. David French has placed the Mesopotamia campaign in the broader context of British strategy in 1915, demonstrating how concerns for British prestige in the Muslim world encouraged senior leaders in London and India to support the offensive plans of the senior commander in Mesopotamia, Sir John Nixon.[4] Paul K. Davis has focused in particular on Nixon's role in instigating the disastrous advance despite the objections of his subordinate Townshend. According to Davis: "Nixon's blindness and the resulting ignorance in Simla and London forced Townshend's retreat to Kut."[5] Richard Popplewell's examination of British intelligence in Mesopotamia places Nixon in a more sympathetic light, demonstrating how erroneous intelligence reports influenced his decision to advance on Baghdad. Nonetheless, Popplewell shares with Davis, French, and earlier writers the assumption that the superiority of the Ottoman Army at Ctesiphon precluded victory by 6 Indian Division. Popplewell argues that "the deciding factor [at Ctesiphon] was not just the quantity of Turkish troops unaccounted for but also their quality."[6]

Studies of the armies involved in the conflict in Mesopotamia have reinforced the assumption that Townshend's advance on Baghdad was a doomed enterprise. Edwin Latter has noted the deteriorating morale of Indian soldiers during the advance toward Baghdad, as well as the relatively rudimentary tactics employed by British commanders in Mesopotamia.[7] Kaushik Roy has highlighted the logistical shortcomings that hindered Townshend's advance.[8] Edward Erickson's recent study of Ottoman military effectiveness has provided significant new insights into the capabilities of Townshend's adversary at Ctesiphon.[9] By emphasizing Ottoman defensive prowess, however, Erickson's work lends support to the existing interpretation of the battle as an inevitable British defeat.

One of the key proponents of this interpretation was Charles Townshend himself. In communications with Indian military authorities during the siege, Townshend asserted that Sir John Nixon had compelled him to advance on Baghdad against his better judgment. He expanded upon this argument in his 1919 memoir, portraying Ctesiphon as an ill-advised engagement, brought about by the incompetent decisions of his superiors. According to Townshend: "Personally I had no doubts in my mind as to the extreme gravity of the results of this advance – an offensive undertaken with insufficient forces, and not only that, but an offensive undertaken in a secondary theatre of the war, where our strategy should have been to have remained on the defensive with minimum forces sufficient for that purpose. All my study indicated disaster to me."[10]

Townshend's version of events influenced the report of the Mesopotamia Commission, and it has been integral to historians' understanding of this period. Significantly, however, this interpretation diverts attention from the actual battles of Kut-al-Amara and Ctesiphon, and particularly Townshend's conduct of them. Reconstructing these engagements is no easy task, given the destruction of unit war diaries during the siege of Kut. Nonetheless, it is essential if we are to understand fully the genesis of the siege. Using a variety of sources, including memoirs, the report of the Mesopotamia Commission, the correspondence of the British official historian, F. J. Moberly, and the account of an Ottoman staff officer, this chapter challenges the prevailing view that the British offensive was destined for failure, culminating in the siege and surrender of Kut. It will argue that Charles Townshend's attitude toward the offensive was more complex than he subsequently claimed. While he had genuine concerns about his ability to capture Baghdad, he was confident that he could defeat Nurettin in battle, furthering his career in the process. Townshend's performance on the battlefield, however, did not match his aspirations. After struggling to influence events at the Battle of Kut-al-Amara, he took a more direct role in commanding his force at Ctesiphon, but his decisions under fire undermined its success and contributed to heavy casualties, sapping his confidence even as his chances of victory increased.

THE ADVANCE ON BAGHDAD AND
THE BATTLE OF KUT-AL-AMARA

In order to assess Townshend's command in this period, it is important to understand his relationship with Sir John Nixon. Historians have generally accepted Townshend's assertion that pressure from the reckless Nixon compelled him reluctantly to embark on an offensive about which he had serious reservations.[11] There is some truth to this claim. Nixon clearly pressed Townshend to undertake an advance that both officers recognized to be fraught with danger. Moreover, Townshend believed that Nixon hoped to claim credit for victory while leaving him to take the blame for defeat. Townshend did not simply acquiesce, however, to the machinations of his superior. Despite its risks, the commander of 6 Indian Division saw an advance on Baghdad as an irresistible opportunity that might vault him from the relative backwater of Mesopotamia to a more prominent posting on the Western Front. He therefore worked assiduously throughout 1915 to highlight the weakness of his force and thereby deflect responsibility for any potential setbacks, while at the same time portraying himself to senior Indian military and political leaders as the principal architect of an offensive that he believed would ultimately end in victory.

Townshend's efforts began during his convalescence in India during the summer of 1915, when he advised Sir Beauchamp Duff of the hazards associated with an advance up the Tigris with a single division.[12] Townshend expressed similar sentiments in a letter to Lord Curzon upon his return to Mesopotamia. On 4 September Townshend wrote the former viceroy of India, informing him that "we are dangerously weak in Mesopotamia" and that the enemy "may be superior to us in numbers." Much like he had promised victory to Duff, however, Townshend predicted success in his letter to Curzon. He continued, "If I can get them on the run . . . I shall hammer them I hope all the way to Baghdad." Confident of victory, he contrasted his allegedly underappreciated exploits with the stalemate in France, commenting derisively, "All the generals in France are given knighthoods after each indecisive combat where not one of them has had to manoeuvre one yard! A double company commanders' war in trenches & mines & rabbit warrens. Here at least *we do advance*."[13]

The Battle of Kut-al-Amara fell short of Townshend's highest expectations. On 28 September 6 Division, comprising approximately 11,000 combatants, attacked the Ottomans just downriver from Kut. The Ottoman commander Nurettin had taken charge after Townshend's capture of Amara in June and had spent several months preparing new defenses. Thus, for the first time in the war, Townshend faced "a properly orga-

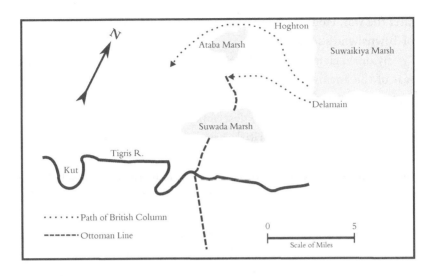

2.1. *The Battle of Kut-al-Amara, 28 September 1915*

nized trench system" extending for more than five miles on both sides of the river, anchored by impassable marshes.[14] Given the scale of the enemy position, Townshend planned to divide his force into two columns. Column "B," a single infantry brigade under Brigadier-General C. I. Fry, would hold the enemy in place with a frontal attack against Ottoman positions just north of the Tigris. Meanwhile, Column "A," comprising two and a half infantry brigades and the cavalry, all under Major-General W. S. Delamain, would turn the enemy's left flank by pushing through a gap between the northern end of the Ottoman line and the nearby Ataba marsh, which had apparently receded northward since the construction of the position.[15] Friction diminished the impact of this turning movement. Part of Column "A," the 17th Infantry Brigade under Brigadier-General F. A. Hoghton, mistakenly advanced around the north side of the Ataba marsh, increasing the length of its march and delaying by several hours its engagement with the enemy. Moreover, upon encountering strong enemy positions, Hoghton proved reluctant to advance without reinforcement, further diluting Townshend's intended concentration of force against the Ottoman left flank. As Sir John Nixon's chief of staff, Major-General George Kemball, related after the war, Hoghton's delay was "disastrous to the complete success of Townshend's scheme."[16]

By dusk, elements of 6 Division had established themselves in the rear of the enemy positions, forcing Nurettin to initiate a withdrawal under the cover of darkness.[17] In his memoir, Townshend portrayed the battle as an outright victory, describing it as "one of the most important in the history of the British Army in India."[18] In reality, however, 28 September proved frustrating for Townshend. Rather than routing the enemy, his force had allowed the Ottomans to retire intact. Moreover, throughout the battle he had struggled to discern, let alone influence, the course of events. While the relatively small scale of his previous engagements in the spring of 1915 had enabled him to lead from the front, Townshend spent the Battle of Kut in a wooden observation tower several miles from the front, his view marred by mirage and sandstorms. As the battle progressed, he received sporadic and increasingly infrequent information from his subordinates. A lack of telephone cable forced Townshend to rely solely on aerial reconnaissance reports after 11 AM, and for three full hours during the afternoon he received no news whatsoever.[19] The commander of 6 Indian Division thus passed the day waiting apprehensively as the misdirection and the apparent hesitancy of Hoghton's 17th Brigade impeded the timely execution of his plan.

Townshend also had to contend with an uninvited guest in the form of Sir John Nixon, who chose to observe the battle at his side. In his study of the Mesopotamia campaign, A. J. Barker has suggested that "Townshend's personality was such that the presence of his commander made no difference."[20] It is difficult to believe, however, that the proximity of his superior, who was eager for victory, did not add to Townshend's frustration as he waited impatiently for news from the front. In personal correspondence Barker himself acknowledged that during the autumn of 1915, Nixon "was breathing down Townshend's neck the whole time. All the time he was sending optimistic messages back to India and to London and pressing Townshend very hard."[21] Nixon's deployment of his chief of staff, Kemball, to observe the battle at Delamain's headquarters compounded Townshend's anxiety. Nicknamed "the Flammenwerfer" in postwar correspondence, Kemball apparently acted as Nixon's prod, egging on ostensibly hesitant field commanders.[22] His presence at a subordinate headquarters closer to the front likely diminished Townshend's sense of control over the battle. It is therefore not entirely surprising that he admitted in his memoir: "No one knew – I am sure none of my staff did – how very anxious I had been over the success of this turning attack, with its unaccountable delays."[23]

Upon discovering that Nurettin had abandoned his positions on 29 September, Nixon urged Townshend to pursue the retiring enemy force. Despite encountering multiple delays embarking troops onto ships and then negotiating the shallow waters of the Tigris, Townshend obliged for several days. On 3 October, however, after reaching the town of Aziziya, 60 miles upriver from Kut, he halted. Townshend had legitimate reasons to interrupt his advance. Aerial reconnaissance indicated that the Ottomans were establishing themselves in strong defensive positions at Ctesiphon, just below Baghdad. Even if his force managed to dislodge them, it would be left in a weakened state hundreds of miles from its base at Basra, vulnerable to Ottoman counterattacks as well as hostile elements of the indigenous population.[24]

To make matters worse, upon arriving at Aziziya, Delamain informed Townshend of his doubts regarding the reliability of at least some of his Indian troops, who had retired in disorder during the Battle of Kut-al-Amara. It is possible that this led Townshend to overestimate the fragility of his Indian units, which comprised approximately three-quarters of the total strength of his force. In postwar correspondence Delamain indicated that his concerns were based primarily on the actions of a single battalion, when in fact the morale and performance of Indian soldiers in Mesopotamia seems to have varied significantly depending on factors such as caste, religion, and ethnicity.[25] Townshend's worries, however, were not entirely groundless. As explained in the previous chapter, a variety of factors were contributing to the erosion of discipline and morale in Indian battalions in Mesopotamia by the fall of 1915.

While Townshend had legitimate reasons for concern regarding the vulnerability of his force and the morale of its Indian units, his decision to halt stemmed in no small part from a fear of his own culpability for any setbacks that might occur if he continued his "pursuit" without explicit orders from Nixon. H. A. Holdich, the chief of staff of Delamain's

16th Brigade, related after the war that "Nixon irritated Townshend in many ways with the object (as we thought) of driving him to take the bit between his teeth and advance without orders. T. was too leery to be caught out like that!"[26] Thus, upon reaching Aziziya on 3 October, Townshend sent a lengthy telegram downriver to Nixon articulating his reservations about continuing the pursuit. He also requested an order "in writing over Sir J. N.'s signature."[27] The commander of 6 Indian Division received a reply the same day directing him to develop a plan to "open the way to Baghdad."[28]

In his memoir, Townshend claimed that he had serious doubts about the success of the advance, and argued that Nixon "should have taken command himself." Nonetheless, he resolved to comply with the directive despite his misgivings.[29] In reality, however, the receipt of a written order from Nixon seems to have assuaged many of Townshend's concerns. Significantly, Townshend wrote to senior figures in England in early November, predicting victory in his next battle. Rather than attempting to shift responsibility to Nixon, he emphasized his own autonomy in planning and executing the advance. On 3 November he informed Lord Lansdowne that he intended "to attack Ctesiphon and occupy Baghdad in ten days, that he again had the command and that it was his own plan."[30] On 7 November he again informed Lord Curzon of the unfavorable odds he faced, explaining: "I shall have just 11,000 combatants & 28 guns. Nureddin has got reinforcements & is at least as strong as I am and in a very strong position just like Kut al Amara astride of the Tigris." Despite these disadvantages, Townshend emphasized that his aim was to "drive the Turks into the river itself if I can & occupy Baghdad." He was sufficiently confident in his ability to do so that he asked Curzon to facilitate his transfer to Europe "when I have occupied Baghdad."[31] Townshend likely believed that conveying timidity or indecision would not help elicit Curzon's support. If he genuinely doubted his ability to defeat Nurettin, however, it made little sense to make his transfer to the Western Front contingent upon the capture of Baghdad, effectively treating victory at Ctesiphon as a foregone conclusion. That Townshend was willing to do so is indicative of his continued confidence.

Notwithstanding this confidence, Townshend's recognition of the vulnerability and weaknesses of his force influenced his planning of the battle. In specific terms, it led Townshend to believe that decisive victory was possible at Ctesiphon only if he struck quickly. To compensate for his lack of numerical superiority and the perceived fragility of his Indian units, Townshend devised a plan that contemporary military planners might recognize as a rudimentary "effects-based operation." Unable to rely on sheer numbers or firepower to destroy the enemy force, he proposed to execute a series of rapid, precisely timed attacks at distinct locations throughout the enemy's position in order to create confusion and panic in the Ottoman command system.

Townshend clearly underestimated the size of the Ottoman force at Ctesiphon, which consisted of over 30,000 troops, including at least 18,000 infantry. He also misjudged the quality of the troops that had joined Nurettin since Kut. Rather than receiving piecemeal reinforcements to fill the depleted ranks of 35 and 38 Divisions, Nurettin was joined by 45 and 51 Divisions, both composed of Anatolian soldiers with better training and much higher morale than the Arab conscripts on whom he was forced to rely previously.[32] Nonetheless, Townshend's plan recognized the weaknesses in the Ottoman position. Nurettin had spent nearly two months preparing two defensive lines on the left bank of the Tigris around Ctesiphon, but his only line of retreat across the Diyala River to his rear was exposed to envelopment.[33] Townshend thus divided 6 Indian Division into three columns, each under one of his brigade commanders. On Townshend's left, a "Minimum Force," comprising the 17th Brigade and the divisional artillery under Hoghton, would commence the attack at 6:30 AM on 22 November. Supported by fire from barges and naval vessels on the Tigris, Hoghton was to advance boldly with the intent of convincing the enemy that his column constituted the main thrust of the British attack.[34] In Townshend's words: "By making a great display and fight, he should induce [the enemy] to use up his reserves." At 7:30, a "Turning Attack," comprising the 18th Brigade under Brigadier-General W. G. Hamilton, would strike the enemy's left flank. This force would be supported on its right by a "Flying Column," comprising the 6th Cavalry Brigade, which was attached to Townshend's force, as well as an infantry battalion. Under the command of Major-General Sir Charles Melliss, this force was to attack the enemy's left flank and rear, "seriously menacing his line of retreat."[35]

With the enemy fully occupied on either flank, Townshend's "Principal Mass," consisting of the 16th and part of the 30th Brigade under Dela-main, would deliver the decisive blow against a position on the right of the Ottoman front that Townshend dubbed "Vital Point" or "v.p." "I hoped," Townshend explained in his memoirs, "either to throw the Turks into the Tigris or to compel them to a disastrous flight across the Diala River."[36]

Given that speed was essential to the success of Townshend's plan, it is notable that he did not assign an independent role to the 6th Cavalry Brigade, commanded by Brigadier-General H. L. Roberts. The military historian A. H. C. Kearsey criticized the amalgamation of the cavalry with an infantry battalion in Melliss's column, arguing: "The Cavalry Commander had not a free hand to operate against the flanks and communications of the opposing forces. He was not given a position on the northern flank from which, on his own initiative, he could have exerted a decisive influence on the battle either by pursuit or by operating rapidly against some point of strategic importance."[37] According to A. J. Barker, Townshend subordinated Roberts to Melliss, commander of the 30th Infantry Brigade, because he "did not trust" the cavalry commander.[38] Townshend's memoir supports this interpretation, criticizing the 6th Cavalry Brigade for its apparent inaction at the Battle of Kut-al-Amara and afterward. At Kut, Townshend complained, "Even if the cavalry had been sent to menace the rear of the Turks it should have sufficed to put them on the move; but I could never ascertain where the cavalry had gone and what they were doing." When the cavalry encountered an enemy force at Al Kutuniya as Townshend's force moved up the Tigris a month later, he lamented, "Had our cavalry charged, the enemy's cavalry and camel corps and guns must have been either destroyed or captured. However, Brigadier-General Roberts, in command of the cavalry brigade, assured me that most unfortunately the terrain on our extreme right was absolutely impossible to charge over, and thus the enemy got away with impunity."[39]

Townshend's postwar views were not simply a product of his frustration at the outcome of the campaign. Other participants shared his low opinion of Roberts. Major J. E. Bridges, an officer in Roberts's brigade, provided the following lukewarm assessment: "He is not a brilliant

Cavalry leader, but fairly sound, and a most charming man socially."[40]
In a postwar interview, Henry Rich described his own encounter with
Roberts during the Battle of Shaiba in April 1915, at which Rich served
as a messenger for Melliss, the senior British commander involved in
the engagement. Unable to locate the cavalry in the midst of the battle,
Melliss sent Rich to locate Roberts and deliver the pointed personal message, "For God's sake do something." Rich eventually discovered that the
cavalry commander "had knocked off for lunch." As he recalled, "There
was the general and his staff sitting against the limbers of the guns, who
were the only people taking any part in the battle in the cavalry brigade,
having their lunch baskets in front of them."[41]

While Rich's anecdote suggests that Townshend had legitimate reason to doubt Roberts's initiative, it also hints at a more general problem
facing commanders in Mesopotamia and elsewhere in this period: that
of integrating cavalry into combined-arms operations. On one hand,
cavalry required considerable independence in order to fulfil its reconnaissance, exploitation, and pursuit roles. On the other hand, if it was to
play a meaningful role in offensive operations, cavalry required directions more specific than an admonition to "do something." Indeed, the
increased lethality of the early-twentieth-century battlefield could be
deadly for cavalry units that attempted to intervene on the battlefield
without precise directions. This had been demonstrated during the battle at Kut in late September. Operating "in the blue," out of contact with
Townshend and his brigade commanders, Roberts's cavalry had been
mistaken for the enemy and shelled by the 6 Indian Division artillery.[42]
Faced with the challenge of managing a cavalry brigade that had hitherto proven of limited value in offensive operations, Townshend opted
for a short leash. Given Roberts's apparent limitations, this decision is
understandable. Nonetheless, as a postwar study of the Mesopotamia
campaign by the Quetta staff college observed, the attachment of an
infantry battalion "must have been a drag on the Cavalry Brigade."[43] In
effect, Townshend's decision hobbled the fastest, most mobile element
of his force, thus limiting his ability to generate the rapid, decisive attack
necessary to induce the retirement of a stronger enemy force.

Sacrificing the speed of the cavalry to obtain greater control over its
movements forced Townshend to rely more heavily on timing. In more

specific terms, the success of Townshend's plan depended on his ability to orchestrate precisely the attacks of his three columns. In order to achieve the intended effect on the enemy commander, he could initiate the Turning Attack only once the frontal attack by Hoghton's Minimum Force had attracted the enemy's attention, and he could unleash his Principal Mass only once Nurettin had focused on his threatened left flank. The Battle of Kut-al-Amara, however, had demonstrated the difficulty of directing separate formations from a command post several miles behind the front line. In an attempt to enhance his control over his force at Ctesiphon, Townshend decided to move his headquarters forward, so that he could observe more of the battle directly and issue timely instructions to his subordinates.

The commander of 6 Indian Division was certainly not the only senior officer to struggle with a sense of detachment caused by the unprecedented scale of operations and the limitations of real-time communications in the opening campaigns of the First World War. In 1914, British commanders such as Sir John French and Sir Douglas Haig attempted to overcome this detachment by visiting the front lines in the midst of battle. Townshend's response was more extreme, however, in that he intended not just to observe the battlefield briefly, but to exercise command from the front. This approach enabled him to respond to events more rapidly than he had at the battle of Kut-al-Amara. While the scarcity of telephone cable and the mirage precluded reliable communication by phone or heliograph, Townshend could send and receive information to his subordinates using messengers more quickly than had been possible at Kut. Moving forward also reduced opportunities for Nixon or Kemball to interfere with his conduct of the operation. Significantly, however, it also threatened to warp Townshend's perspective of the battle. Given the flatness of the terrain around Ctesiphon and the distorting tendencies of the mirage, it was impossible to observe the entire battlefield. Moreover, as French and Haig had both discovered, proximity to live fire could narrow a decision maker's perspective dramatically.[44] Developments in Townshend's immediate vicinity could therefore have a disproportionate influence over his decisions regarding the entire operation. Thus, while the limitations of 6 Indian Division's communications system left him with few more effective means of con-

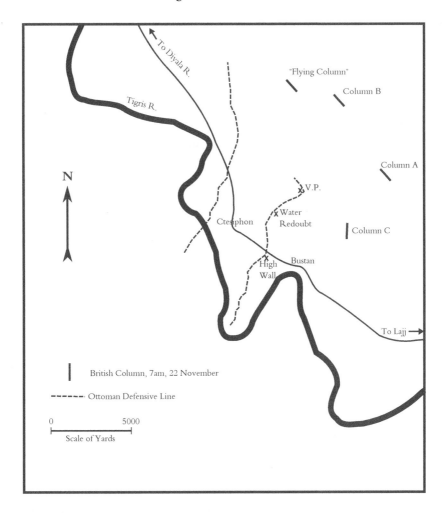

2.2. *The Battle of Ctesiphon, 22–25 November 1915*

trolling his force, Townshend's approach actually held the potential to undermine his efforts to achieve his intended effect upon the enemy.

THE BATTLE OF CTESIPHON

Townshend's location, along with his belief in the necessity of a rapid victory, influenced his decisions from the outset of the Battle of Cte-siphon. On the morning of 22 November, the commander of 6 Indian

Division established his headquarters with the divisional artillery, just behind Hoghton's Minimum Force, or Column C. (See map 2.2.) Townshend certainly planned to achieve a decisive victory. Prior to the battle, his staff issued detailed maps of enemy positions at Ctesiphon and the city of Baghdad, accompanied by instructions detailing "the methods to be adopted to push the enemy through and out of the city."[45]

Hoghton began his advance on schedule at 6:30 AM, but by 7:40 he had encountered no opposition. Meanwhile, Hamilton, on the right flank, was growing impatient. At 7:45 AM, he sent a message to Townshend asking permission to commence his advance. Despite the fact that Hoghton's diversionary attack had yet to make an impact, Townshend agreed, and the Turning Attack by Hamilton's Column B began at 8:30. Shortly afterward, Delamain, commanding the Principal Mass or Column A, observed what appeared to be the rearward movement of enemy forces and asked permission to initiate his own advance against V. P. Townshend consented, and by 9 AM, the ostensibly decisive attack had been unleashed.[46] Apparently convinced that the enemy was about to collapse, Townshend moved forward to join the Principal Mass. This bold initiative undoubtedly encouraged the troops, but it almost certainly undermined Townshend's ability to control the battle. As B. T. Reynolds, a British artillery officer at Ctesiphon, observed in a postwar history of the battle, "Townshend was now in a position where superhuman judgment and coolness would be required to avoid being influenced by events within his immediate and restricted circle of vision."[47]

On the morning of 22 November Townshend did not possess these qualities in sufficient measure. Around 11 AM, he received a message from Hoghton suggesting that the Principal Mass had advanced too rapidly, leaving the Minimum Force unable to dislodge the enemy forces in front of it.[48] Townshend responded by ordering Hoghton to move immediately to the right in order to support the ostensibly decisive attack by Delamain's Principal Mass. This was among the most controversial decisions of the battle, and the rationale behind it remains unclear. It likely stemmed in part, however, from Townshend's lack of confidence in Hoghton. Whatever the reasons for the slow pace of Hoghton's advance at the battle of Kut in September, it had subsequently tarnished his reputation in the upper ranks of 6 Indian Division. Kemball observed after the war, "T[ownshend] was never cordial to poor Hoghton afterwards!"[49]

From the rather narrow perspective afforded by Townshend's position at the front, it likely seemed that Hoghton was once again vacillating while the Principal Mass was heavily engaged and on the verge of inducing an enemy retirement. His decision, however, had unfortunate consequences for the entire force. Townshend's order required the Minimum Force to break off its engagement with the enemy and traverse an open plain in full view of Ottoman positions. An officer in Hoghton's brigade, W. C. Spackman, described this movement: "It is a great tribute to our troops and their officers that the extremely difficult manoeuvre of changing the direction of its attack to half right in mid-career was rapidly performed but it inevitably resulted in some confusion and intermingling of units, carried out as it was under increasing Turkish fire."[50] Thus, Hoghton's brigade joined the Principal Mass, but at considerable cost. As B. T. Reynolds argued, "Had Townshend been able to view the battle as a whole from further back, he would probably have allowed Hoghton to go ahead and capture the trenches in his immediate front before moving north to join Delamain's men. As it was, a certain amount of time was saved, but Hoghton's brigade had suffered crippling casualties."[51] As the official historian of the Mesopotamia campaign, F. J. Moberly, related in postwar correspondence, Hoghton's flank march "was responsible for heavy losses which directly affected the result" of the battle.[52]

By early afternoon on 22 November, 6 Indian Division had also inflicted significant casualties on the Ottomans, but Townshend's attack had not induced the collapse he expected. On the contrary, resistance stiffened as enemy infantry counterattacked and artillery bombarded British and Indian units that had captured parts of the Ottoman defensive line. This resistance was undoubtedly due in part to the size of the Ottoman force, which exceeded Townshend's expectations. At least as important, however, was the fact that the Ottoman command system did not respond as he expected to his orchestrated attack. While Townshend's location left him highly sensitive to the ebb and flow of the fighting, Nurettin remained well insulated from the front. His headquarters stood more than six miles from the front line, while the mirage made it impossible to see even two miles in the direction of the battle. Telephone lines laid between Ottoman headquarters and lower formations quickly broke down, forcing commanders to rely on messengers who frequently lost their way. According to the Turkish historian Muhammad Amin, who served on Nurettin's staff at Ctesiphon, "In this area, presenting no accidents of ground to serve as a guide, mirage ridden by day and obscure by night, it was an extraordinary piece of luck if a man succeeded in going and returning a few kilometres or sometimes a few hundred metres without making detours and losing his way."[53]

Thus, it appears that the Ottoman command system was not sufficiently sensitive to recognize the subtleties of Townshend's attack, let alone respond to them. Townshend assumed that Nurettin would react to the attacks of his three columns in sequence, shifting his forces to meet them as they occurred. After responding to pressure from Hoghton's column on his front, Nurettin would interpret the attack by Hamilton's Turning Attack as a repetition of Townshend's flanking movement at Kut-al-Amara, and accordingly send as many forces as possible to stop it. This would leave his center relatively vulnerable to the attack by the Principal Mass. In reality, Nurettin's headquarters does not appear to have noticed Hoghton's attack before becoming aware of Hamilton and Melliss's flanking movement. Nor did Nurettin react to the flank attack before Townshend unleashed the Principal Mass. As a result, rather than attacking a weakened Ottoman center, Delamain struck the strongest point in the enemy line, well defended and supported by reserves.[54]

Townshend's attacks took a heavy toll on Nurettin's force. By the end of 22 November, Amin described 38 and 45 Divisions as "crushed," while 51 Division "had lost extremely heavily."[55] The events of the day also shook the confidence of the Ottoman commander, who was forced to abandon the formidable front line of a defensive position he had spent weeks constructing. According to Amin: "It was an irreparable loss for the commander-in-chief that his first line of defence prepared and strengthened with the efforts of months and from all the local sources which the district could furnish should be captured by the enemy with such ease in the course of a few hours."[56] At least one observer, B. T. Reynolds, believed that if Townshend had renewed his attack on 23 November, Nurettin "would have withdrawn the remains of his army across the Diyala in the morning."[57]

The events of the day, however, had an even greater impact on the commander of 6 Indian Division. Townshend's plan had failed to overwhelm the Ottoman command system in the way that he had hoped. Moreover, by early afternoon on the 22nd the attack had lost momentum as the enemy counterattacked. At this point he observed the unsettling spectacle of able-bodied soldiers retiring from the fight. Townshend argued in his memoir that "it was evident that all control must have been lost owing to very heavy casualties amongst the British officers of Indian units. Here were hundreds of Indian soldiers streaming to the rear, because there were not enough white officers to keep them steady and in hand."[58] Whether or not Townshend's assessment of its causes was correct, this voluntary retirement was significant in that it seemed to confirm his worst fears about the fragility of his force.

The condition of 6 Indian Division at the end of the day extinguished the remaining confidence of its commander. When the fighting subsided at dusk, Townshend remained at the front, where he was witness to scenes of chaos and abject misery. While the divisional staff had planned for the transport of wounded soldiers forward into Baghdad, the failure of the attack on the 22nd forced them to improvise, collecting the unexpectedly large numbers of wounded at v.p. In his memoir Townshend recalled: "If I live a hundred years I shall not forget that night bivouac at 'v.p.' amongst hundreds of wounded, who were being brought in, loaded on commissariat carts, by which they were collected for hours during the night."[59] It is tempting to dismiss this account as an exaggeration intended to justify Townshend's subsequent decision to retreat. B. T. Reynolds, however, described the situation at v.p. in similar terms. According to Reynolds:

> When I got there the confusion was far worse. Guns, teams, transport, prisoners, and hundreds of wounded were all collected together in a narrow space, cut up in all directions by a maze of trenches and pitted with shell holes. The trenches were choked with dead. Hoghton and Hamilton were sorting out men from every regiment in the force, and setting them to clear out and man a line facing the Turks. In the midst of this confusion I found Townshend and the remains of his divisional staff, working by the light of a hurricane lamp, writing orders for the morrow.[60]

The disorganization and suffering around him almost certainly reinforced Townshend's concerns about the vulnerability of his force. As
Reynolds explained, "He knew that the Turks had been heavily reinforced. As the casualty reports came in he saw that his own ranks had
been sorely depleted. His mind must have turned to the long line of
communications – some 350 miles of river – between him and the sea,
with a bare two brigades to guard and keep it open until such time as
reinforcements could arrive from overseas."[61] Surrounded by casualties
and faced with an apparently defiant enemy, Townshend elected not to
renew the attack, ordering his division to concentrate at the Tigris to
secure ammunition, food, and water.

From 23 November the tempo of the battle slowed considerably as
both forces reorganized. According to W. C. Spackman, the medical
officer of the 48th Pioneers, part of Hoghton's 17th Brigade, "The picture was far from reassuring. We had lost 60% in dead and wounded.
Of our ten British officers, four had been killed and four wounded, and
all of the Indian officers except one had become casualties. The fighting force engaged was about 10,000 and the casualty list was later given
officially as 4,593. Behind us we had almost no reserves, and reinforcements were only just reaching Basra nearly 500 miles away by river."[62]
The failure of the previous day's attack and the heavy losses suffered
by 6 Indian Division depleted Townshend's enthusiasm for offensive
operations. Nurettin proved to be more resilient, but he struggled to organize and execute an attack. It was not until early in the afternoon of the
23rd that Nurettin recognized the abatement of Townshend's offensive.
Apparently owing to poor communications and faulty intelligence, the
Ottoman counterattack developed slowly and largely missed its target.
Unaware that Townshend's force had moved southward, 51 Division, the
strongest formation in Nurettin's force, "lost its way in the dark and never
even found an enemy." The other Ottoman formations suffered heavily
attacking entrenched units of 6 Indian Division, which remained capable
of mounting a stubborn defense.[63]

The morning of 24 November saw little activity on either side as
both commanders waited pensively for the other to act. With several aircraft at his disposal, Townshend likely had a better understanding of his
enemy's position than Nurettin, who relied on the infrequent and often

inaccurate reports of observers on the ground. Neither method of gathering intelligence proved entirely accurate, however, and exhaustion and apprehension led both commanders to interpret reports in the bleakest possible light. Given the condition of his force and the continued presence of the enemy, Townshend apparently concluded during the 24th that he had no choice but to retire, and issued orders for the withdrawal of his division on the morning of 26 November. Sir John Nixon advised against a withdrawal, observing, "At the present moment the enemy does not apparently realize your state, and they themselves are apprehensive of being attacked by you."[64]

Nixon was correct. Late in the evening of 24 November, Ottoman headquarters received a false report that Townshend was once again advancing. By this point, heavy casualties and the desertion of large numbers of rear-echelon troops had weakened the Ottoman force considerably. Moreover, Nurettin and his staff had struggled to respond to Townshend's initiatives for more than sixty hours with limited information and even less sleep. Their reaction to his apparent renewal of the offensive was therefore less than sanguine. According to Amin, "The terror and confusion aroused at HQ with the rapidity and effect of a thunderbolt by this frightful news is quite impossible to describe or picture."[65] Nurettin and his staff were aware that the abandonment of the Ctesiphon position would be devastating to the morale of their force and would encourage unrest among the inhabitants of the region. As Amin explained, "to fall further back and take refuge in the Diala line might cause the disruption and mutiny of certain tribes and elements only too glad of any opportunity and would cause a terrible despondency in the minds of all."[66] In addition, the Ottoman staff had little confidence that they could hold the Diyala line, which was much weaker than the Ctesiphon position. Nonetheless, despite the potentially catastrophic consequences of a retreat, Nurettin ordered an immediate retirement across the Diyala.

The Ottoman commander eventually regained his composure. On the morning of the 25th when subsequent reports revealed no movement by Townshend's force, the Ottoman commander ordered the reoccupation of his original position. Townshend, however, never regained any semblance of the confidence that had animated him on the first morning of the battle. Assuming that the enemy advance indicated the arrival of substantial Ottoman reinforcements, Townshend expedited the retirement of his force, and 6 Division initiated a hasty withdrawal on the evening of 25 November.

CONCLUSION

Given the numerical superiority of Ottoman forces at Ctesiphon, it is tempting to conclude that Charles Townshend's retirement to Kut-al-Amara was a foregone conclusion. Certainly this is what Townshend implied from 1916 onward, as he argued that he conducted the advance with a single division against his better judgment. In fact, from his return to Mesopotamia in August 1915 until the first day of the Battle of Ctesiphon, Townshend believed that he could inflict a decisive defeat on an Ottoman force of equal or greater strength. Even as his force became increasingly vulnerable after the inconclusive Battle of Kut-al-Amara, he remained confident that he could achieve victory at Ctesiphon using a series of carefully orchestrated frontal and flanking attacks that would overwhelm the enemy's command system and force Nurettin to initiate a panicked withdrawal. Townshend's plan, however, contained a flaw inherent in contemporary "effects based operations" in that it assumed that the enemy would react in a predictable manner to specific actions, despite the fact that these actions were executed in a chaotic environment and interpreted by the enemy through the crude filter of an imperfect intelligence-gathering apparatus.[67] Townshend's decision to command from the front exacerbated this problem. Driven by his belief in the necessity of a rapid victory due to the fragile morale of his force, as well as his experience at the Battle of Kut-al-Amara, Townshend attempted to minimize delays in the transmission of orders by accompanying his columns into battle. Influenced by the events unfolding directly in front of him, Townshend expedited the pace of his operation, making it even more difficult for the enemy to detect, let alone respond to, the separate attacks of his three columns. In the process, he made costly decisions such as directing Hoghton's entire brigade to traverse the battlefield under enemy fire. Thus, by the end of 22 November, his force had suffered heavily, but failed to provoke Nurettin's withdrawal.

Townshend may well have achieved greater success had he executed his plan more gradually, allowing each column to engage fully with the enemy before initiating the attack of the next. This would have allowed the Ottoman command system more opportunity to react to the attack in the way Townshend intended. Even if it did not induce the collapse of Nurettin's army on the first day of the battle, it would likely have been less costly to 6 Indian Division, leaving Townshend more able to continue the offensive on subsequent days. The Ottoman numerical advantage was not decisive. The enemy was much stronger than Townshend expected, and as Edward Erickson has demonstrated, Nurettin was capable of mounting effective counterattacks. That said, the Ottoman commander was certainly not convinced that he held a significant advantage. Ottoman intelligence, which was just as bad as Townshend's, drastically overestimated British strength at 20,000 troops.[68] Under the impression that he was outnumbered, Nurettin proved increasingly nervous throughout the battle, as demonstrated by his potentially disastrous retreat to the Diyala on the night of 24–25 November. Given the shakiness of the Ottoman commander, it seems possible that had Townshend orchestrated his attack more effectively on 22 November 1915, he may very well have compelled Nurettin to abandon his last strong defensive position below Baghdad, undermining Ottoman control over the local population in the process.

To point out Charles Townshend's mistakes is not to exonerate his superiors, who grossly underestimated the difficulties of capturing Baghdad with little more than a single division. Indeed, even if Townshend had won a quick victory on 22 November, occupying Baghdad for any significant period was beyond the capabilities of his force. Nonetheless, Townshend had an opportunity at Ctesiphon to defeat Nurettin and throw the Ottoman army in Mesopotamia into disarray. Had he done so, 6 Indian Division may have reached Baghdad, loosening significantly the Ottomans' hold on the region and compelling them to divert resources from elsewhere in an attempt to reestablish it. At the very least, a victory would have eliminated the perceived necessity of a rapid retirement, almost certainly sparing Townshend's force the fate that ultimately befell it at Kut-al-Amara.

THREE

RETREAT FROM CTESIPHON

25 NOVEMBER–7 DECEMBER

TOWNSHEND'S FORCE WITHDREW FROM THE BATTLEFIELD AT Ctesiphon on the evening of 25 November. Eight days later, after marching more than 90 miles with the enemy in pursuit, 6 Indian Division reached Kut-al-Amara. There Townshend decided to halt. Over the next four days, Ottoman forces approached the town and gradually established positions around it while British and Indian troops prepared defenses. On 7 December the Ottomans surrounded Kut-al-Amara completely and the siege began. Influenced by Townshend's memoir of the campaign, modern historians have generally assumed that the commander of 6 Indian Division resolved to defend Kut well before he reached the town. Arthur J. Barker has argued that "probably Townshend had intended to fall back and stand at Kut from the moment he realized that the Turks were on the march."[1] Russell Braddon has alleged that while Townshend initially anticipated only a short retreat from Ctesiphon, by 27 November his formative experience at Chitral had led him to fix his sights on Kut. There, surrounded on three sides by the Tigris, "he could sit out another siege; and, when he was relieved, a hero again, he would take command of an adequate force, seize Baghdad, become its governor . . . and who knew what else?"[2] In the most recent history of the war in Mesopotamia, the historian Charles Townshend challenges Braddon's interpretation. Nonetheless, he agrees that the commander of 6 Indian Division chose Kut as his objective during the initial stages of his retreat from Ctesiphon.[3]

This assumption has discouraged scholars from examining this period in detail. If Townshend resolved to defend Kut during the Battle of Ctesiphon or shortly afterward, then the siege appears to have been almost unavoidable. A careful assessment of Townshend's retirement from Ctesiphon as well as the Ottoman pursuit of his force reveals a more complex picture. This period was characterized by uncertainty, as the commanders on both sides struggled to discern the whereabouts and intentions of their adversary. Townshend initially intended to make only a short withdrawal from Ctesiphon, but his unplanned engagement with the enemy on 1 December led him to initiate a sustained retirement. When he finally reached Kut, the exhausted commander of 6 Indian Division was convinced that his force could go no further. By the time he reconsidered his decision to halt, neither Nixon nor the Ottomans would permit a further withdrawal.

WITHDRAWAL FROM CTESIPHON, 25–30 NOVEMBER

There is little evidence that Charles Townshend expected a lengthy retirement, let alone a prolonged siege, when he withdrew his force from the battlefield at Ctesiphon. On the morning of 25 November he decided to initiate a "leisurely" march to Lajj at approximately 2 PM the next day.[4] Townshend was aware of the potentially corrosive effects of a retirement on the morale of his already beleaguered force. He therefore issued communiqués to his British and Indian troops explaining that he wished to withdraw to Lajj primarily to shorten his supply lines. While enemy units on the right bank of the Tigris could disrupt the transport of food and supplies up the river to Ctesiphon, Lajj offered a more secure position downriver where 6 Indian Division could await reinforcements that would enable it to resume the offensive.[5] Given Townshend's concerns about the morale of his force, he had little to gain by issuing these communiqués if he actually anticipated a longer retirement. To abandon Lajj after publicly extolling its virtues could undermine the already fragile confidence of his soldiers and raise questions about his own leadership.

When aerial reconnaissance reports arrived later on the afternoon of 25 November indicating that Nurettin was about to assume the offensive, Townshend decided to expedite his withdrawal, directing his force to march that evening. He remained content, however, to retire to Lajj, just six miles downriver. Thus, the force departed around 7:30 PM on the

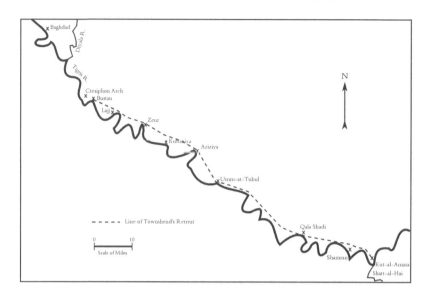

3.1. *Townshend's Retreat from Ctesiphon, 25 November–3 December 1915*

25th and arrived at Lajj at approximately 1 A M on the 26th.[6] The division
spent 26 November preparing for an extended stay. According to B. T.
Reynolds, the troops "started to make themselves comfortable and put
the place in a state of defence."[7] Townshend was not complacent. At
9:10 A M on 27 November he wired Nixon expressing concern about the
proximity of the enemy to his new position. He also noted that both Lajj
and his supply depot 22 miles downriver at Aziziya were subject to flooding during the winter, thus implying that he might have to withdraw even
further if reinforcements did not arrive quickly. Nonetheless, neither the
Ottomans nor the rising Tigris seem to have caused him great concern,
as he informed Nixon that he intended to remain at Lajj for a week until
available rations for his Indian troops were exhausted, before moving on
to Aziziya where even more supplies were available.[8]

Later that morning, however, cavalry and aerial reconnaissance reports indicated that approximately 12,000 Ottoman infantry along with
400 cavalry were advancing toward Lajj. In his memoir, Townshend
contended that this news convinced him of the necessity of withdrawing
all the way to Kut-al-Amara, over 60 miles downriver from Aziziya. In

his words: "I began to see that there was no halting on the Baghdad side of Kut-al-Amara, if the enemy really intended an offensive with large forces. If he once hooked on to my little force I should be pinned down and surrounded."[9] This assertion may have been a retrospective attempt to justify Townshend's subsequent retreat to Kut. There is no other evidence to suggest that he had made this decision on 27 November. Nonetheless, for Townshend this was the first indication that Nurettin was willing to leave prepared positions and take the offensive. It appears to have shaken his assumption that 6 Indian Division would be able to reorganize and await reinforcements in close proximity to the enemy. Therefore, upon learning of Nurettin's unexpected advance, Townshend quickly issued orders for an immediate withdrawal to Aziziya, in the process abandoning "a considerable quantity of stores."[10]

The force arrived in Aziziya between 4 and 10 AM on the morning of the 28th. While this was an onerous march, it appears to have been the result of prudence rather than panic on Townshend's part. If Nurettin had any intention of advancing, Lajj was simply too close to the Ottoman force at Ctesiphon to allow 6 Indian Division to reorganize, let alone await the arrival of the nearest significant reinforcements, which were not expected to arrive until mid-December. Aziziya was the closest point downriver where there were sufficient rations and supplies available to sustain his division for an extended period. Townshend therefore hoped that it offered a temporary sanctuary where he would be able to await the arrival of reinforcements out of Nurettin's reach.

On 28 November, however, these hopes began to evaporate. According to Townshend, upon arriving at Aziziya he was "disagreeably surprised to find only six days' supplies there, instead of the twenty days' British and seven days' Indian I had reckoned on."[11] To make matters worse, the morale and discipline of his force was beginning to fray, with soldiers looting stockpiles of supplies in the town. T. A. Chalmers, the commander of a hospital boat accompanying the force, observed significant disorder on the 28th. As he related in his diary, "The scene of confusion this afternoon when sepoys and Tommies were looting kits, stores, jams etc., was like a riot."[12] Townshend appreciated the tenuous nature of his position at Aziziya and began to consider seriously the possibility of retiring as far downriver as Kut, but he continued to doubt Nurettin's stomach for offensive action. He explained in a 4 PM telegram to Nixon, "I expect he will advance to Zor [Zeur], but if he moves from that place to attack me here I shall refuse battle and fall back to Kut in all probability." Nonetheless, he continued, "personally I do not think he will fight below Zor so far away from his beloved entrenchments at Ctesiphon."[13]

The Ottoman commander quickly proved Townshend wrong. On the afternoon of 29 November, the commander of 6 Indian Division received an aerial reconnaissance report indicating that the main body of the enemy force had reached Zeur, with an advanced guard occupying Al Kutuniya, just six miles from Aziziya. Townshend clearly recognized that the Aziziya position was no longer tenable, but he was still not convinced that Nurettin posed an immediate threat to his force. The commander of 6 Indian Division ordered his force to conduct a relatively short withdrawal to Umm-at-Tubul, less than eight miles to the southeast, commencing at 9 AM the next morning.[14] In addition, when General Nixon sent a message later that evening asking "what troops can you spare" to help neutralize Arab and Ottoman forces interfering with the corps commander's party below Kut, Townshend dispatched the entire 30th Brigade along with a cavalry regiment and artillery, all under the command of Major-General Melliss. Thus, 6 Indian Division and its associated shipping departed Aziziya on morning of the 30th. While Melliss's force continued toward Kut, the rest of the division reached its objective "about midday."[15] By this point, Townshend's ultimate intent was to retire well beyond Umm-at-Tubul to Qala Shadi, approximately 30 miles further downriver. There his force would establish an "entrenched camp" in order to cover the concentration of reinforcements at Kut, another 20 miles down the Tigris.[16] In his memoir, Townshend acknowledged that his division could have marched much further on 30 November, but he claimed that the senior naval officer attached to his force, Captain Nunn, had advised him that Umm-at-Tubul represented the furthest point attainable by his shipping due to the difficulties associated with navigating the river. If 6 Indian Division outpaced its ships, some of them "would surely fall into the hands of the enemy."[17]

Historians have challenged Townshend's assertion. According to F. J. Moberly, Nunn categorically denied making such an assessment and in fact pointed out to Townshend that by stopping at Umm-at-Tubul early in the afternoon on the 30th, the ships had wasted several hours of daylight during which they might have continued moving downriver. A. J. Barker has argued that Nunn limited the journey of his ships because he believed that Umm-at-Tubul was the furthest point attainable by Townshend's exhausted troops.[18] Regardless of the exact nature of the misunderstanding between Townshend and Nunn, it is unlikely that Townshend would have halted at Umm-at-Tubul and allowed his force to sit idly during the afternoon of the 30th had he genuinely believed that it was in imminent danger. Nor would he have detached such a significant component of his force, under one of his most trusted commanders, in response to Nixon's general query regarding the availability of troops. Despite growing evidence of a sustained enemy pursuit, Townshend was content to halt relatively early on 30 November, with only a weak force of 6,000 infantry, 1,250 cavalry, and 26 guns at his disposal.[19]

ENCOUNTER AT UMM-AT-TUBUL

Given the heavy losses suffered by the Ottomans at Ctesiphon and the initial hesitancy of Nurettin's pursuit, Townshend's relative nonchalance is not entirely unfathomable. Ottoman casualties totalled 9,500 during the period 22–24 November, more than double the number incurred by 6 Indian Division. One of the two newly arrived Anatolian formations, 45 Division, had lost up to 60 percent of its strength.[20] While losses were not as heavy in 35 and 38 Divisions, the two formations composed of Iraqi conscripts, their discipline was apparently suspect in the aftermath of the battle. In his account of the campaign, the staff officer Muhammed Amin complained of "the state of disorder" of 38 Division in the initial stages of the Ottoman advance from Ctesiphon. According to Amin, "The men had taken off their boots and nether garments and hung them over their shoulders and were marching barefoot with limbs unconstrained in small separate groups."[21]

Consequently, Nurettin made little effort to pressure Townshend's force in the immediate aftermath of the battle at Ctesiphon. The Ottoman force arrived at Lajj only on 28 November, a full day after Townshend had withdrawn from the town in response to reports of approaching enemy forces. Upon learning that the British had moved on to Aziziya,

Nurettin continued his advance on the evening of the 28th to Zeur, just under ten miles downriver from Lajj.[22] The next day, Ottoman cavalry harassing British ships on the Tigris encountered resistance from British cavalry. Apparently reluctant to risk an engagement with the rest of Townshend's force, Nurettin halted at Al Kutuniya, less than ten miles from Zeur and well short of Aziziya.[23] The Ottoman force did not reach Aziziya until 2.30 PM on 30 November. Upon their arrival, however, Nurettin and his staff encountered evidence of a panicked British departure, with ammunition, food, firewood, officers' belongings, and even official documents left behind. According to Amin, "All of these matters and especially the official papers having been thrown about haphazard, scattered and abandoned, there being no time to destroy them, showed with what haste and hurry the enemy had evacuated the place and gone off."[24]

While it was not an accurate gauge of Townshend's disposition on the afternoon of the 30th, the detritus left by 6 Indian Division emboldened the Ottoman commander. At 4:30 PM, Nurettin ordered his force to continue on to Umm-at-Tubul immediately. Nurettin undoubtedly believed that he had to expedite his advance in order to inflict a decisive defeat upon Townshend's force before it was reinforced, but in his eagerness to attain a quick victory, he was taking a significant risk. With less than an hour before dusk, the Ottoman commander was pushing his troops into unfamiliar territory in the dark without even the benefit of maps.[25] While reconnaissance aircraft had joined the Ottoman force on 27 November, they were of no use at night. Thus, Nurettin had to rely on his cavalry and the reports of Arabs in the vicinity for intelligence regarding the whereabouts of his enemy.

These same sources had proven woefully inadequate in detecting Townshend's movements at Ctesiphon, and they were even less effective on the night of 30 November. As the Ottoman force began its advance from Ctesiphon, Nurettin had directed his cavalry brigade to "push on in pursuit of the British."[26] Subsequent reports from the cavalry describing Townshend's retirement led the Ottoman commander to believe that it remained in contact with the enemy. After beginning 30 November in the vicinity of Aziziya, however, the cavalry brigade had inexplicably fallen behind the rest of the Ottoman force as it advanced on the same town. From this vantage point, the cavalry mistook Nurettin's army for

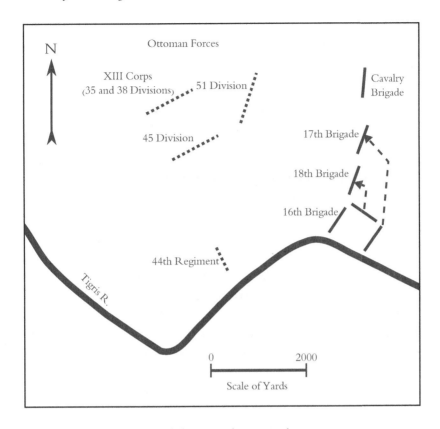

3.2. *The Encounter at Umm-at-Tubul, 30 November–1 December 1915*

6 Indian Division, sending erroneous reports regarding the whereabouts of the enemy that can only have perplexed the Ottoman commander. The Ottoman cavalry brigade continued to wander after dark on the 30th, and eventually returned to the now empty town of Aziziya, where a cornucopia of abandoned British supplies diverted the Ottoman troopers, who "passed the night in drunkenness among this priceless display of plunder."[27]

The misdirection of his cavalry left Nurettin moving forward on the evening of the 30th without an advanced guard to detect the presence of the enemy. To make matters worse, despite the confusing reports received from the cavalry brigade, he continued to believe, or perhaps hope, that it remained in front of his main force. Thus, around 7 PM, when the Ottoman commander and his staff spotted camp fires approximately two miles ahead, they deduced that they were approaching their own advanced guard. A burst of small arms fire at about the same time was a more ominous indicator of hostile forces in the vicinity, but the shield ostensibly provided by the cavalry screen led Nurettin to attribute the bullets to mischievous Arabs rather than elements of Townshend's division. Shortly afterward, however, a reconnaissance party ascertained that the campfires belonged to the British, and Nurettin directed his artillery to open fire. In response, British ships on the Tigris turned searchlights toward the source of the bombardment. After identifying the Ottoman force, the British quickly extinguished both the lights and the campfires.[28]

By continuing on from Aziziya to Umm-at-Tubul, Nurettin had in fact caught up with Townshend's force. The two armies spent the night of 30 November little more than two miles from one another. Fortunately for 6 Indian Division, faulty intelligence, the play of chance, and the Ottoman commander's own assumptions left him unaware of the opportunity that had suddenly presented itself to his force. Surmising that it had encountered a weak enemy rearguard, Nurettin ordered 51 Division to dispatch a single regiment to drive it away. In the darkness, however, the assigned unit, the 44th Regiment, was unable to locate the enemy. After moving between the two forces without detecting either, it eventually reached the Tigris, where it spent the night. A second party sent to locate the 44th Regiment returned just after midnight, reporting that it had taken fire from an unidentified source. In light of erroneous reports from local Arabs indicating that Townshend's force had withdrawn "to a distance of 3 or 4 hours march," Nurettin and his staff concluded that the second party had been fired upon by the missing 44th Regiment. Apparently convinced that no enemy forces remained in the immediate vicinity, Nurettin ordered his force to halt until well after daylight the next morning.[29]

While Townshend had initially underestimated the threat posed by the enemy advance, he discerned more quickly than his Ottoman counterpart the implications of the sudden encounter on the evening of the 30th. The brief salvo of enemy shells and the sound of cart or gun wheels moving in the darkness convinced the commander of 6 Indian Division that the main body of Nurettin's force was in close proximity.[30] Among Townshend's subordinates, the recognition that their enemy was upon them induced profound pessimism. In a postwar interview, Henry Rich, then a lieutenant in the 120th Infantry, recalled, "During the night there was a sound of wheels and we could see the camp fires of the Turks all round us, and there I like many others of the force decided that is where we finish."[31] The commander of 6 Indian Division kept his composure. He quickly recognized that it would be impossible to retire before daylight. His shipping would be unable to navigate the Tigris in darkness, and the movement of his army would almost certainly attract the attention of the enemy. Townshend therefore resolved to attack at dawn, in the hope of buying time to enable his ships and transport to escape. The force had camped alongside the river with the three remaining infantry brigades, the 16th, 17th, and 18th, forming a semicircle around the transport. Townshend directed these three brigades to form a line and advance at daybreak, with the cavalry brigade moving forward on their right flank. He also sent a message to Melliss, camped ten miles downriver, to return immediately to Umm-at-Tubul. Townshend's plan was similar to that which he had employed at Kut-al-Amara in September. He intended to hold the enemy in place with a frontal attack by one of his infantry brigades, while the other two infantry brigades and the cavalry turned Nurettin's left flank. If Melliss arrived in time, his brigade would also attack the Ottoman left.[32]

Given that Townshend did not know the exact location of Nurettin's army, much less its left flank, the likelihood of 6 Indian Division implementing this scheme successfully was small. Ultimately, however, Townshend did not require the flawless execution of his plan to extricate his force. The division was active well before daylight on 1 December. By 6:30 AM, the three infantry brigades had moved into line with the cavalry brigade moving forward on their left. Meanwhile the transport was moving off in the direction of Kut. At approximately 6:45 the two armies became visible to one another. In his memoir of the campaign, the medical officer W. C. Spackman described the sight that materialized to the northwest of the British position: "A very large and well-ordered camp with lines of white tents, horses and mules being groomed or led off in strings to the river. In fact a busy camp at its morning chores and getting ready for a leisurely start all unsuspecting and at a range of 2,500 to 3,000 yards!"[33]

The enemy had not been caught entirely unawares. As early as 6 AM, the Ottomans had detected the movement of British forces in front of them, and Nurettin ordered 51 Division on his left flank to attack, with the adjacent 45 Division advancing in support on the right. When daylight broke these forces had begun to move toward Townshend's force. In response, Townshend expedited his own attack, directing the infantry to move forward and the cavalry to outflank the advancing 51 Division while the artillery opened fire on the Ottoman camp. According to the official historian, the British guns had a "great and immediate effect," halting the advance of 51 Division and forcing 45 Division into a rapid retirement.[34] The artillery wreaked even greater havoc on XIII Corps, which had camped in rear of 45 and 51 Divisions. The sudden barrage killed the commander of the corps and wounded the commanders of 35 and 38 Divisions, which comprised it. Several other senior officers were also killed or wounded. Thrown into disarray and deprived of leadership, the troops of the two divisions began retiring back toward Aziziya.[35]

The artillery barrage left the Ottoman force extremely vulnerable. According to Amin, the British fire "totally disorganised the 13th A[rmy] C[orps] and 45th Division and kept them for hours out of the battle."[36] Only 51 Division, on the Ottoman left, managed to hold its position. Despite the onset of enemy artillery fire, Townshend observed the action calmly. According to E. O. Mousley, an artillery officer present at Umm-at-Tubul, "One could not help but feel the keenest admiration for General Townshend, so steady, collected and determined in action, so kind, quick and confident. There, totally indifferent to the shell fire, he stood watching the issue, receiving reports from the various orderly officers and giving every attention to the progress of the transport.... More than once I caught a humorous smile on the General's face as some shell just missed us."[37] G. W. R. Bishop, a "galloper" who carried messages between Townshend's headquarters and 16th Brigade, commented, "I was struck by his immaculate appearance and utter calm and detachment, although standing periodically in the gun fire, and with the Turks 1000 yards or less away."[38]

Recognizing the enemy's confusion, Townshend seized the opportunity to extricate his force. By 8:30 AM, all of his transport and shipping had left Umm-at-Tubul and the three infantry brigades were withdrawing from the battlefield. The Cavalry Brigade followed shortly afterward.[39] Assuming Townshend's retreat to Kut to have been inevitable, modern historians have not examined the engagement of Umm-at-Tubul in significant detail. Writers contemporary to the event, however, have argued that it was an opportunity that the commander of 6 Indian Division failed to grasp. B. T. Reynolds, an artillery officer present at Umm-at-Tubul, contended in a postwar article that "it is obvious that fortune was holding out both hands to Townshend and offering him the opportunity of a lifetime. Had he let the action develop, it is as certain as anything can be that he would have crushed the scattered battalions of the 51st Division, the only part of the Turkish army to stand up to him, and dealt . . . a blow that would have sent . . . [Nurettin] scuttling back behind the Diyala."[40]

The *Official History* was more charitable toward Townshend. Moberly's account acknowledges that the battle at Umm-at-Tubul was "an action that had been forced upon him, and which he did not desire." In explaining Townshend's decision to break off the engagement, however, Moberly comments that Townshend "probably did not realize" the disorganization and demoralization of the Ottoman force, thus implying that he missed a chance to inflict a significant defeat on the enemy.[41] The official historian went further in private correspondence, suggesting in a letter to the military historian W. D. Bird, "that if Townshend had pressed his advantage then, he'd have completely knocked into the Turkish pursuit."[42]

These criticisms suggest that if Townshend had possessed sufficient patience to allow the full implementation of his plan, he might have won a more significant victory, forcing Nurettin into a hasty retreat. Townshend's conduct of operations at Ctesiphon may be susceptible to this criticism, but at Umm-at-Tubul there is little evidence that he intended to inflict a decisive defeat on the enemy. Townshend knew neither the strength nor the disposition of the hostile force that had unexpectedly arrived in his vicinity on the evening of 30 November. He was also without an entire infantry brigade and one of his most trusted commanders.

While he had quickly recalled Melliss, Townshend had no idea when the 30th Brigade would actually arrive at Umm-at-Tubul. Moreover, the fact that he directed his transport and shipping to start moving before daybreak suggests that he had no intention of holding his position, let alone advancing. Overall, given Townshend's lack of knowledge of his enemy's capabilities and his eagerness to dispatch his transport, it seems reasonable to accept Townshend's assertion in his memoir that his principal aim was "to extricate myself from the clutch of the enemy."[43]

Even if Townshend had allowed his infantry brigades to continue their advance, it is unlikely that he would have discerned the opportunity to achieve more decisive results. After the initial shock of the British artillery bombardment, Ottoman resistance intensified. While the bulk of Nurettin's force fell back, elements of 51 Division checked the advance of Townshend's cavalry on their left flank. The 44th Regiment, which had camped along the Tigris after failing to find 6 Indian Division the previous night, quickly detected 6 Indian Division in the daylight and opened fire, destroying two British gunboats on the river. In addition, despite its misadventures on the night of the 30th, Nurettin's cavalry "suddenly" appeared on the battlefield the next morning, strengthening the threatened flank of 51 Division. Thus, Townshend's force withdrew from Umm-at-Tubul under "heavy enemy gunfire."[44] Nor did the pressure cease once the force left the battlefield. Nurettin's artillery and cavalry harassed the retiring units until around midday, compelling Townshend to order his own mounted troops and batteries to cover the retreat. According to E. O. Mousley: "Gradually we out-distanced the enemy, the Cavalry Brigade keeping him back. Once they caught us and sent shells wildly over our heads. The Turks don't know enough about the science of gunnery. If their fuses had been more correct our casualties could not have failed to have been more heavy."[45]

THE DECISION TO DEFEND KUT-AL-AMARA

While enemy pressure dissipated by the afternoon of 1 December, the encounter at Umm-at-Tubul had injected a newfound sense of urgency into Townshend's conduct of the retirement. After breaking contact with Nurettin's force, 6 Indian Division marched steadily throughout the day. Even at sunset Townshend resisted entreaties from his brigade commanders to allow the troops to stop briefly and drink from the Tigris. As he recalled, "I said, 'Once these men get down to the river bank, we shall not collect them for hours. They will lie by the water, drink, and fall asleep like logs. I do not know that the Turks are not a few miles behind.'" Only at Qala Shadi, 36 miles from Umm-at-Tubul, did the commander of 6 Indian Division agree to a halt. According to Townshend, the troops, "lay down on the road in column and slept in ranks as they were – and I had *no food* to distribute!" [46] While the last units of the division did not arrive at Qala Shadi until early on the morning of 2 December, Townshend ordered the retirement to resume at daybreak. The increasingly fatigued and hungry troops marched another 18 miles on the 2nd, arriving at Shamran, about 6 miles west of Kut, during the afternoon. There they received rations and spent the night.

Even on 2 December, Townshend's defense of Kut was not a foregone conclusion. During the afternoon, the commander of the Kut garrison, Brigadier-General J. C. Rimington, met with Townshend at Shamran and expressed his doubts regarding the wisdom of holding the town. As Rimington explained in a postwar article, Kut was located on a peninsula surrounded on three sides by a loop in the Tigris. Thus, the Ottomans had only to establish positions along the base or "neck" of the peninsula in order to trap Townshend's force, after which they could bypass it entirely and move down the river. Rimington contended that 6 Indian Division would be less vulnerable to encirclement at Es Sinn, where Townshend had defeated Nurettin in late September. Just six miles down the Tigris from Kut, the Es Sinn position ran across the Tigris with the Suwada, Ataba, and Suwaikiya marshes complicating any attempts to outflank it from the north. South of the Tigris, old canals and riverbeds slowed the movement of large forces, as British commanders would discover in early 1916. Holding Es Sinn, Townshend's force could threaten the advance of Ottoman forces further down the Tigris, or down the Shatt-al-Hai, which ran south from Kut toward Nasiriya, on the Euphrates. Rimington also made clear that he could quickly evacuate ammunition and supplies from Kut. On the evening of 29 November he had wired Townshend explaining that he could "lift and place below Es Sinn the whole of stores at [the] Advanced Base in 48 hours." [47]

Having received no reply from Townshend by 2 December, Rimington reiterated at their meeting that he had 30 *mahelas,* "400 or 500 men of the garrison and at least 400 or 500" local civilians available to move supplies and ammunition down the Tigris to Es Sinn. While Rimington acknowledged that the weakened 6 Indian Division would have difficulty holding the entrenchments at Es Sinn, he argued that Townshend's force could probably have resisted pressure from the exhausted and depleted Ottoman force until Major-General George Younghusband's 28th Brigade arrived to reinforce it in mid-December.[48]

By the time he reached Shamran, however, the commander of 6 Indian Division had decided to make a stand at Kut-al-Amara. After listening to Rimington's arguments at their meeting on the afternoon of 2 December, Townshend informed the garrison commander that he intended to halt. When Townshend entered Kut the next morning, Rimington's subordinate, Lieutenant-Colonel S. de V. Julius, approached Townshend's staff with the suggestion that 6 Indian Division continue retiring downriver so that they might unite with the 28th Brigade. According to Julius, however, he was informed that "there is nothing we don't know about the lines of communication, and we don't want to hear any more."[49] On the morning of the 3rd, Townshend sent a message to Nixon and issued a communiqué to his troops explaining his decision. In his memoir Townshend detailed the strategic benefits of the Kut position, emphasizing that it enabled his force to prevent the Ottomans from pushing further down the Tigris or down the Shatt-al-Hai, while covering the concentration of reinforcements to the south.[50] He acknowledged the possibility of retiring to Es Sinn, from which Rimington believed 6 Indian Division could achieve the same objectives without being surrounded. Nonetheless he maintained that his force was too weak to hold the Ottoman entrenchments there, and that it would be "enveloped and overwhelmed in a decisive battle in three or four days' time."[51] Moreover, he argued that his force was "too exhausted to move a yard further at the moment," let alone evacuate supplies from Kut to Es Sinn.[52] In his memoir Townshend placed great emphasis on the fatigue of his force, which had repelled the enemy at Umm-at-Tubul and then completed two long marches with little food or rest. He recalled, "Never have I seen anything like the exhaustion of the troops after we reached

Kut. The great bulk of the Indian troops would not move at all, although I got the British to work on 4th December, just as the Turkish advanced guard came into sight!"[53]

A variety of sources support Townshend's assertions regarding the condition of the soldiers and sepoys of 6 Indian Division. According to the *Official History*, "the troops were so weary that it required constant effort to keep them going, in spite of the fact that they knew they could expect no mercy from the Arabs."[54] Officers involved in the retirement had similar recollections. In 1970, Henry Rich surveyed other survivors of the siege of Kut regarding Townshend's command decisions before and during the siege of Kut. Several respondents attested to the fatigue of the troops and horses upon reaching the town. According to H. G. Thomson, who commanded an artillery battery, "The officers and men of the How [itzer] Battery and their teams were completely exhausted on reaching Shamran Camp."[55] Warren Sandes, a captain in the divisional Bridging Train, went further, declaring, "I think that when we reached Kut from Ctesiphon we were *exhausted* not merely tired. We needed at least a week's rest."[56] Historians have generally agreed with Townshend's assessment. According to A. J. Barker, "the one factor of paramount importance" in Townshend's decision to halt at Kut was the fact that "his men needed rest there and then."[57] In his recent history of the war in Mesopotamia, the historian Charles Townshend accepts the justification offered by his namesake, contending that "all the accounts of the men of the 6th Division stress their exhaustion."[58]

Many members of Townshend's force, however, maintained that the condition of the troops was more easily remediable. H. S. Soden, a wireless operator attached to the division, commented, "They were not exhausted, only tired and hungry."[59] Royal Flying Corps Captain T. R. Wells agreed, adding that "two days' rest and good food would have put them on their feet again."[60] J. J. Bouch expressed similar sentiments, commenting: "At such times its [*sic*] surprising what 24 hours' rest can do to a man. A fag, a few mugs of hot tea and some sleep and a good swear."[61] According to John Mellor, a lieutenant in the 1/Oxford and Buckinghamshire Light Infantry, "Certainly in British units they were normal after a day's rest. . . . The Indian troops appeared more exhausted, but we thought this largely emotional."[62] Mellor's recollections echo

Townshend's comments regarding the condition of the Indian troops, but others painted a different picture. Brigadier-General W. S. Delamain, commanding the 16th Brigade at Kut, contended that both the British and Indian troops under his command were able to continue the retirement after a single day's rest.[63] Officers in close contact with the Indians concurred. R. V. Martin, a medical officer in the 22nd Punjabis, recalled, "As regards the condition of the Indian troops, I would say they were in very good shape on arrival." Martin acknowledged that there were stragglers. Nonetheless, he maintained that "any men I picked up on retreat were mostly Gurkhas. They were no good marching."[64] Rich himself remembered Gurkhas falling behind during the retirement from Umm-at-Tubul, but as he explained, "They had done an extra march to us. We offered to help them or carry their rifles or anything like that but the little men would have none of it. They just solidly went on."[65]

The relatively modest casualty list incurred by 6 Indian Division during the retirement also suggests that it largely retained its cohesion upon its arrival at Kut. According to the official history, Townshend's force lost 37 killed, 281 wounded, and 218 missing at Umm-at-Tubul and during the subsequent retreat on 1–2 December.[66] The majority of those killed and wounded likely became casualties during the engagement with the Ottomans on the morning of the 1st. Even if most of those listed as missing disappeared during the subsequent retreat, they still represent a relatively small proportion of Townshend's force. Moreover, the fact that 6 Indian Division immediately began preparing defenses upon entering Kut also suggests that the troops were not completely spent upon their arrival. According to W. C. Spackman, "My own unit, the 48th Pioneers, were tired and hungry after bringing the Divisional Transport Column 50 miles from Umm-at-Tubul to Kut in 30 hours, but certainly few of us were 'exhausted'—we set to and dug like hell to prepare the defences."[67] This required sustained effort. G. L. Heawood, another lieutenant in the 1/Oxford and Buckinghamshire Light Infantry, recalled "never ending digging and night duties over the first three weeks at Kut."[68]

The historian Townshend is correct in pointing out that "forced marches under enemy pressure" impose greater demands than digging trenches.[69] Nonetheless, the recollections of officers involved in the retreat from Umm-at-Tubul, the moderate casualty list, and the sustained labor the troops commenced immediately following their arrival at Kut indicate that 6 Indian Division was not yet at the limit of its endurance when it marched into the town on the morning of 3 December. British and Indian soldiers alike were undoubtedly fatigued, but given food and a few hours rest, they almost certainly could have continued their retirement, particularly given the slackening of the Ottoman pursuit following the unexpected skirmish at Umm-at-Tubul. After suffering nearly 750 casualties on the morning of the 1st, Nurettin paused, losing track of Townshend's force entirely for approximately forty-eight hours. By 4 December the main body of the Ottoman force had reached Shamran, two days behind 6 Indian Division. Here it was forced to halt to await the arrival of supplies.[70] Ottoman forces did not close off the neck of the Kut peninsula on the night of 6 December, and they did not surround the town completely until the next day.[71] Thus, it is likely that 6 Indian Division could have completed the relatively short march to Es Sinn and saved a substantial proportion of the ammunition and supplies stockpiled at Kut, as Rimington and Julius suggested.

Contrary to Townshend's assertion in his memoir, it is also doubtful that Nurettin's force was capable of quickly "enveloping" and "overwhelming" 6 Indian Division in the Es Sinn position. When it finally reached Kut, the Ottoman army was tired, depleted by attrition, and suffering from low morale. The arrival of 52 Division from Baghdad around 9 December bolstered Nurettin's strength by about 4,600 combatants, to a total of approximately 19,000. Without maps of the area, however, or adequate ammunition for its artillery, the Ottoman force was capable of executing only rudimentary frontal assaults across open ground.[72] According to Edward Erickson, these tactics "allowed the British and Indian soldiers to maintain deadly fields of fire against which the Turkish attacks foundered" when Nurettin attacked Kut on 10–11 December. Thus, the attacks "failed to make much of an impression" on Townshend's force. [73] The Es Sinn position was certainly not impregnable, but neither was it as vulnerable to encirclement as the town of Kut. Rimington certainly believed that Townshend's force could have resisted any attacks that the enemy was capable of mount-

ing against it until mid-December. This may have allowed the arrival
of reinforcements in the form of the 28th Brigade, which Nixon had
initially ordered to proceed to Kut as quickly as possible.[74] At the very
least, retiring to Es Sinn would have delayed Nurettin's encirclement
of 6 Indian Division, altering subsequent decisions by commanders on
both sides and potentially changing the course of the entire campaign.

It is not particularly productive to speculate further regarding the
ultimate outcome of the retirement had Townshend continued to Es
Sinn. It is sufficient to conclude that Townshend's decision to halt at
Kut was neither the only, nor even the best, option open to him on
3 December. Why then did he resolve to defend the town, eschewing
other alternatives? Fatigue undoubtedly influenced his decision. Since
arriving at Umm-at-Tubul on the afternoon of 30 November, the commander of 6 Indian Division had planned and executed an attack on
Nurettin's force, broken contact with the enemy in the midst of their
engagement, and then completed an extended retirement with very little
rest. If this ordeal left his troops tired, it must have taken an even heavier
toll on the fifty-four-year old Townshend, who had returned to India
due to illness as recently as the previous summer. Townshend's distant relationship with his Indian subordinates also contributed to his
decision. The commander of 6 Indian Division had expressed concern
about the quality of Indian reinforcements that had joined his force in
October, and the performance of Indian soldiers at Ctesiphon had exacerbated his concerns. When Indian troops wavered during the retreat
from Umm-at-Tubul, it would have been all too easy for an exhausted
commander with a limited grasp of the morale and condition of specific
Indian units to conclude that they all were on the verge of collapse. In
addition, Townshend's expectations regarding the arrival of reinforcements encouraged him to downplay the dangers of remaining at Kut.
On 27 November Nixon had informed him that the 28th Brigade would
reinforce 6 Indian Division around 15 December, with two additional
brigades arriving "as soon as possible" afterward.[75] With his force apparently close to disintegration, Kut appeared to the exhausted Townshend
to be a haven in which he could rest and feed his troops while awaiting
the imminent arrival of relief.

Over the next seventy-two hours, however, Townshend began to recognize this haven as a trap. On 5 December he received a message from Nixon indicating that a relief force might not reach him for two months. By this point 6 Indian Division and its commander had eaten, slept, and recuperated considerably since their arrival at Kut. With the prospect of a prolonged siege, defending the town was no longer essential or desirable. Thus, Townshend replied the next morning proposing that his division retire all the way to Ali Gharbi, more than 50 miles further down the Tigris. He now claimed that he could save "most of the ammunition . . . and bring away heavy guns."[76] With Ottoman forces closing in on the town on 6 December, it is doubtful that 6 Indian Division could have withdrawn from Kut without significant casualties, let alone evacuated the supplies, ammunition, and guns in the town. In addition, while Sir John Nixon had initially given Townshend considerable latitude in deciding where to halt, by the 6th he had accepted Townshend's earlier arguments that his force should stand at Kut in order to prevent Ottoman forces from moving down the Shatt-al-Hai while covering the assembly of British reinforcements down the Tigris. He therefore directed Townshend to remain at Kut, assuring him two months was an "outside limit" and that Younghusband's force would reach Shaikh Saad, about 40 miles downriver, within a week.[77] By 7 December the opportunity to withdraw had disappeared, as Ottoman forces invested Kut and began digging trenches along the base of the peninsula.[78]

CONCLUSION

It is tempting to view the siege of Kut-al-Amara as an inevitable outcome of the Battle of Ctesiphon, or even as an attempt by the ambitious and frustrated Townshend to replicate his earlier success in defending Chitral in 1898. In reality, the defense of Kut was the result of an accumulation of often hasty decisions made by a fatigued commander in the context of ambiguous information regarding his own army and that of his enemy. Initially, Townshend intended to make only a short withdrawal from Ctesiphon in order to await reinforcements and supplies that would enable him to resume the offensive. Growing evidence of a sustained enemy pursuit compelled the commander of 6 Indian Division to continue its retirement further than he had initially planned, but even on 30 November, Townshend remained relatively confident that he could reorganize his force without Nurettin's interference. The unexpected engagement with the Ottomans at Umm-at-Tubul proved to be a rude awakening. In its aftermath Townshend accelerated dramatically the pace of his withdrawal in order to elude his adversary. By the time 6 Indian Division reached Kut, with its tempting stockpiles of food and ammunition, the troops were tired and hungry. Exhausted himself, and concerned about the morale of his Indian units, which he had long suspected, Townshend resolved to halt rather than risk the disintegration of his own force, or the sudden reappearance of an enemy that he previously had underestimated. As Townshend and his troops recovered from their ordeal, it became apparent that the enemy pursuit had subsided. Moreover, Townshend became increasingly aware of the shortcomings of the Kut position. By the time he resolved to resume his retirement, however, neither Nixon nor Nurettin would oblige him.

In his recent history of the Mesopotamia campaign, the historian Charles Townshend has characterized the retreat from Ctesiphon as his namesake's "finest hour." This may be true of the engagement at Umm-at-Tubul. Faced with the sudden appearance of an enemy army of unknown strength and disposition, Townshend quickly devised and successfully executed a plan to extricate his own weakened force. Nonetheless, Townshend's earlier underestimation of Nurettin's pursuit may have left him unable to inflict a more significant defeat on the Ottomans. Had he taken more seriously the threat posed by the enemy on 30 November, he would almost certainly have retained the 30th Brigade. With Melliss's force at his disposal, Townshend would have had greater strength and confidence to capitalize on the enemy's confusion on 1 December. Nor was Townshend's conduct in the aftermath of Umm-at-Tubul beyond reproach. In particular, his decision to halt at Kut on 3 December allowed the Ottomans to regain contact with 6 Indian Division and gradually surround it without opposition. While the Es Sinn position had its own manifest limitations, it was almost certainly attainable, and it was less vulnerable to encirclement. Occupying Es Sinn may not have enabled the survival of 6 Indian Division, but it is difficult to imagine it producing a worse outcome than that which ultimately transpired. Given the condition of Townshend and his force on 3 December, as well as his expectation of rapid relief, Townshend's decision to hold Kut is understandable. The events that followed, however, resulted from this and earlier decisions by the commander of 6 Indian Division.

FOUR

OUTSET OF THE SIEGE

DECEMBER 1915

FOLLOWING TOWNSHEND'S DECISION TO HALT AT KUT-AL-
Amara, 6 Indian Division began preparing defensive positions around
the town. The force occupying Kut comprised the three original infantry
brigades of 6 Indian Division as well as Melliss's 30th Brigade. It also
included the 10th Brigade of the Royal Field Artillery, three additional
batteries, several individual guns and a machine gun section, the 48th
Pioneers, a bridging train, and three companies of sappers, as well as
assorted medical and communications personnel. Accompanying these
combatants was a numerous and diverse array of Indian followers including cooks, servants, drivers, and sweepers. The strength of the entire
garrison totaled approximately 300 British officers, 2,850 British other
ranks, 8,250 sepoys, including Indian officers, and 3,500 followers. Despite its apparent exhaustion on 3 December, Townshend's force quickly
managed to construct a trench system to the north of Kut that helped it
repel Ottoman attacks from 9 to 12 December. It also withstood another
more serious attack on the 24th. Ottoman efforts to breach Townshend's
defenses and capture the town subsided after Christmas as the enemy
began shifting units down the Tigris to meet approaching British forces
sent to relieve 6 Indian Division. Faced with growing evidence that
Nurettin had no intention of conceding Kut to the relief force, Townshend remained hopeful that the force would reach the town as quickly
as possible. As the New Year arrived, the commander of 6 Indian Division and his subordinates looked forward to the imminent conclusion
of the siege.

This period saw 6 Indian Division repel the only serious enemy attacks on Kut that occurred during the entire siege. Nonetheless, historians have questioned Townshend's decisions during this period, focusing in particular on his apparent failure to prepare for a protracted engagement. While Townshend ordered the construction of defenses around Kut, he did not take a thorough inventory of the food available in the town for the sustenance of his force. As a result, the commander of 6 Indian Division underestimated significantly the length of time that his besieged garrison could survive. This underestimate encouraged Sir John Nixon and the commander of the relief force, Lieutenant-General Sir Fenton Aylmer, to expedite and intensify their efforts to relieve 6 Indian Division in January, with disastrous results. As the members of the Mesopotamia Commission concluded in 1917, "the neglect of General Townshend to intimate his true position as regards supplies was one of the main factors in the hurried advance."[1] Historians have also questioned Townshend's decision to allow Kut's 6,000 inhabitants to remain in the town rather than evicting them at the outset of the siege. As A. J. Barker commented in his study of the Mesopotamia campaign, "It may have been humane to let them remain, to eat up their own grain and that of the besieged force, but when the consequences of that decision are assessed in terms of soldiers' lives, it may seem that it would have been preferable to expel many more."[2] In the most recent history of the campaign, the historian Charles Townshend has even challenged the humanitarian benefits of his namesake's decision, pointing out that the civilians who remained inside Kut would be exposed "to direct artillery bombardment and possibly worse."[3]

Major-General Townshend's formative experience at Chitral, as well as his extensive study of military history, had undoubtedly given him an appreciation of the importance of managing his resources carefully during a siege. His decisions in December 1915 are therefore puzzling. According to Russell Braddon they reflected Townshend's ambition and professional jealousy. In his words: "Unless . . . he was relieved within two months, command of the second corps which by then would have been concentrated in Mesopotamia would almost certainly go to his junior, Major-General Gorringe, who then would become a lieutenant-general and deny Townshend not only his promotion but also the command of that force which would eventually take Baghdad."[4]

Townshend certainly believed that a prolonged siege would hinder his career advancement, but his consequent desire to escape Kut and resume offensive operations is not the only factor that influenced his decisions in December 1915. Despite his sobering experience at Ctesiphon, Townshend shared the conviction common among senior British military officers in this period that the relief force would be able to reach Kut in short order. He therefore saw little need to prepare for a lengthy siege. As the month progressed, the arrival of additional Ottoman forces and the tenacity they displayed in their attacks on Kut suggested that the relief of the town might take longer than initially expected. At the same time, however, Townshend became increasingly concerned about the loyalties of Kut's civilian population as well as the morale of his Indian subordinates. Thus, even as imminent relief began to appear less likely, Townshend became increasingly convinced that it was a necessity. As a result, he pressed Nixon and Aylmer to initiate relief operations as quickly as possible.

TOWNSHEND'S DECISIONS AT THE BEGINNING OF THE SIEGE

Charles Townshend made his initial decisions regarding the defense of Kut in the context of what he later termed Sir John Nixon's "absolute promise of relief" within two months at the latest.[5] Townshend's own experiences in the fall of 1915 had demonstrated the inhibiting effect of friction on offensive operations in Mesopotamia. They had also indicated the increasing effectiveness of Nurettin's army. Townshend nonetheless accepted Nixon's optimistic timeframe without reservation, for several reasons. First, despite mounting evidence to the contrary, Townshend, like Nixon, remained confident that a British force of sufficient strength would be able to reach Kut without serious difficulty.[6] The rationale for this assumption is not entirely clear, but in his memoirs Townshend admitted that he assumed that news of the arrival of British forces at Basra would "cause the Turks to hesitate and halt in their counter-offensive."[7] In addition, senior officers in Mesopotamia and India believed that even if the Ottomans attempted to hold Kut, Townshend's occupation of the town prevented them from moving large forces and heavy artillery down the Tigris to stop a relief force. They also assumed that Nurettin lacked the time and means to establish the type of prepared defensive positions to which they attributed Ottoman success at Ctesiphon.[8]

Secondly, while Townshend's calculations regarding his career trajectory in early December may not have reached the level of specificity alleged by Russell Braddon, the commander of 6 Indian Division believed that his best route to a promotion and possibly even a post on the Western Front was through victories on the battlefield. Trapped inside Kut, he could only watch from the sidelines as other commanders distinguished themselves, a depressing prospect for a restless personality like Townshend. In addition, the possibility of enduring a lengthy siege with demoralized Indian troops likely evoked unpleasant memories of Chitral. While Townshend had outlasted his enemy in 1894, he remembered at least some of his Indian subordinates as a hindrance on his ability to do so. Thus, Townshend's decisions in early December reflected his conviction that a rapid conclusion to the siege was possible and eminently desirable.

In the words of the historian Townshend, "Kut was an unbeguiling place to be stuck in."[9] The town was located at the south end of a "featureless and flat" peninsula approximately two miles long and one mile wide, surrounded on three sides by the meandering Tigris.[10] According to one survivor of the siege, "The sandy desert stretched right up to the town, the only relief from the monotony of the landscape being a grove of date palms."[11] Aside from a mosque, several wool-presses, a bazaar, and a flour mill, the settlement itself consisted primarily of single-story mud houses separated by streets that served as repositories for sewage and household garbage.[12] According to the senior medical officer attached to 6 Indian Division, the town was "the most insanitary place that the British force had occupied in Mesopotamia."[13] In the early twentieth century, Kut was a center for the grain trade in the surrounding region. The vast majority of its approximately 6,000 inhabitants were Arabs, but the town was also home to smaller groups of Jews, Sabeans, and Nestorian Christians.[14]

Notwithstanding its hygienic and aesthetic drawbacks, the town had become a supply depot in support of 6 Indian Division's abortive advance on Baghdad in the fall of 1915. In addition to a recently constructed military hospital, Kut held substantial stockpiles of rations in early December. At the outset of the siege, Townshend ordered all food in the town to be requisitioned. A relatively quick search revealed two months' rations for British and Indian troops as well as additional stockpiles of grain, flour, and atta, the lentil or chickpea flour issued to Indians for the preparation of chapattis. In addition, the inhabitants of Kut possessed enough food to last three months, at least some of which they were willing to sell to the town's military governor, Colonel Taylor.[15] The commander of 6 Indian Division was sufficiently satisfied with this result that he did not press his chief supply and transport officer, Lieutenant-Colonel A. S. R. Annesley, to search private homes in Kut for additional stockpiles of food. Nor did he emphasize the importance of securing the foodstuffs already discovered.

As a result, a substantial quantity of food spoiled or disappeared in the initial stages of the siege. After discovering "2 or 3 mounds of barley waiting to be shipped" in the village of Yakusub, just across the Tigris from Kut, officers of the 120th Rajputana Infantry notified 6 Division headquarters immediately. Townshend's staff did not make arrangements to collect the grain, however, until at least six weeks later, at which point much of it was no longer edible.[16] In his account of the Mesopotamia campaign, the British political officer Arnold T. Wilson alleged that "extra rations were supplemented by extensive pilfering and even pillaging of the ration dumps by British and Indian soldiers when they first reached Kut, conduct which General Townshend seems to have winked at or ignored."[17] The commander of the Royal Field Artillery Brigade inside Kut, Colonel H. N. Maule, wrote in his diary that bags of food were "built into fortifications . . . as well as looted indiscriminately."[18] Even the local inhabitants were able to secure foodstuffs from military stockpiles. According to Major A. J. Anderson, commander of the Volunteer Artillery Battery, local merchants sold jam and condensed milk, which they had obtained "due to looting which took place in the early days of the siege, when the supply park on the river bank was a pandemonium on the return of the Division from Ctesiphon."[19] Ultimately, the divisional supply and transport personnel were responsible for securing all available food supplies in the town. Townshend admitted in his memoirs, however, that he did not draw "special attention" to his initial orders to do so, at least in part because he did not yet believe that the siege would be prolonged.[20]

This belief also influenced Townshend's treatment of Kut's inhabitants at the outset of the siege. In his memoir, the commander of 6 Indian Division maintained that he initially intended to expel the town's civilian population, but Percy Cox, the chief political officer attached to the Indian Expeditionary Force in Mesopotamia, convinced him that the women and children of the town "would perish in the desert from hunger and the bullet of the desert Arab." Mindful of the impact of such a humanitarian disaster on Britain's reputation with the Arab population of Mesopotamia, Townshend decided to allow the vast majority of civilians to remain in the town, expelling only 700–800 men who were not residents of Kut. Townshend later claimed that he "bitterly regretted" this decision, as the civilian population hoarded and ultimately consumed a significant proportion of the food available in the town. He also suspected local civilians of passing information to the enemy.[21]

In light of the ultimate outcome of the siege, Townshend's decision to allow local civilians to remain in their homes appears questionable. In early December, however, to do otherwise would have appeared difficult, politically hazardous, and probably unnecessary. Following his arrival at Kut on 3 December, Townshend had only a limited opportunity to reduce the town's population. Once the Ottomans invested Kut on the 7th, the departure of civilians and military personnel alike became impossible. Between 3 and 7 December, Townshend sent several hundred sick and wounded soldiers downriver. At Nixon's request, he dispatched Roberts's 6th Cavalry Brigade downriver to meet the relief force. The remaining soldiers capable of working were occupied with the task of preparing defenses around the town. Given Townshend's expectation that relief would be forthcoming within two months, the diversion of significant numbers of soldiers to expel the town's civilians did not seem to be an urgent necessity. In early December there appeared to be ample food for soldiers and civilians alike. Moreover, if the siege ended before food supplies in Kut were depleted, the expulsion and subsequent deaths of thousands of civilians would have been seen as an avoidable tragedy, damaging British prestige in Mesopotamia and elsewhere in the Muslim world. Thus, in early December it made little sense to evict the civilian population.

Local civilians also provided a badly needed source of labor for what quickly became Townshend's overriding priority: the construction of defensive positions across the north end of the Kut peninsula. The preparation of defenses did not begin in earnest until several days after 6 Indian Division's return to Kut-al-Amara. In his memoir, Townshend claimed that while his British troops were able to work on 4 December, the Indians "lay down and could do nothing but sleep and eat for two days!"[22] It is doubtful, however, that the exhaustion of the Indian troops delayed significantly the construction of defenses around the town. By the 5th Townshend was having second thoughts about remaining at Kut. It is therefore likely that he did not direct the bulk of his force to start building defensive positions until after Nixon rejected his appeal to retire to Ali Gharbi on the 6th. By this point, the approach of Nurettin's army made the construction of defenses a matter of some urgency. Fortunately for Townshend's force, the Tigris protected Kut on three sides, acting as a moat some 250–450 yards wide.[23] At the north end of the Kut peninsula, however, there were no serious obstacles to obstruct the advance of the enemy. When the British established a supply depot at Kut earlier in the fall, they had envisioned attacks only by "Arabs unsupported by artillery." To counter this threat, they had constructed a mud-walled fort on the banks of the Tigris northeast of the town and a line of four blockhouses stretching across the 2,700-yard neck of the peninsula. In the words of the Royal Engineer Captain E. W. C. Sandes, the commander of 6 Indian Division's bridging train, such defenses were "eminently suited for defence against savages, but useless against artillery."[24]

With Ottoman forces approaching, soldiers, followers, and levies of local Arabs began constructing a more robust trench system. D. A. Simmons, a lieutenant in the 2/Dorsetshire Regiment, recalled after the war, "Although no two points were more than two miles apart within our defences I believe that eventually there were nearly thirty miles of

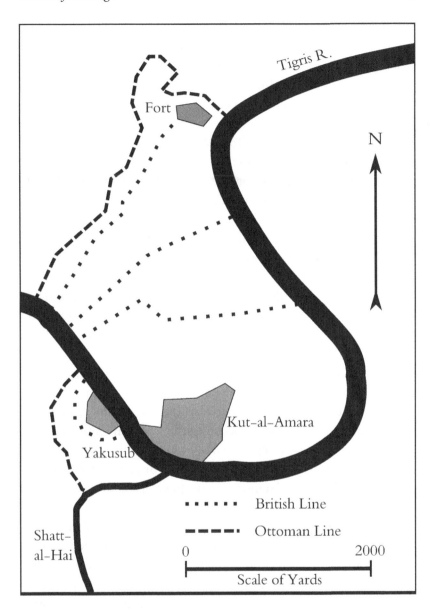

4.1. *Kut-al-Amara, December 1915*

trenches dug."[25] Townshend's force constructed a "first line" of trenches extending across the neck of the peninsula, anchored by four redoubts that replaced the blockhouses. While the fort at the east side of the peninsula was isolated and difficult to reinforce, it contained substantial quantities of supplies, it overlooked the Tigris, and it served as an excellent vantage point for directing 6 Indian Division's artillery, which was located inside the town of Kut. Townshend therefore decided to hold the fort, enclosing it behind the first line. Roughly parallel to the first line, the troops constructed a "second line" several hundred yards closer to the town. Subsequently they also dug a "middle line" between the first two lines.[26] Five communications trenches extended northward from the town of Kut to these three lines. On the western end of his position, Townshend decided to occupy and fortify the village of Yakusub on the right bank of the Tigris. Known to the British as "Woolpress," the village was isolated and difficult to resupply, but it commanded the junction of the Tigris and the Hai, and its occupation protected the town of Kut from direct enemy fire.[27] Townshend deployed his force as follows: Hoghton's 17th Brigade occupied the northeast sector of the Kut position, which included the fort and the eastern halves of the first, middle and second lines. Delamain's 16th Brigade held the northwest sector, which consisted of the western halves of the first, middle, and second lines. Hamilton's 18th Brigade occupied the southern sector, with two battalions occupying "Woolpress" village while the other two performed picket duty in the town of Kut.[28] Melliss's 30th Brigade formed Townshend's "General Reserve," stationed in the town of Kut by day and north of it by night.[29]

Survivors of the siege remembered its opening weeks as an exhausting ordeal. In addition to digging trenches, Townshend's force had to prepare gun emplacements, move shells and ammunition, string barbed wire along the trenches, lay cable between Townshend's headquarters and those of the four infantry brigades, and perform a variety of other tasks to ready the town for defense. According to Ernest Walker, a field ambulance driver attached to 6 Indian Division, the soldiers "dug day and night for a month."[30] As Lieutenant G. L. Heawood of the Oxford and Buckinghamshire Light Infantry recalled, "There was no rest. The company I commanded was nearly all old regular troops of many years' service and tough. But I remember a tough regular soldier of them breaking down and crying as he tried to dig one afternoon."[31]

Nurettin's force invested the Kut position well before its defenses were completed. To the north, Ottoman troops pushed forward as close as possible to Townshend's first line and began establishing their own trench system across the neck of the Kut peninsula. They also began moving around the eastern and western flanks of the peninsula, threatening Townshend's line of retreat.[32] The Ottomans subjected the British and Indian troops to small-arms and artillery fire as they tried to work. According to D. A. Simmons: "Our trenches were far from complete and it was asking for a bullet through your head to stand upright, so we couldn't do much by day except sit in the bottom of the trench and get covered with dust every few minutes as a bullet hit the parapet."[33] Fortunately for the Kut garrison, its embryonic trench system was sufficient to thwart Nurettin's first attempts to take the town by force. As his army completed its investment of the Kut position on 7 December, Nurettin sent a formal letter to his British counterpart demanding the surrender of 6 Indian Division and pointing out that its presence inside Kut endangered the town's civilian inhabitants, in contravention of the laws of "civilized warfare." The next day Townshend replied with a characteristically bombastic refusal in which he argued that the Ottoman commander was "curiously and extraordinarily in error in imagining that the defence of a town was against the laws of war; that there was no battle of any consequence in Europe and no siege that did not include the attack or defence of a town or village; and that his friends the Germans not only always occupied towns and villages, but did so in a manner peculiar to themselves."[34] Nurettin responded by ordering the continued artillery bombardment of Kut as well as the initiation of infantry attacks on the morning of the 9th.

Since the Battle of Ctesiphon the Ottoman soldiers had endured privations equal to, if not greater than, those of their opponents in 6 Indian Division. In addition to suffering heavy casualties, they had marched as far as Townshend's force while experiencing ongoing shortages of food and supplies. Their morale was therefore shaky as they prepared to assail their enemy's defensive positions around Kut.[35] Moreover, the Ottomans did not have enough ammunition to launch an artillery bombardment of sufficient strength to suppress their enemy's defensive fire.[36] To make matters worse, the Ottoman commander initially made no attempt to focus the attack, simply directing Halil Bey's XVIII Corps, comprising 45 and 51 Divisions, to advance over open ground against the entirety of Townshend's first line. Not surprisingly, these efforts made little progress, stalling by 8:30 A M on 9 December.[37] Nurettin ordered the resumption of operations the same afternoon, directing XVIII Corps to attack the fort at the northeast end of the British line in conjunction with units of XIII Corps, which was on the right bank of the Tigris to the east of the Kut position. When this effort also failed, Halil Bey ordered 45 Division to assault the British left flank instead. This was the only Ottoman infantry attack on the 9th that was recognized as such by the British. According to the *Official History*, it was "quickly checked by the British rifle, machine gun and gun fire, and then brought to a complete halt."[38] When attempts to renew the attack the next morning also failed, Nurettin suspended his efforts to break through the British defenses around Kut, opting instead for "regular siege methods" intended to compel the surrender of Townshend's force by making it impossible to survive inside the town. To this end, Ottoman forces attempted to capture the British position at Yakusub on 12–13 December. Possession of the village would enable them to fire on soldiers and civilians inside Kut who attempted to draw water from the Tigris, effectively cutting off the town's water supply. These attacks, however, failed to make a significant impression on the two battalions holding Yakusub.[39]

The initial flurry of Ottoman attacks failed to achieve their immediate objectives. Despite the nascent state of Townshend's defenses, Nurettin's troops were unable to penetrate or capture any of them. In their attempts to do so, they suffered over 1,100 casualties, while their adversaries sustained less than 750.[40] Nonetheless, the enemy pressure concerned Townshend for two reasons. First, while the Ottoman XVIII Corps made no headway in its attacks, the threat posed by XIII Corps on the right bank of the Tigris east of Kut compelled the commander of 6 Indian Division to abandon his only bridge across the river. Initially constructed near the fort to facilitate the evacuation of the Cavalry Brigade on 6 December, the bridge was moved south of Townshend's second line and closer to the town of Kut on the 8th. After Melliss, commanding the General Reserve, determined that his force would be unable to prevent the enemy from crossing the bridge at night and establishing a foothold inside Kut, Townshend decided to dismantle it the next day. Constructed out of local watercraft and spare lumber, the bridge was too small and fragile to enable the rapid evacuation of Townshend's entire force. Nonetheless, its loss was psychologically significant. On 6 December, the route down the Tigris had remained open, and Sir John Nixon had referred to the possibility of resupplying the Kut garrison from Shaikh Saad. Just three days later, Townshend's only potential escape route and lifeline had been severed. This may not have surprised the commander of 6 Indian Division, who had predicted on the 4th that the enemy would surround Kut and move downriver.[41] Nonetheless, it certainly did not lift his spirits.

A second source of concern was the rate of casualties incurred by 6 Indian Division in the opening days of the siege. Unaware that Nurettin's force suffered higher losses in this period, or that Ottoman shelling and infantry attacks represented a concerted effort to capture Kut, Townshend understandably grew concerned about the depletion of his force. On 13 December he informed Lieutenant-General Fenton Aylmer, who had just taken command of all British forces on the Tigris, that he was incurring casualties at a rate of "150 to 200 a day." In light of the apparent fact that desultory shelling and isolated infantry attacks were taking an unsustainable toll on his division, Townshend maintained that a "determined assault" on Kut represented a "great danger" to his force.[42]

Ottoman pressure on Kut subsided from 14 to 23 December, thanks largely to the influence of the new commander of the Ottoman 6th Army, the German Field Marshal Colmar von der Goltz. Seventy-one years of age in 1915, von der Goltz had been recalled from retirement in 1914 and appointed military governor of German-occupied Belgium. In 1915 he went to Turkey, and in October the Ottoman minister of war, Enver Pasha, appointed him commander of the newly formed 6th Army, comprising all Ottoman forces in Mesopotamia. On 12 December von der Goltz visited Nurettin, now designated commander of the "Iraq

Group," at the latter's headquarters upriver from Kut. There he quickly took measures to rein in his Ottoman subordinate. The German commander doubted that Nurettin could take the town by assault. He instead favored the starvation of Townshend's division while the bulk of the 6th Army repelled British forces sent to relieve it. He also hoped to make gains in Persia, detaching nearly 2,000 of Nurettin's troops as well as several machine guns and artillery pieces for this purpose.[43]

As a result, Nurettin suspended his attacks on Kut. Contrary to von der Goltz, however, he continued to believe that its swift capture was necessary in order to open the Tigris and enable the shipment of sufficient troops and supplies downriver to defeat the assembling British relief forces. Therefore, in apparent defiance of his superior, Nurettin ordered the resumption of attacks on the town on 24 December. Learning from his experiences earlier in the month, the Ottoman commander focused specifically on the fort at its eastern extremity, from which his enemy was able to direct fire against Ottoman units all along the neck of the Kut peninsula. Nurettin believed that the capture of the fort would neutralize this flanking fire and enable XVIII Corps to overwhelm the entire British first line. [44] At approximately 6:30 AM on Christmas Eve, the Ottoman artillery opened first against the village of Yakusub, the town of Kut, and the entire first line, but its primary target was the mud-walled fort. By 11 AM shelling had destroyed large sections of the fort's north wall, its northeast wall, and the bastion between them. Just as the commander of the newly arrived Ottoman 52 Division ordered his infantry to advance, however, a temporary shortage of ammunition weakened the supporting artillery barrage. This enabled British artillery and machine guns to fire on Ottoman trenches, while British and Indian units repelled the infantry attack with rifle fire, grenades, and even bayonets.[45]

Nurettin ordered the resumption of the attack as soon as possible. It took several hours, however, for 52 Division to organize another assault on the fort. When the Ottoman infantry again moved forward darkness had fallen, but the moon soon illuminated the battlefield, leaving them vulnerable to enemy fire.[46] While the Ottomans managed to fight their way into the remnants of the bastion, inflicting heavy losses on the defenders, they were thwarted by the arrival of the 48th Pioneer Battalion, which had been preparing defenses behind the fort. The Ottomans made a last attempt early on Christmas morning, but it achieved little success. Thus, according to the official historian, "Christmas Day dawned on a definite Turkish repulse, and, as it turned out, on their last serious attempt to take Kut by assault."[47]

Once again, Nurettin had failed to breach the defenses around Kut, and incurred heavy losses in attempting to do so. Estimates of Ottoman casualties on 24 December vary significantly, from Muhammed Amin's tally of 913 to Moberly's estimate of "at least 2000." They far exceeded those of 6 Indian Division, however, which suffered a comparatively modest 315 casualties. Moreover, the battle for the fort took a heavy toll on Nurettin's cadre of officers. In the night attack alone, the units involved lost at least three battalion commanders and nine company commanders.[48] The commander of the 6th Ottoman Army was evidently not impressed. Upon learning of the costly attempt to take the town, von der Goltz issued instructions that "casualties were not to be incurred in attacks unlikely to lead to decisive results."[49] While it is unlikely that the Christmas Eve attacks were the only factor that influenced his opinion of Nurettin, it is significant that von der Goltz replaced him less than three weeks later with the commander of XVIII Corps, Halil Bey.

TOWNSHEND'S GROWING ANXIETY

Initially, the failure of the Ottoman attacks buoyed Townshend's spirits. After observing the movement of large enemy forces on 26 December, he wired to Nixon and Aylmer, "Nur-ud-Din must now know of large British forces arriving at Ali-al-Gharbi; he would be foolish to try and fight a battle with relieving force, he knows he must be beaten and could never shake off our pursuit on left bank and that of our gunboats. Then his best division has suffered heavy losses in its repulse from the fort." Townshend concluded optimistically, "I think his repulse on December 25th and our concentration at Ali-al-Gharbi has caused his retirement."[50] Over the next forty-eight hours, however, he came to a more somber conclusion. Yakusub suffered from heavy fire on the nights of the 27th and 28th. Meanwhile, additional Ottoman forces passed Kut on their way downstream. Thus, on 29 December, Townshend surmised to his superiors that the enemy was actually strengthening its defensive positions below Kut.[51]

This recognition heightened Townshend's concerns about the reliability of his Indian subordinates, an issue that the Christmas Eve battle had brought into sharp relief. While Hoghton's 17th Brigade had held the fort, some of its Indian units had retired under enemy fire during the first Ottoman attack. In particular, three companies of the 119th Infantry had abandoned their positions along the eastern wall of the fort after all but two of their British officers had become casualties. Major A. J. Anderson, commanding the Volunteer Artillery Battery, managed to rally the sepoys of the 119th and drive the enemy back from the eastern wall, but only with a great deal of support from his own troops. According to W. C. Spackman, the members of the Volunteer Artillery Battery were Anglo-Indians from Calcutta, "nicknamed the 'Buchanans,' the Black and White Battery, after a well-known brand of whisky." Spackman characterized them as "a gallant, friendly lot, and so devoted to the 'motherland' they had never seen." Although they were not trained as infantry, they provided crucial support to the wavering troops of the 119th. According to Spackman: "There resulted a desperate hand-to-hand struggle during which a Volunteer (Eurasian) Artillery Battery fought gallantly at literally point-blank range, using also bombs and anything they could lay hands on in their efforts to assist the sorely pressed sepoys." After their shaky performance, the three companies of the 119th played no role in the fierce fighting on the evening of the 24th, their trenches taken over by British troops from the Oxfords.[52]

The historian Charles Townshend has argued that the psychological impact of this episode on officers already uneasy about the morale of their Indian troops had "an enduring influence on the conduct of the siege."[53] While the retirement of the 119th on Christmas Eve was certainly a cause for concern, it was actually just one of a series of troubling developments in December that indicated the deterioration of morale and discipline in Indian units. The apparent exhaustion of his Indian troops was one of the key factors that led the commander of 6 Indian Division to halt at Kut at the beginning of the month. The end of the retreat from Ctesiphon, however, did not lead to an immediate improvement in Indian morale. On the contrary, incessant digging and enemy attacks gave the sepoys no time to recover. Many showed little enthusiasm for the task of preparing defensive positions. Lieutenant H. S. D. McNeal, an artillery officer at Kut, commented after the siege "that the trenches that had been dug by the British infantry were far more advanced than those worked on by the native troops with the exception of the 2/7th Gurkhas."[54] Others attempted to avoid frontline service entirely. In a 9 December telegram Townshend complained to Nixon, "I have 800 sick and wounded and am convinced there should not be more than 300 at the outside." In his memoir Townshend attributed the high number to "a considerable amount of malingering among the Indian troops, whose tails are decidedly down."[55] Such behavior raised fears about the reliability of sepoys in combat. On 13 December, Brigadier-General Hoghton "begged" Townshend to replace one of his Indian battalions, "as it was so shaken he could not rely on it."[56] Respecting Hoghton's experience with Indian troops, the commander of 6 Indian Division withdrew the battalion, presumably the 22nd Punjabis, even though he did not have British troops available to replace it.[57]

Townshend attributed disciplinary problems in Indian units largely to the shortage of British officers in Kut. Of 317 British officers in 6 Indian Division at the Battle of Ctesiphon, 130 were killed or wounded. Seventy-five of these officers were members of Indian battalions. The retreat from Ctesiphon and the Ottoman attacks during the first month of the siege exacerbated this shortage. For example, seventeen British officers were killed or wounded on 24 December alone. In several battalions, the number of officers reached critical levels. Even at the outset of the siege the political officer Arnold T. Wilson recounted that "the 110th Mahrattas had 1 officer, the 104th Rifles 2; the 66th Punjabis 117th Mahrattas and the 2/7th Gurkhas 4 each."[58] The fact that many of these remaining British officers were inexperienced compounded the disciplinary problems created by heavy losses. In his diary, Reverend Harold Spooner, the chaplain attached to the Kut garrison, recalled his 26 December visit to the 66th Punjabis: "The only British officers left were Colonel Moore and two IARs, Bishop and Ubsell."[59] So desperate was the shortage of British officers in December that Townshend apparently offered commissions to British noncommissioned officers (NCOs) who agreed to transfer to Indian battalions. The idea was quickly abandoned, probably due to the recognition that most British NCOs had neither a grasp of Indian languages nor experience commanding sepoys.[60] Nevertheless, the fact that it was even considered indicates the level of concern that prevailed regarding morale and discipline in Indian units even at the outset of the siege.

Despite the ongoing shortage of officers, Townshend noted an improvement in Indian morale in mid-December, a development he attributed to a communiqué he issued on the 16th. It is more likely that this trend resulted from the temporary suspension of Ottoman attacks on the Kut garrison, but in any case it proved to be short-lived. The collapse of the 119th Infantry on Christmas Eve demonstrated that problems of morale and discipline were not limited to the 22nd Punjabis. During the following week, additional evidence emerged that malaise was spreading among the Indian units of Townshend's force. In late December, the Ottomans initiated a propaganda campaign aimed specifically at the sepoys, throwing leaflets attached to rocks into the trenches outside of Kut. Written in several Indian languages, the documents exhorted the Indians "to rise and murder their British officers and join their brothers the Turks, who would pay them better and give them grants of land."[61]

E. W. C. Sandes contended that the Ottoman campaign "failed completely."[62] It is nonetheless significant that the appearance of the leaflets coincided with the first recorded incidents of sepoy desertions from Kut. Two sepoys, from the 22nd and 66th Punjabis respectively, went over to the enemy on the night of 27–28 December. Two nights later at least two more deserted. On 1 January, a sepoy from the 103rd Light Infantry, which had defended the fort stubbornly on Christmas Eve, attempted to desert but was captured and executed.[63] At the same time, British authorities began to encounter Indian soldiers with self-inflicted wounds. In his memoir Townshend recalled the discovery of more than a dozen sepoys in a single battalion "who shot off their fingers and pretended they had been wounded."[64] While Townshend did not identify the unit in question, a 29 December directive from Major J. B. K. Davie, the divisional deputy assistant adjutant-general, informed Townshend's brigade commanders that "several cases have been detected of men of the Double Company 99th Infantry, attached 76th Punjabis, shooting off their 'trigger' fingers. They endeavor to prevent the powder scorch and burn from showing by binding a piece of cloth round finger and hand. The General Officer Commanding the division directs you to make it clear to all concerned that this evil must be stopped by the adoption of measures of the utmost severity."[65] By the end of the first month of the siege, Townshend's anxiety about his Indian subordinates had grown significantly. Concerns about exhaustion and low morale in Indian battalions had evolved into fears of widespread desertion, self-mutilation, and perhaps even mutiny. In reality, serious disciplinary problems appear to have been limited to a relatively small proportion of Indians in Townshend's division in this period. Even during the sustained enemy attacks of 24 December discipline had collapsed only in three companies of one battalion. Given Townshend's longstanding concerns about his Indian subordinates, and his reluctance or inability to differentiate between them, the commander of 6 Indian Division saw the incidents that occurred in December as evidence of widespread disaffection.

As Townshend's worries about his subordinates grew, so too did his unease regarding the civilian population of Kut. In general terms, the commander of 6 Indian Division recognized the importance of maintaining British prestige in Mesopotamia and elsewhere. While his decision to allow the inhabitants of Kut to remain during the siege resulted partly from his confidence that it would end quickly, it also reflected his concerns regarding the negative political repercussions that would result if he evicted Kut's women and children at the beginning of winter. Nonetheless, Townshend, like many British military officers in Mesopotamia, had little goodwill toward the local population. Since the beginning of the war, British political officers in Mesopotamia had worked to maintain cordial relations between the army and local civilians, but as 1915 progressed, this became increasingly difficult. Contrary to the expectations of British officials, many of the Arab tribes declined an opportunity to "take part in breaking the Turkish yoke," instead remaining neutral or even siding with their Ottoman rulers against the British.[66] Moreover, the robbery and mutilation of dead and wounded soldiers by local Arabs did little to endear the locals to British and Indian military units. In his memoir, Arnold T. Wilson described the growing divergence of opinion between British officers and their civilian counterparts regarding Arab atrocities against battlefield casualties:

Incidents such as these . . . came within the experience of practically all members of the [British] civil administration employed in Mesopotamia outside the large towns: that they should have been able, nevertheless, to put some trust in the Arab tribes, and to gain their confidence in large measure, is an indication of the spirit that animated them. All alike were convinced that if conditions could be moulded aright men would grow good to fit them. Yet the Army, staff and regimental officers alike, could scarcely be blamed for regarding Arabs, collectively, as incorrigible thieves and murderers, faithless and mercenary. Again and again they found the wounded slaughtered, the dead dug up for the sake of their clothes and left to the jackals.[67]

At the outset of the siege, Townshend directed the two political officers present in Kut, Sir Percy Cox and Gerard Leachman, to depart downriver. This left him without an experienced advisor to assist in his dealings with the local population.[68] Townshend's knowledge of Mesopotamia and its inhabitants was largely limited to his own experiences in 1915, which had left him with a deep distrust of the civilian population. As a result, he took a hard line against disorder and suspected sabotage inside the town. In response to looting by local inhabitants in the initial stages of the siege, the commander of 6 Indian Division tried and executed twelve men who had been caught stealing British supplies. Faced with evidence of sniping from inside the town, Townshend imprisoned several civic leaders as hostages, threatening to shoot them "if there was the least sign of treachery."[69]

The executions likely helped deter further looting. Townshend's decision to imprison civic leaders, however, was probably counterproductive. By removing from public circulation many of the most prominent figures in the town, the commander of 6 Indian Division deprived himself of potential allies who might have helped him influence, or at least communicate with, the local population.[70] Clear lines of communication were important because British preparations to defend Kut inevitably created resentment among local inhabitants, who objected when they were drafted to move supplies, or when their homes were destroyed to create roads through the town.[71] Civic leaders may well have served as intermediaries, limiting disaffection among local civilians and informing Townshend of unrest among the population. Given the absence of these leaders, and the language barrier between the local inhabitants and the soldiers of 6 Indian Division, there is no evidence of substantive communication between the two groups. In the resulting vacuum of information regarding the local population, British suspicions flourished. Townshend and other officers became convinced that civilians were passing information to the enemy. According to Sir John Mellor, then a lieutenant in 6 Indian Division: "We knew pretty well that they were doing it all the time.... It was almost impossible to stop."[72]

In reality, there is little evidence of collaboration between local civilians and the enemy outside Kut. The Ottomans actually made a practice of shooting civilians who attempted to escape in order to force them to remain in Kut and draw down Townshend's supplies more quickly. They also fired on women who attempted to collect water from the Tigris. When the siege ended, the Ottomans tortured and executed prominent citizens as collaborators.[73] Nonetheless, in the context of escalating enemy pressure and deteriorating Indian morale during the month of December, Townshend was haunted by the specter of an insurrection by local civilians in conjunction with an enemy attack. He related in his memoirs, "It was certain that the consequences might be serious if the enemy should induce them to rise in the night when an attack was in progress on our northern front."[74] Thus, according to Ronald Millar, Townshend "issued orders that all officers and men were to carry arms when moving around Kut and that working parties must have an armed escort. He forbade any troops from entering the Arab coffee shops."[75] Rather than diminishing as 6 Indian Division established itself in the town, Townshend's suspicion grew as the siege continued through December.

PARALYSIS OF COMMAND

The first month of the siege saw the Ottomans repeatedly defy the optimistic assumptions of Charles Townshend and his superiors. Not only did Nurettin invest Townshend's position at Kut, he initiated multiple attacks in an effort to capture the town. Moreover, despite suffering heavy losses on 24 December, the Ottomans maintained their positions around Kut while moving thousands of soldiers down the Tigris to oppose the approaching British relief force. Collectively, these initiatives suggested that while they were unable to overwhelm 6 Indian Division's defensive perimeter, the Ottomans were determined to maintain their grip on the town. As the month passed, however, Charles Townshend became convinced that disaffection among the local population and his Indian subordinates posed a more serious menace than the enemy surrounding him. In his memoir, Townshend argued that throughout the siege, he "never ceased to take every means possible of raising the *moral* of the Indian troops."[76] His sole method, however, was the distribution of communiqués to the troops, praising their conduct and exhorting them to remain resolute in their defense of Kut. While the communiqués initially had a positive impact on many soldiers, at least some of the messages suggested that relief was imminent. On 7 December, for example, Townshend informed his subordinates that the relief force would reach Shaikh Saad within a week.[77] He did not specify when it would reach Kut, but communiqués such as this contributed to the widespread belief that the siege would be over by the end of the month, if not earlier. As D. A. Simmons related in his memoir of the siege, "Most people thought we were bound to be relieved by Christmas or the New Year at the latest."[78] When the relief force did not materialize as expected, soldiers and sepoys became increasingly cynical. According to Henry Rich, the communiqués were initially useful in sustaining morale, but later became "a source of amusement and often irritation. We were selective when it came to translating them to our Indian soldiers."[79]

Beyond his communiqués the commander of 6 Indian Division did not introduce substantive measures to boost morale among his Indian subordinates. Earlier in his career Townshend had relished personal leadership of his subordinates, but he had little contact with the sepoys under his command at Kut. According to W. C. Spackman, the medical officer attached to the 48th Pioneers, "Townshend was to us at that time a remote figure, almost unknown and rarely seen in the camps and trenches." R. V. Martin of the 22nd Punjabis commented that Townshend "knew nothing of his Indian troops. He never saw them."[80] In addition to lifting the spirits of the sepoys, visiting Indian units might have alleviated some of Townshend's pessimism regarding their morale and discipline. The artillery commander H. N. Maule, who worked at Townshend's headquarters inside the town of Kut, remarked in his diary at the end of December, "[Townshend] practically never steps out, which is a great pity as the men never see him and he never sees things for himself."[81]

Sequestered in his headquarters, the commander of 6 Indian Division became captive to his fears regarding his Indian subordinates and the local population. As a result, he grew progressively more reluctant to take active measures to prepare for a prolonged siege if they threatened the fragile equilibrium that prevailed inside his defensive perimeter. Thus, even in late December Townshend did little to consolidate or conserve the food available inside Kut. After learning at the outset of the siege that the town contained enough food to feed his garrison and the civilian population for approximately two months, Townshend did not press for a house-to-house search in order to determine the maximum period his force could hold the town without starving. Initially this decision may have stemmed in part from Townshend's confidence in an early relief. Even as this possibility became more remote, however, his growing concern regarding the tenuous relationship between 6 Indian Division and Kut's civilian population deterred him from ordering the forcible entry of private homes and the confiscation of food.[82] Nor did he close the town bazaar and seize the foodstuffs that local merchants sold to the soldiers.[83] Such a measure threatened to provoke the ire of local merchants while depriving sepoys of a traditional means of supplementing their rations.

Moreover, Townshend made no effort to limit the rations issued to his troops in the first month of the siege. Given the fatigue affecting soldiers after the retirement from Ctesiphon and the strenuous work labor required to prepare trenches, the distribution of full rations was undoubtedly justified during the first three weeks of December. Once the defenses around Kut, were completed, however, the soldiers became largely sedentary. According to Sir John Mellor, "by the end of December, particularly after we had defeated the Christmas Eve attack we were sufficiently dug in. There was very little work for anybody to do, and therefore we could have gone on half rations straight away and people would have been no worse for it."[84] Nevertheless, the *Official History* relates that soldiers in Kut received full rations throughout the month of December. Sepoys ate particularly well. According to J. J. Bouch of the 5th Hants Howitzer Battery, "to keep their morale up they were given far bigger rations for a much longer time than we were."[85] This was certainly the case in the 120th Rajputana Regiment. According to Henry Rich, "for roughly the month of December we had a ration and a quarter."[86]

Townshend's anxiety regarding Indian morale also deterred him from relieving the beleaguered 17th Brigade after the 24 December attacks. While Delamain's 16th Brigade and Melliss's 30th Brigade alternated in holding the northwest section of Townshend's defenses for the rest of the siege, Hoghton's formation, which had borne the brunt of enemy pressure in December, held the northeast section without relief. In light of Townshend's concerns regarding Indian morale, particularly in the 17th Brigade, his rationale for forcing Hoghton's troops to remain at the front is not immediately clear. As Ronald Millar has explained, however, Townshend reasoned that "hostile bullets made better supervisors than sergeants."[87] The commander of 6 Indian Division evidently feared that removing Hoghton's unreliable Indian units from the front line and freeing them from the discipline imposed by the proximity of the enemy would lead them to deteriorate even further. Allowing them to mingle with other Indian units behind the front lines might also spread disaffection throughout his force. Given the losses already suffered by Hoghton's brigade, this decision might have had disastrous consequences had the Ottomans mounted another assault on the fort. Nonetheless, Townshend proved willing to run this risk in an effort to maintain the fragile morale of his force.

Reluctant to prepare for a protracted siege, Townshend increasingly placed his hopes in the diminishing prospect of a rapid relief. Thus, even as the difficulties facing the relief force became clearer, the commander of 6 Indian Division urged Aylmer and Nixon to expedite their operations. As early as 9 December, just two days after the Ottomans surrounded Kut, Townshend wired Nixon asking for relief within ten to fifteen days. He repeated this request to Aylmer on the 12th, explaining the following day that he was concerned that his Indian troops would not be able to withstand a determined enemy assault on the town. At this point, Aylmer expected two more Ottoman divisions, totaling approximately 14,000 men and thirty-three guns, to join Nurettin's force, estimated at 15,000 men and fifty-four guns, by early January. Intelligence reports suggested that two additional divisions would arrive by the end of January. In light of these expectations and Townshend's alarming reports regarding the deterioration of morale in his force, Aylmer concluded that "he should attempt to relieve Kut by the 10th January if possible."[88]

As Ottoman attacks subsided after 14 December, Townshend noted an improvement in Indian morale. This, combined with reports that von der Goltz was planning an invasion of Persia that would divert Ottoman reinforcements away from Kut, lifted his spirits temporarily. The 24 December attacks, however, combined with its subsequent conclusion that the Ottomans were moving forces downriver from Kut to meet the relief force, led him to wire Aylmer on the 29th, expressing his hope for relief before 10 January. Aylmer responded the next day, indicating his willingness to begin the advance toward Kut with less than a full division "should your condition absolutely require it." If possible, however, Aylmer preferred to wait until he had a full corps comprising two divisions and a cavalry brigade under his command. As he explained to Townshend, "It is essential to postpone our actual methodical advance as long as possible, as hurry means inevitable want of organization, and consequently decreased efficiency." [89]

In replying to Aylmer on 1 January, Townshend acknowledged the benefits of assembling the entire relief force before advancing up the Tigris, but not before sending two separate messages detailing the casualties suffered by his force as well as the appearance of troubling indicators of collapsing morale among his Indian units such as desertion and self-mutilation. According to the *Official History*: "The news conveyed in these telegrams added greatly to the anxiety already felt by General Aylmer lest Kut should fall before he could effect its relief."[90] As a result, Aylmer initiated the advance of the relief force well before it was fully assembled. He ordered Major-General George Younghusband, commanding 7 Indian Division and the 6th Cavalry Brigade, to advance up the Tigris on 4 January, before the arrival of 3 Indian Division, the second infantry division assigned to the relief force. Moreover, 7 Indian Division advanced without adequate medical and transport personnel and equipment, a signal company, or even its divisional staff. Nixon and Aylmer recognized the shortcomings of the force, but given the impend-

ing arrival of additional Ottoman forces and the apparent crisis of morale inside Kut, they believed "that it was imperative to relieve General
Townshend without further delay."[91]

CONCLUSION

Charles Townshend's force recovered relatively quickly from the retirement from Ctesiphon. The soldiers of 6 Indian Division established a
network of defensive positions around Kut and repelled two concerted
efforts by the enemy to take the town by assault. Despite these successes,
Townshend became increasingly convinced that he faced growing dangers inside of Kut, in the form of deteriorating morale among his Indian
subordinates and the hostility of the local population. Thus, even as it
became increasingly evident that the Ottomans intended to maintain
their grip on the town, the commander of 6 Indian Division became
increasingly hesitant to take measures to prepare for a prolonged siege
if they affected Indian units or local civilians. Largely isolated in his
headquarters, the commander of 6 Indian Division saw a rapid conclusion to the siege as the only solution to his predicament. As a result, he
convinced his superiors to initiate relief efforts prematurely. The urgency
of Townshend's requests may have resulted in part from growing exasperation as he watched other commanders arrive in Mesopotamia to
embark on offensive operations against the enemy, potentially earning
accolades that he coveted for himself. Frustrated ambition, however,
does not explain his reluctance to initiate preparations for a prolonged
siege, or even to visit his Indian units. As had been the case earlier in the
fall of 1915, Townshend's decisions in December were largely a reflection
of the gulf that existed between himself and his Indian subordinates.
In January 1916 these decisions would have grave consequences for the
soldiers of the relief force.

FIVE

OPERATIONS OF THE RELIEF FORCE

JANUARY 1916

TOWNSHEND'S REPEATED WARNINGS REGARDING THE deterioration of his division and the arrival of additional Ottoman forces in the vicinity of Kut compelled the rapid dispatch of a relief force up the Tigris in early January 1916. Under the command of Lieutenant-General Sir Fenton Aylmer, this force assaulted Ottoman positions below Kut three times in January before heavy casualties forced it to suspend offensive operations and await reinforcements. The initiation of Aylmer's advance without sufficient shipping, artillery, ammunition, bridging equipment, rations, medical personnel and supplies, and even staff officers contributed significantly to his inability to break through Ottoman positions below Kut. The Mesopotamia Commission concluded that the force's failure was "mainly due" to the haste with which it was assembled. Historians have echoed this conclusion. In the words of A. J. Barker, "Aylmer's expedition, like all other hastily improvised expeditions, was foredoomed."[1]

While material and personnel shortages certainly had a detrimental impact on the operations of the relief force, they are not sufficient to explain its inability to relieve 6 Indian Division in January 1916. A largely overlooked but equally significant deficiency was that of experience in its upper ranks. Aylmer and other senior commanders in the relief force had no previous operational experience during the First World War. The perceived necessity of relieving 6 Indian Division as quickly as possible forced them to initiate offensive operations with little preparation. They consequently struggled to execute coordinated attacks against an entrenched enemy equipped with modern weapons. Any lessons they

drew from the failure of their initial attempts came at the cost of heavy
casualties and deteriorating morale that weakened the force progressively, leaving it increasingly incapable of breaking through enemy positions below Kut.

THE BATTLE OF SHAIKH SAAD, 6–8 JANUARY

On 10 December 1915, Fenton Aylmer took command of the newly constituted Tigris Corps, comprising all British forces operating on the Tigris including Townshend's division and the nascent relief force. Aylmer
had won the Victoria Cross during the Hunza-Nagar campaign on the
North-West Frontier in 1891. Coincidentally, he had also been part of the
force that had relieved the besieged Townshend at Chitral in 1895. None
of Aylmer's previous experiences, however, left him especially well prepared for the task of saving Townshend again in 1915. Adjutant-general
of the army in India until he left for Mesopotamia in 1915, Aylmer had
not commanded troops on active operations during the First World War.
To his credit, he quickly recognized the difficulty of the task that he
faced. In response to Townshend's 11 December telegram requesting
relief in ten to fifteen days, Aylmer emphasized the risks associated with
a rapid advance and advised him that the longer 6 Indian Division could
hold out, "the greater would be the probability of successful relief operations."[2] By late 1915, two Indian infantry divisions and at least four additional infantry brigades were en route to Mesopotamia. While the two
divisions of the Indian Corps that had served on the Western Front since
1914, 3 (Lahore) Indian Division and 7 (Meerut) Indian Division, made
their way from France, three infantry brigades from the subcontinent
and another from Egypt also sailed to Basra.[3] Aylmer anticipated that
7 Indian Division, an additional infantry brigade, as well as an Indian
cavalry brigade would be ready to advance up the Tigris from Ali Gharbi
by early January. Nonetheless, he hoped to wait a further three weeks
until the arrival of 3 Indian Division and the other brigades bolstered
the relief force further.

British intelligence reports, however, indicated that the Turkish force
around Kut would consist of four divisions comprising nearly 30,000
troops by early January, with two additional divisions arriving between

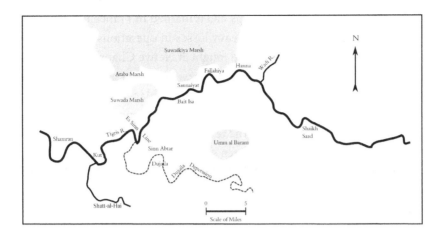

5.1. *Tigris Corps Area of Operations, January–April 1916*

20 and 27 January. Meanwhile, Townshend estimated that casualties would reduce his effective strength of 7,800 rifles by nearly one-third by the middle of the month. He also warned of increasing despondency and unrest among his Indian troops. In light of these factors, Aylmer decided to expedite relief operations in an attempt to reach Kut by 10 January. According to the official historian, "while he realised that to advance with only part would delay the concentration of the remainder and would prejudice his chances of obtaining a decisive victory, General Aylmer realised that the essential point was to ensure General Townshend's timely relief."[4]

The consequent necessity of initiating operations as quickly as possible led to the assembly of the relief force before Indian units en route from Europe had even arrived. Thus, while a force bearing the name "7 Indian Division" had assembled at Ali Gharbi by early January 1916, it bore virtually no resemblance to the formation of the same name that had fought on the Western Front. Of the twelve battalions that comprised the division as it advanced from Ali Gharbi on 3 January, only three had served in Europe. One of these, the 125th (Napier's) Rifles, had been withdrawn from the Western Front to Egypt after fighting with 7 Indian Division at the Battle of Festubert in May 1915. The other two battalions from the Indian Corps had remained in France until the autumn, but both had sustained heavy losses in operations on the Western Front. The 2nd Leicesters had fought at Neuve Chapelle, Festubert, and Givenchy before suffering nearly 50 percent casualties at the Battle of Loos in late September. The 1st Seaforth Highlanders had also fought at Neuve Chapelle, Festubert, Givenchy and Loos in 1915, suffering particularly heavily at Festubert.[5] The rest of the battalions in 7 Indian Division in early January 1916 had been scavenged from garrisons in India, Egypt, and elsewhere in the Middle East.[6] Thus, at the outset of the advance from Ali Gharbi, the majority of the soldiers in the relief force had never participated in large-scale offensive operations against an organized enemy in Mesopotamia or anywhere else.

To make matters worse, the relief force advanced without crucial supplies, including signalling equipment, ambulances, stretchers, wound dressings, drugs, tents, clothing, firewood, and adequate rations. In addition, it had neither land transport nor adequate bridging materials, which meant that it could not maneuver away from the Tigris and could cross it only with difficulty. Even artillery, seemingly essential for attacks against enemy entrenchments, was also deficient in the initial stages of Aylmer's relief operations.[7] Moreover, the force suffered from shortages of essential personnel, including medical staff, supply and transport troops, and sappers and miners.[8] Experienced staff officers, crucial for coordinating the operations of this hastily assembled force, were also in exceedingly short supply. The staff of the Indian Corps had remained in Europe after Sir John Nixon indicated that he would not require its services in Mesopotamia. According to the *Official History,* this forced Aylmer to rely on officers with "insufficient or no training in staff work and some appointments at first could not be filled at all."[9] The staff of 7 Indian Division was still en route from France at the beginning of January, and did not join the relief force until the 10th of the month. Thus, its newly appointed commander, Major-General Sir George Younghusband, also had to improvise.[10] In his autobiography, Younghusband praised his makeshift staff, contending that "fate was again kind to me and produced out of the blue two excellent staff officers, none better." Lieutenant-Colonel A. M. S. Elsmie, "was one of the cleverest officers in the Army, and a skilled staff officer of the highest brand." Major E. W.

Costello, "was not only first class at his job, but was one of those heavenly persons who keep their eyes fixed on the silver lining of the blackest cloud."[11]

Nonetheless, this lack of trained staff officers was particularly significant given the inexperience of the senior commanders of the relief force. Younghusband had spent the previous year in Egypt in command of the 28th Brigade. Like Aylmer he had yet to participate in active operations during the First World War. The three brigade commanders in Aylmer's division were Lieutenant-Colonel A. H. Dennys, temporary commander of the 19th Brigade, Major-General George Kemball, who had taken command of the 28th Brigade following his replacement as Sir John Nixon's chief of staff in late December, and Brigadier-General G. B. Rice, who had accompanied the 35th Brigade from India. Kemball was the best prepared of any of the senior officers in Aylmer's force, as he had been involved in the planning of the abortive advance on Baghdad and had observed Charles Townshend's operations at Kut and Ctesiphon. Dennys had served on the Western Front, but his perspective had been that of a battalion commander. Rice does not appear to have held an operational command prior to arriving in Mesopotamia. The fact that none of these officers had worked together during the war added to the difficulty of their task as they struggled under severe time constraints to devise and disseminate plans to attack an enemy of uncertain strength and location.

By 3 January, 7 Indian Division and the 6th Indian Cavalry Brigade had assembled at Ali Gharbi. In an effort to initiate the advance as quickly as possible, Aylmer directed Younghusband to lead this force forward the following day while he awaited the arrival of an additional infantry brigade. Intelligence reports indicated that an enemy force approximately 2,500 strong was holding a line on both sides of the Tigris three miles southeast of Shaikh Saad.[12] Younghusband believed that the Ottoman units on the right bank were vulnerable because their positions lay in front of the village of Shaikh Saad, which sat in a loop of the Tigris with no bridges across it. He therefore intended to use the 35th and 19th Brigades as a diversion to occupy Ottoman forces on the left bank while his most cohesive formation, Kemball's 28th Brigade, supported by the 6th Cavalry Brigade and the eighteen guns of the 9th Brigade RFA, drove the enemy forces on the right bank back into the loop. With these forces trapped and ostensibly defeated, he would be able to enfilade the enemy units on the left bank, forcing their retreat.[13] As he approached Shaikh Saad on the afternoon of 5 January, Younghusband therefore ordered his force to attack in this fashion the next morning.

Meanwhile, however, Aylmer had received word from Townshend that large enemy columns were moving downriver past Kut-al-Amara. A single air reconnaissance flight on the afternoon of the 5th seemed to confirm Townshend's report, indicating the presence of more than 10,000 Ottoman troops in the previously identified positions below Shaikh Saad.[14] In light of this information, Aylmer attempted to restrain Younghusband until he arrived in the vicinity late the next day to take command of the relief force. On the evening of 5 January he informed his subordinate that he did not want to risk even a "modified check" in the opening engagement of the relief operation. Aylmer nonetheless instructed Younghusband to "hold [the] enemy to his position with suf-ficient vigour as to make him show his hand until my arrival with re-mainder of [the] Corps."[15] This directive left the commander of 7 Indian Division and his makeshift staff nonplussed. To draw a force entrenched in defensive positions into a prolonged engagement that revealed its strength and dispositions without incurring significant casualties in the process appeared to be a prohibitively difficult task. Unable to conceive of a better means of accomplishing it than the advance he had already planned, Younghusband forwarded a copy of his existing orders to his superior. He also sent a telegram to Aylmer explaining that he intended to advance with the intention of "pinning the enemy to his position to this side of Shaikh Saad if he holds on."[16]

The *Report* of the Mesopotamia Commission criticized Younghus-band for disregarding Aylmer's directions, "which were not to commit himself, but merely to hold the enemy."[17] In postwar correspondence with Moberly, however, the acting chief of staff of 7 Indian Division, A. M. S. Elsmie, maintained that Aylmer acknowledged receipt of Younghus-band's plan without comment. Therefore, "it was naturally assumed that he approved of the orders issued."[18] Given the confusion that likely pre-vailed as Aylmer hurried toward Shaikh Saad with a makeshift staff, it is possible that he never saw his subordinate's orders for 6 January. Even so,

his initial directions to Younghusband left considerable room for interpretation. Given their ambiguity, and the possibility that a late alteration
to his original order might cause confusion among the inexperienced
troops under his command, Younghusband's decision to adhere to his
original plan is understandable.

This plan also had a very real prospect of success. At Shaikh Saad,
the relief force faced the Ottoman XIII Corps, comprising 35 and 52 Divisions, under Nurettin's command. Ottoman accounts disagree regarding the strength of the force facing 7 Indian Division on 6 January, but it
is clear that a significant proportion of XIII Corps had not arrived in the
vicinity when the battle began. The number of Ottoman troops around
Shaikh Saad on the 6th totaled anywhere from 3,000 to 8,000, the majority of whom were part of 35 Division. This formation had recently been
reinforced by units of the recently disbanded 38 Division, but its troops
consisted entirely of Iraqi conscripts who had suffered heavily at Ctesiphon and Umm-at-Tubul in late November.[19] It was therefore deemed to
be of "secondary value" by Ottoman officers. Moreover, the bulk of this
force was on the left bank, with only an infantry regiment, a 400-strong
camel regiment, and an undisclosed number of "Arab irregulars" facing
Kemball's force on the right bank in front of Shaikh Saad.[20] Given that
the 28th Brigade and the 6th Cavalry Brigade comprised more than
4,500 troops in total, Kemball almost certainly had a numerical advantage of at least 2:1.[21] With eighteen guns on the right bank, he also had
an advantage in terms of artillery, as the entire Ottoman force at Shaikh
Saad had only fifteen, most of which were likely on the left bank. Thus,
Kemball enjoyed considerable local superiority on 6 January.

That morning, however, fog delayed Kemball's advance and left him
unable to locate Ottoman positions. This effectively negated the impact
of the British artillery and left the infantry vulnerable to fire from un-
anticipated enemy positions. Attempting to outflank the enemy's right,
units of the 28th Brigade discovered that the Ottoman line extended
further than originally thought. As a result they themselves came under fire from their left flank.[22] On the left bank, the 35th Brigade also
incurred losses as it attempted to divert the enemy from Kemball's attack. Recognizing the difficulty of advancing into the dark against an
entrenched opponent, Younghusband called operations to a halt late

in the afternoon. Nonetheless, Kemball remained optimistic, and he convinced his superior to shift an additional battalion to the right bank to support a renewed attack the next morning.[23] After learning of the extent to which Younghusband's force had engaged the enemy, however, Aylmer sent orders late on the evening of the 6th, directing the suspension of further attacks until he arrived on the 7th with the 21st Brigade, half of the 9th Brigade, an additional cavalry regiment, and several artillery pieces.[24]

The commander of the Tigris Corps undoubtedly considered that the addition of these reinforcements would increase his chances of breaking through at Shaikh Saad. He likely also believed that he could coordinate operations more effectively once he joined the bulk of his force. Ultimately, however, Aylmer delayed the attack on 7 January and dispersed its impact. It was not until 10 AM on the 7th that Aylmer issued new orders. Rather than adhering to Younghusband's existing plan, the corps commander directed "a simultaneous attack on both banks" to begin just two hours later.[25] While Kemball was to continue attacking on the right, Younghusband was ordered to take command of the 35th, the 19th, and the newly arrived 21st Brigade and advance against the enemy positions on the left bank of the Tigris. With just two hours between the distribution of Aylmer's order and the beginning of the attack, Younghusband and his staff struggled to reposition the units under their command. In particular, two artillery batteries were unable to get across the lone bridge over the Tigris before noon, forcing Younghusband to use a battery of howitzers instead.[26] In addition, there was no time to reconnoiter the enemy positions on the left bank, which had been strengthened by the arrival of nearly 3,000 seasoned troops of the Anatolian 52 Division on the evening of the 6th.[27]

The result, according to Elsmie, was "a hopeless fiasco."[28] As was the case on the right bank the previous day, advancing units on the left were unaware of the location of enemy positions. Younghusband had directed the 35th Brigade to move forward along the river while the 19th Brigade advanced on its right and turned the enemy's flank. It soon became clear, however, that the Ottoman line extended further from the river than anticipated, as units of the 19th Brigade came under enemy fire from their right. This forced the 19th Brigade to move in that direction in an effort to locate the Ottoman flank. This in turn created a gap between the 19th and 35th Brigades, forcing Younghusband to send two battalions of the 21st Brigade forward to fill it. As the afternoon progressed the 19th Brigade made the unpleasant discovery of an extensive network of enemy lines behind the first one, extending further from the river. As Younghusband explained in an after-action report, "The enemy's front line trenches extended for over three miles inland from the river and were connected with his supports and reserves by numerous communication trenches all well dug in. Other trenches some distance from the left of those mentioned were placed so as to enfilade our advance, whilst another line was echeloned back to the Turkish left, from three to five miles in rear, so as to guard against any wide turning movement on that flank."[29]

Moreover, enemy forces in these positions began to move around Younghusband's right flank, necessitating the dispatch of the rest of 21st Brigade and one of the delayed artillery batteries. By late afternoon, the force on the left bank had suffered significant casualties. According to the divisional war diary: "The 3 brigades had put all their men into the fight and were not in a position to push home their attack unless reinforced."[30] With no additional reserves available, Younghusband called a halt to the attacks.

Kemball achieved more success on the right bank on 7 January, capturing two lines of enemy trenches, killing "over 300" Ottoman troops and taking 600 prisoners. His brigade suffered heavy losses in the process, however, and with the bulk of the force engaged on the other side of the Tigris, he had no reinforcements to sustain the advance. After the war, Elsmie lamented Aylmer's alteration of the original plan to concentrate against Ottoman forces on the right bank on the 7th. He maintained, "It is my firm belief that had Aylmer not interfered with Younghusband's orders, but allowed the attack on the right bank to be pushed home after an artillery bombardment by the guns on both banks, the 28th Brigade would have had a considerable succes[s] and the three brigades on the other bank would have been intact for further operations."[31] By the morning of 8 January Aylmer seems to have come to a similar conclusion. Rather than resuming the attack on both banks, he reverted to Younghusband's original plan, ordering the force on the left bank to

hold its positions while the 28th Brigade continued its advance toward
Shaikh Saad.[32] By this point, however, even Kemball proved hesitant to
attack. The units of the 28th Brigade had suffered significant casualties
over the preceding two days, and as he informed Aylmer, even those who
remained healthy "much needed food, rest and water."[33] Nor was the rest
of the force in any condition to support further attacks on Shaikh Saad.
According to Moberly, "On both banks, owing to reorganisation of units,
readjustment and consolidation of positions, the search for wounded and
escorting carts, etc., the troops had been fully occupied for most of the
wet and cold night, and the morning of the 8th January found officers
and men very tired."[34]

Aylmer and Younghusband hoped to alleviate the suffering of the
35th Brigade, which had endured particularly heavy losses, after dark
on the 8th. Their overworked and inexperienced staff officers, however,
did not have a clear idea of the exact locations of the formations under
their command. Nor were the conditions on the ground conducive to
finding them at night. According to the divisional war diary, "Arrangements for the relief had to be made in the darkness; it was impossible to
take compass bearings etc., nor, owing to the fire swept ground and the
proximity of the enemy, could units call to one another or show lights.
Our trenches were well concealed, all men under cover and not easy to
locate by daylight."[35] Thus, the relief attempt failed, and the beleaguered
35th Brigade remained in its positions overnight.

While rain and fog inhibited aerial and other forms of reconnaissance on the morning of the 9th, it gradually became clear that the Ottomans had evacuated their positions. Aylmer ordered the force forward, and by evening, 7 Indian Division occupied Shaikh Saad without
further opposition. The enemy's withdrawal was not entirely voluntary.
The Ottoman force incurred more than 2,000 casualties from 6 to 8
January, and its morale was low as it withdrew on the night of the 8th.[36]
Moreover, the German field-marshal Colmar von der Goltz, commanding Ottoman operations in Mesopotamia, was sufficiently perturbed
by the outcome of the engagement that he sacked Nurettin and promoted Halil Bey to command XIII Corps.[37] Nonetheless, Shaikh Saad
was a modest victory at an exorbitant price. The relief force suffered
approximately 3,790 casualties in its attempts to dislodge the Ottomans

from the vicinity of Shaikh Saad, but it was unable to prevent them from retiring intact to a formidable new position along the Wadi stream further up the Tigris.[38] After the war, Sir John Nixon's chief of staff, A. W. Money, identified Aylmer's conduct of operations at Shaikh Saad as one of the principal reasons for the failure of the relief force to break through to Kut-al-Amara.[39] Personnel and supply shortages, as well as the stubbornness of the Ottoman defenders, certainly contributed to this failure. By canceling his subordinates' plans on short notice, however, and instead initiating an attack on both banks of the Tigris on 7 January, Aylmer missed a brief but real window of opportunity to drive the enemy forces out of the Shaikh Saad position and pursue them up the Tigris. As an Ottoman staff officer admitted after the war, pressure from the British would have prevented 35 and 52 Divisions from establishing positions at the Wadi. The relief force ultimately compelled the Ottomans to abandon Shaikh Saad, but the casualties it sustained in the process obviated an aggressive pursuit and left it significantly weaker as it attempted to dislodge the enemy from another line of prepared defensive positions.

THE WADI

The relief force spent 10, 11, and much of 12 January engaged in what the 7 Indian Division war diary euphemistically described as "reorganisation."[40] The force certainly benefited from a pause in operations, as it allowed the attachment of individual battalions that had arrived during or after the battle at Shaikh Saad to their respective brigades. It also enabled the permanent staffs of the 9th and 21st Brigades as well as 7 Indian Division to take charge of the operations of their respective formations. Nonetheless, the lull in activity was also necessary to address the rapid deterioration of morale in the Tigris Corps. In early 1916, the Mesopotamia campaign had little prestige in the eyes of British soldiers. Even those languishing on garrison duty in Egypt had recoiled upon learning of their despatch to Mesopotamia. Younghusband recalled in his memoirs, "I have never known such intense gloom settle on a body of soldiers as it did on us when that order came."[41] This view was shared by soldiers arriving from Europe, who comprised an increasing proportion of the

relief force after Shaikh Saad. According to Moberly, those who had previously served in France regarded the campaign as a "side show."[42] The
absence of basic amenities that soldiers took for granted on the Western
Front, such as full rations and regular leave, further diminished soldiers'
enthusiasm for service in Mesopotamia. As Lieutenant-Colonel F. I.
Bowker, commanding the 1/4th Hampshire Regiment, remarked in a
January 1916 letter to his wife, "Fellows from France wish themselves
back there & those from Egypt long for the Suez Canal again."[43]

Resentment was especially acute among Indians. As was the case
in Townshend's force, some Muslim soldiers had qualms about facing
an Islamic enemy and fighting near sites of religious significance. Moreover, sepoys struggled to supplement their meager rations in Mesopotamia. For Indians who had previously served in France, their arrival in
the new theater was a particularly rude shock. Some Indian units had
fought in Europe since October 1914, suffering heavy casualties in the
process. The loss of familiar officers and comrades, along with the fact
that many wounded soldiers rejoined their units rather than returning
to India, progressively eroded the morale and cohesion of Indian battalions. The decision to remove 3 and 7 Indian Divisions from the Western
Front in late 1915 stemmed in large part from consequent concerns about
their continued effectiveness.[44] According to the British war correspondent Edmund Candler: "The original plan had been that the Lahore and
Meerut Divisions were to reorganise in Egypt. But Townshend's investment at Kut had altered the whole situation. Reinforcements were to be
pushed through without delay, though we knew nothing about this."[45]
In a letter to Lord Kitchener, Sir Walter Lawrence, commissioner for
Indian hospitals in England and France, expressed concern regarding
this unexpected redeployment of already demoralized Indian troops. As
Lawrence stated, "It might be a very dangerous thing if their destination
were only disclosed to them when they reach Aden."[46]

Although Lawrence's gravest fears never materialized, the unexpected reassignment to Mesopotamia came as an unpleasant surprise
to the sepoys. The austere conditions they faced upon their arrival compounded their disaffection. To make matters worse, Indians serving in
Mesopotamia received less pay than they had received in France.[47] Not
surprisingly, Indian soldiers disliked the new theater of operations. Sol-

diers' letters indicate that even those without religious qualms about the campaign found that service in Mesopotamia compared unfavorably with Europe. One observed that the fighting in Mesopotamia was "much more severe than against the Germans," perhaps because the hastily deployed relief force fought without the elaborate defensive fortifications and the artillery support that Indian units had in France.[48] Others commented on the Spartan conditions they faced in the new theater. One Sikh wrote to a comrade still in Europe, "In France there was no lack of anything. It has remained for us to encounter the greatest of difficulties in this place. There is no sign of milk or sugar, and for drink we have nothing but water of the Dijah (Euphrates)."[49] Another lamented: "We are marching every day, and have the greatest difficulty about water. There are no trees to be seen anywhere. The misery we are enduring here is as great as the comfort we enjoyed in France."[50]

The utter inadequacy of medical care during and after the battle at Shaikh Saad intensified disaffection throughout the relief force. According to A. J. Barker: "provision had been made for only about 250 casualties and when the time came these arrangements had to cater for over 4,000."[51] In the absence of ambulances or even stretchers, wounded soldiers remained on the battlefield in wet and cold conditions for hours or even days before being collected. According to Captain J. C. Catty, adjutant and quartermaster-general of the 69th Punjabis, some soldiers with fractured legs resorted to crawling four to five miles in order to receive medical care.[52] Soldiers' prospects did not improve significantly once they finally reached makeshift field hospitals. There was insufficient space to accommodate casualties, and those not lucky enough to secure a spot in a tent or on a river boat requisitioned for medical purposes were forced to lie in the open. The cavalry officer J. E. Bridges related one case in a 16 January letter to his father: "A gunner officer was badly wounded on the 7th. He was carried to hospital and laid down outside it. No one came near him (perishing cold and wet). The next morning he came to (can't say he woke up) and finding he could get up and that no one seemed likely to attend to him, he crawled back to his own lines."[53] The number of casualties overwhelmed the handful of trained medical personnel accompanying the relief force. In his recent account of the siege of Kut, Patrick Crowley describes three medical officers attending to 1,200 sick and wounded on 7 January. Thus, casualties received little care other than rudimentary first aid before being crammed onto boats and sent down the Tigris to Basra.[54] T. A. Chalmers, captain of a make-shift "hospital auxiliary boat" in January 1916, commented in his diary regarding the plight of newly arrived soldiers who became casualties at Shaikh Saad. He reflected:

> Will the wounded at Shaik[h] Saad ever forget that action? Here were troops who had been a year in France where within an hour of being wounded you were in a hospital tent with all the attention required and within 24 hours were in England in a hospital with all modern improvements for comfort and saving life. Here you crawled or got a lift in a jolting cart to a flag post on a river and on arriving there you must sit, lie or stand in the mud in the rain all night as there are no tents up and no food to be got and no attendents [sic].[55]

The Ottoman withdrawal from Shaikh Saad, however, did not re-duce the sense of urgency animating the operations of the relief force. While Townshend's fears of a collapse of Indian morale inside Kut had apparently diminished since the end of December, he had not fully re-gained his confidence in his subordinates. When Aylmer raised the pos-sibility of 6 Indian Division conducting a sortie from Kut in an attempt to divert Ottoman forces away from the relief force, Townshend de-murred, commenting, "my troops now are naturally not the same men: they will defend well, but to leave trenches and cross open demands spirit and *élan*." Moreover, Townshend continued to emphasize the im-portance of prompt relief, predicting the arrival of an additional Otto-man corps on 20 January as well as the depletion of his food supplies by the beginning of February.[56] The Ottoman decision to halt at the Wadi also encouraged Aylmer to press forward quickly. Three and a half miles west of the Wadi stream lay the Hanna defile, a narrow passage between the Tigris to the south and the Suwaikiya marsh to the north. With its flanks anchored by these two bodies of water, an Ottoman defensive line across the defile could be broken only by a costly frontal assault. By halting 35 and 52 Divisions at the Wadi, however, rather than retiring all the way to the defile, Halil Bey presented Aylmer with a second op-portunity to turn his flank.[57] Thus, a variety of factors encouraged the commander of the Tigris Corps to resume his advance despite concerns about morale.

On 12 January, therefore, Aylmer issued orders for an advance against enemy positions at the Wadi. In comparison to the attacks at Shaikh Saad, this advance was carefully planned and orchestrated. An aerial reconnaissance flight on the 12th surveyed the enemy position, determining that Ottoman lines extended two and a half miles up the Wadi from its junction with the Tigris.[58] In recognition that they would be in action for an extended period if all went well, soldiers were given two days' rations and were followed by carts carrying drinking water.[59] On the night of the 12th the force moved toward the Wadi. On his left, Aylmer directed the 28th Brigade to take up positions near the junction of the Tigris and the Wadi the next morning. While Kemball's force held the Ottomans to their positions in this vicinity, 7 Indian Division, now comprising the 19th, 21st, and 35th Brigades, supported by the 6th Cavalry Brigade, would move to the north in an effort to outflank the Ottoman line and cut off the enemy's line of retreat up the Tigris.[60]

In its initial stages the attack developed smoothly. The 21st Brigade moved northward and crossed the Wadi by 9:30 AM without encountering opposition. Assuming it had cleared the enemy flank, Younghusband ordered the brigade to advance toward the Hanna Defile. By noon, however, it became clear that Ottoman positions extended behind the Wadi line, and during the afternoon the 21st and 19th Brigades became engaged with enemy forces that were "facing North and fighting on an East and West line."[61] This opposition intensified throughout the afternoon, as the 28th Brigade, holding positions 3,000 yards from the Ottoman 35 Division on the other side of the Wadi, was unable to exert significant pressure on that force. This enabled Halil to transfer reserves to his threatened left flank.[62] By late afternoon, Aylmer had recognized the necessity of pressuring the Ottoman right flank along the Tigris and consequently directed the 9th Brigade, now under Elsmie, to support an advance by the 28th Brigade. Kemball, however, initiated this advance just after 4 PM, without waiting for the 9th Brigade to arrive. Attacking across open ground with ranges marked by the enemy, the units of the 28th Brigade suffered heavily, incurring 648 casualties including three of four battalion commanders, without even crossing the Wadi.[63] By the time Elsmie reached Kemball's headquarters the advance had collapsed. Elsmie described the scene when he arrived:

I reached Gen Kemball just after dark. He had again been impetuous. His orders were to hold the enemy, but he asked to be allowed to attack and he threw
in the whole brigade without looking what he was doing. When I reached him
everything was in a state of chaos. Kemball was in the [Chittab] fort, which is
only a mud enclosure. This place was a hospital as well as his headquarters. The
place was crowded with wounded and dying. Few medical appliances. Raining
again and everything in an awful state. Kemball had no idea where his brigade
was. I could get no definite orders from him, except incoherent statements that I
was not doing my share of the work and so on. When I asked him where to take
my brigade, he waved his hand and said "I don't know, somewhere out there." It
was a pitch dark night, and if his brigade was out of his hand I had no intention
of losing mine. At last I suggested that I should take up a position covering the
fort and that we should await daybreak. He agreed, so I did this.[64]

Elsmie was correct in portraying Kemball's decision to attack as a
rash one, but it seems to have been born out of desperation rather than
ineptitude. The 28th Brigade had hitherto been unable to exert pressure
on the Ottoman force in front of it, let alone prevent Halil from trans-
ferring reinforcements to his embattled left flank. Given that it faced
entrenched enemy positions, significant casualties would have been difficult to avoid in any attempt to divert Ottoman attention from Younghusband's flanking movement. Once darkness fell around 5:30 PM, however, the chances of a successful advance would diminish significantly,
as Ottoman positions would become increasingly difficult to locate. Had
Aylmer ordered the 9th Brigade forward earlier in the day, Elsmie and
Kemball would likely have been able to coordinate an advance by both
of their brigades before dark, forcing a greater proportion of 35 Division
to hold its positions along the Wadi. The hurried attack by the 28th Brigade was too little, too late.

Given the fragile morale of the soldiers in Younghusband's force,
Halil's reinforcement of the Ottoman left flank had a significant impact
on the outcome of the battle. T. A. Chalmers recorded in his diary that
three Afridi Pathans of the 28th Punjabis, part of the 19th Brigade, were
shot on 12 January for declining to advance. According to Chalmers,
"They were made to dig their own graves and permitted to lie down
in them when the time came. They were finished off by Tommies as it
is not advisable to get their comrades to do so."[65] While this example
likely deterred other soldiers from mutiny or desertion the next day, it

also did nothing to raise enthusiasm for attacking. Those who had witnessed the plight of casualties at Shaikh Saad were averse to becoming one themselves, particularly in a campaign for which many had limited enthusiasm. Thus, many soldiers proved hesitant to advance against the sustained enemy opposition they encountered. Although the *Official History* does not discuss the morale of 7 Indian Division at the Wadi, it does note that the 35th Brigade, which spearheaded the flanking movement, did not make "any serious attempts to advance" after dark, even though Younghusband did not order a halt to operations until four hours later.[66] Elsmie maintained that this lackluster advance stemmed from low morale, suggesting that "the troops were so shaken by their useless and fruitless fight on the 6th, 7th and 8th that they did not push in much."[67] Thus, the battle ended with Younghusband's force still two and a half miles from the Tigris, enabling the Ottomans once again to withdraw up the river under the cover of darkness.

HANNA, 21 JANUARY

On 14 January, the headquarters of 3 (Lahore) Division as well as those of the 7th and 9th Infantry Brigades joined Aylmer's force at the Wadi. This enabled the reorganization of the Tigris Corps into two full divisions each comprising three brigades. The force also included forty-six guns and the 6th Cavalry Brigade. Nonetheless, this rearrangement of units did nothing to compensate for their beleaguered condition. The relief force had suffered approximately 6,000 casualties from 7 to 13 January, leaving it with a fighting strength of only 9,000. Given the dearth of medical personnel, many of these casualties were not removed from the battlefield until the 16th.[68] To make matters worse, continued supply shortages left some soldiers without rations for up to forty-eight hours after the battle at the Wadi.[69] Moreover, units of the 35th Brigade found that the enemy had retired to a formidable position stretching across the Hanna defile, with its flanks anchored by the Tigris and the Suwaikiya marsh. Subsequent reconnaissance would reveal that the position was "covered by a wire entanglement and supported by a second trench line a few hundred yards in rear."[70]

While the likelihood of the Tigris Corps relieving Kut in the near future was clearly diminishing, Aylmer remained under considerable pressure to resume his advance as quickly as possible. The British evacuation of the Gallipoli peninsula had freed Ottoman forces at the Dardanelles for service on other fronts, and the British expected two to five divisions to arrive in Mesopotamia within weeks.[71] Furthermore, on the evening of the 15th Aylmer received a reproachful telegram from Townshend, reminding him that "we are now the 15th January, that is to say, the date which you laid down in December as being hazardous to expect me to hold out beyond. I only shut myself up in Kut on the distinct understanding that I was relieved in a month and we have now been six weeks."[72]

Aylmer had no illusions about the difficulty of breaking through the Hanna defile. Late on the 15th he wired Nixon, suggesting that it would be "impossible" to take the first Ottoman line "without losing half the force." He therefore proposed that Townshend break out of Kut and cross the Tigris "with such able-bodied men as he has got" and move down the right bank to meet one of Aylmer's divisions, which would "bring him back here."[73] Nixon, however, refused to entertain the possibility of an escape attempt by Townshend's force. In poor health, the commander of IEFD was about to relinquish his command to Sir Percy Lake, formerly chief of the General Staff in India. If Nixon could not effect Townshend's relief before leaving Mesopotamia, he hoped at least to avoid disaster. Nixon therefore challenged Aylmer's assessment of the strength of the Hanna position, commenting, "I cannot believe that [the] position in front of you can equal in strength those attacked and captured by us in the past which had been in preparation for 4 months."[74]

Thus, Aylmer reluctantly prepared to resume his advance as soon as possible. Weather conditions, however, did nothing to facilitate offensive operations or improve soldiers' morale. Heavy rain and high winds prevailed from 15 to 18 January, exacerbating the challenges Aylmer faced as he planned a hurried attack with a depleted force. The commander of the Tigris Corps initially planned to break through the defile by deploying a portion of his force to the right bank, where it would enfilade the Ottoman line on the left bank and facilitate a frontal assault against it by the bulk of his infantry, but the inclement weather repeatedly thwarted attempts to construct a bridge across the Tigris near the Wadi.[75] Sappers had almost completed a bridge on the 16th when high winds drove a boat into it, "carrying away a considerable portion" of the structure.[76] The sappers rebuilt the bridge the next day, but it promptly broke again on the evening of the 17th. After further efforts to repair the bridge overnight, high winds swamped it the next morning. The current then carried the wreckage down the Tigris, where it impeded the subsequent transport of equipment upriver by boat or barge. Aylmer ultimately managed to ferry the 7th Brigade and two squadrons of cavalry across the river. Artillery pieces, however, proved more difficult to transport.[77] Thus, only fourteen of Aylmer's forty-six guns reached the right bank, limiting the strength of his intended enfilade. According to Moberly, his inability to transfer firepower to the right bank "contributed greatly" to the failure to break through the Ottoman position.[78]

Sustained winds and rain also diminished the impact of the artillery on the left bank, but in different ways. The shortage of ammunition that prevailed throughout Mesopotamia in this period limited the intensity of Aylmer's bombardment of the Hanna position irrespective of other factors. According to Younghusband, "The artillery preparation could only be very meagre, for we only had a few guns and were short of ammunition."[79] The weather, however, limited aerial reconnaissance to only four flights from 17 to 21 January. While the aircraft attached to the Tigris Corps were apparently equipped with cameras in this period, there is no evidence that they were able to identify targets more specific than the two enemy lines at Hanna and the barbed-wire entanglements in front of them.[80] Thus, the guns were unable to maximize the impact of the limited ammunition at their disposal by directing their fire at specific locations.

Aylmer initiated the bombardment of the Hanna position early on 20 January with the intent of launching his infantry attack the following morning. Given the lack of air reconnaissance and the dearth of ammunition, the artillery struggled to suppress enemy fire, let alone destroy the enemy trenches. Aylmer directed Younghusband's 7 Indian Division to advance to within 150–200 yards of Ottoman lines under cover of the bombardment. The divisional war diary complained, however, that "whenever we have attempted to advance heavy fire was opened."[81] As a result, the units of Younghusband's division remained approximately 300 yards from the enemy line at the outset of their attack the next morning. Aylmer had ordered the artillery to resume at 6:30 AM on the 21st. After bombarding the enemy front line for ten minutes the guns would move on to the second line, at which point the infantry would advance. In accordance with Aylmer's directions, Younghusband ordered the 35th Brigade on his left to attack the enemy position near the Tigris, while the 9th Brigade on its right moved forward in support. Although the day began without rain, the weather continued to hinder the operation. Morning mist prevented the observation of artillery fire, compelling Aylmer to delay the bombardment until 7:45 AM.[82] Once the infantry units finally began advancing ten minutes later, they encountered thick mud produced by previous days' rain.[83]

The ineffectiveness of the artillery bombardment, combined with the wet ground, compounded the difficulties of Younghusband's long-suffering infantry. According to Chalmers, "Our men were sent across . . . flat open plain without a vestige of cover and over ground that was sodden with rain to the condition of a bog. They had been out in the rain without blankets or cover night and day and the cold chilled one to the bone. They advanced in extended order under a hail of bullets from machine guns, shrapnel and rifle and were simply decimated before they got to the trenches."[84] Notwithstanding Chalmers's bleak description, about one hundred soldiers from the 35th Brigade managed to capture a portion of Ottoman trenches and hold it for over an hour. To their right, however, the 9th Brigade encountered heavy fire and was consequently unable to provide assistance. The soldiers were subsequently forced to abandon the position in the face of fierce enemy counterattacks.[85]

With the advance stalled by late morning, Aylmer ordered the commencement of another ten-minute bombardment at 12:50 PM, followed by the renewal of infantry attacks against the entire Ottoman line. Shortly after he issued the order, however, heavy wind and rain resumed, increasing the difficulty of offensive operations. Seeing his prospects of victory slipping away, Aylmer attempted to expedite the attacks. At 11:45 AM he sent out a new order directing the artillery bombardment to begin thirty minutes earlier, at 12:20 PM. He also ordered two battalions of the 28th Brigade, in his General Reserve, to move forward to support Younghusband's force. At this stage, however, it was too late for the corps commander to influence the course of the battle. "To avoid confusion," Younghusband flatly refused to alter the original order to begin the bombardment at 12:50. The two additional battalions still arrived too late to assist in the attack. Given the deteriorating conditions and the losses already sustained by the infantry, it is not surprising that this attack failed. According to the divisional war diary, "the ground by this time was very heavy [and] slippery [and] the rifle fire from the Turkish trenches was very heavy."[86]

With little hope of success remaining, Younghusband met with Aylmer's chief of staff, Brigadier-General H. H. Austin, at 3:30 PM, and subsequently ordered his force to retire to the positions it had held on 19 January. Aylmer was initially annoyed by Younghusband's decision, which Austin apparently approved without his authorization. The retirement left 7 Indian Division up to 1,300 yards from the Ottoman line, undermining Aylmer's plan to renew the attack on the 22nd.[87] As the relief force attempted to reorganize on the evening of the 21st, however, it became abundantly clear that it was in no condition to advance the next day. The Tigris Corps incurred 2,741 casualties at Hanna, approximately 30 percent of its remaining strength after the battles at Shaikh Saad and the Wadi. Several battalions had lost more than half their strength, and some were effectively destroyed on 21 January. The 1/4th Hampshires, for example, suffered 81 percent casualties, while the 6th Jats lost 92 percent of their strength.[88] The brigade commanders involved in the attack "were unanimous in the opinion that any offensive on the 22nd by the troops engaged on the 21st was out of the question."[89] While the divisional war diary took pains to emphasize that the condition of Younghusband's formation did not reflect a "want of morale or loss of discipline," there is evidence that disaffection had reached dangerous levels in many Indian units, particularly those that included Muslim sepoys. T. A. Chalmers recorded in his diary that while "Sikhs fought brilliantly" at Hanna, "Muslims would not close."[90] Aylmer went further in the aftermath of the battle, informing Lake that he had "the gravest suspicions" of "very extensive self-mutilation" among Indian soldiers. Similarly, J. C. Catty of the 69th Punjabis recorded in his diary that

40 percent of wounds suffered by Indians in this period were deemed to be "suspicious."[91]

As the relief force attempted to reorganize on 22 January, Sir Percy Lake encouraged Aylmer to resume the offensive as soon as possible. Aylmer, however, retained no illusions about the capabilities of his force. As he conceded frankly to his superior on the 24th, he was "not in a position to reach Kut." Even after the arrival of reinforcements, he continued, "we shall have very little chance of success."[92] Despairing of his ability to relieve Townshend, Aylmer renewed his call for 6 Indian Division to make a sortie from Kut. The failure of the Tigris Corps at Hanna forced Townshend to lower his expectations. Rather than imminent relief, he now faced a choice between attempting to break out of Kut in the face of enemy opposition or reconciling himself to a prolonged confinement among soldiers and civilians he did not entirely trust. Townshend's repeated warnings regarding the morale of his force in December suggest that he had little confidence in its ability to hold out for an extended period. Three weeks into January, however, both his Indian subordinates and the local population remained largely compliant, while the Ottomans had demonstrated that they were intent on preventing the relief of Townshend's force. In this context, an extended siege appeared more palatable than a dangerous escape attempt that would almost certainly be contested.

Thus, on 21 January Townshend finally ordered a thorough inventory of food available in Kut, including a "house-to-house" search of local dwellings.[93] This exercise revealed that in addition to twenty-two days of remaining army rations, there was wheat atta for over thirty days for soldiers and local civilians alike, as well as hundreds of tons of barley that could be ground into flour. Moreover, there were 3,000 horses and mules in Kut, which could also be eaten. Based on the results of this inventory, Townshend argued that he should hold Kut until further reinforcements joined Aylmer downriver. He suggested on the 25th, "I do not see why we should not hold on here for another two months . . . in which case Army Commander could call troops from India or even Australians from Melbourne."[94] Aylmer could not hide his exasperation, commenting the next day, "this new information had it been communicated to me before would certainly have modified much of what I have unsuccessfully attempted to do and what I have proposed."[95] He nonetheless agreed that Townshend should remain at Kut while the Tigris Corps awaited the arrival of reinforcements.

CONCLUSION

Ironically, Charles Townshend's repeated requests for relief in December 1915 contributed significantly to the ultimate demise of his force. Convinced of the necessity of reaching Kut before Townshend's food supply ran out and the morale of his troops collapsed, Aylmer initiated operations without vital personnel, supplies, equipment, and intelligence regarding the strength and location of enemy positions. In addition, the inexperienced commanders of the relief force had no opportunity to become familiar with the tactical conditions they faced or the complexities of coordinating the actions of different formations and arms before commencing offensive operations. Aylmer in particular struggled in his role as a corps commander without a full corps at his disposal. At Shaikh Saad he altered plans developed by Younghusband and Kemball, diminishing their chances of success. At the Wadi his delay in ordering a frontal attack on enemy positions enabled Halil Bey to reinforce his threatened flank.

Aylmer and his subordinates may have learned from each of their engagements. Moreover, the arrival of staff officers and additional units helped compensate for losses incurred at Shaikh Saad and the Wadi. Nonetheless, Aylmer's chances of success diminished as the month progressed. Not only did the enemy retire to increasingly formidable defensive positions, but the morale of his troops deteriorated steadily as they were compelled to make largely unsupported frontal attacks against prepared enemy positions without basic amenities such as rations and warm clothing, or adequate medical care. Thus, while the Tigris Corps was numerically stronger at Hanna than it had been at Shaikh Saad, its chances of relieving Townshend's force had diminished since the beginning of January. The losses it suffered on the 21st rendered it incapable of offensive operations for the foreseeable future. By the end of January

Townshend could only watch helplessly as the enemy consolidated its positions around and below Kut. Thus, when the relief force finally resumed offensive operations in March, reaching Townshend's garrison would be a much more bloody and difficult task than it had been in January. Younghusband concluded in his memoirs, "[The] premature advance was responsible for all the tragedies that followed each other during the next four months."[96]

SIX

DEPRIVATION
AND DEFEAT

FEBRUARY–MARCH 1916

THE DEFEAT OF THE RELIEF FORCE AT HANNA NECESSITATED
an extended operational pause while its commanders awaited reinforcements and devised a new plan to break through Ottoman positions
below Kut. In the meantime, Townshend attempted to manage the expectations of his subordinates inside the town as the siege continued
into its third month. This period of relative inactivity ended on 8 March
when the Tigris Corps attacked Ottoman positions around the Dujaila
Redoubt on the right bank of the Tigris. Existing accounts of this period have focused on the climactic 8 March battle, which contributed
significantly to the ultimate outcome of the siege. The operations of the
relief force in early March certainly warrant careful examination. This
chapter will draw upon unit war diaries as well as postwar correspondence of senior officers in order to explain these operations, particularly
the assault on Dujaila Redoubt. In addition, however, it will also discuss
how Townshend's decisions in this period influenced both the outcome
of the 8 March battle and the morale of the Kut garrison in its aftermath.

UNDER SIEGE: THE KUT GARRISON,
JANUARY–FEBRUARY 1916

The struggles of the Tigris Corps in January convinced Charles Townshend that a delayed relief was not the worst possible scenario that he
faced. Thus, rather than pestering Aylmer to resume offensive operations as soon as possible after the repulse at Hanna, the commander
of 6 Indian Division acknowledged the importance of reorganizing and

strengthening the relief force. When he wired Aylmer on 25 January revealing that his search of Kut had uncovered sufficient supplies to last 84 days, Townshend also conceded that there was only a small likelihood of the enemy attacking Kut, and this would diminish due to expected seasonal flooding of the Tigris in the early spring. Even two weeks later on 7 February, Townshend wired Aylmer and Sir Percy Lake, advising: "If you have any doubts as to result, would it not be wiser to wait and unite all forces before advancing."[1]

Given the state of the relief force after 21 January, Townshend's advice was prudent, if belated. On the 27th, the war diary of 3 Indian Division, which had a fighting strength of only 2,800, described its disarray:

> Bdes [brigades] are to some extent composed of units & staffs unused to one another. They have lost so heavily in 3 actions during past 3 weeks that in some cases battns are reduced to less than 100. Great shortage of B[ritish] O[fficers]; and those still effective largely IAROs of no real experience. Add to this the most unfavourable weather conditions of rain and cold, men always wet, physical exhaustion intensified by constant moves, reliefs and fatigues in heavy wind; and a not over liberal scale of rations; and thin clothing. More movement than essential for any purpose whatever should be avoided till men are rested and to some extent re-organised.[2]

In the opinion of the new commander of IEFD, the need for reorganization extended to the upper ranks of the relief force. On 24 January Lake headed upriver from Basra with his chief of staff, Major-General A. W. Money, to visit Aylmer's headquarters. Money confided in a letter to his wife that day, "We're really going up to see if we can straighten out the mess that Aylmer has got into."[3] Three days later he continued: "I don't think Aylmer is much good for a big show. He is tremendously hard working, but immerses himself in detail instead of leaving the same to his staff." In an effort to ease the burden on Aylmer, Lake appointed Major-General George Gorringe as the new chief of staff of the Tigris Corps on 28 January. Gorringe replaced Brigadier-General H. H. Austin, who, according to Money, "has not been a success."[4] At first glance Gorringe was an unusual choice for a staff position. As commander of 12 Indian Division in Mesopotamia, he had developed a reputation as an aggressive field commander, capturing Nasiriya from the Ottomans in July 1915. According to T. A. Chalmers, commander of the Tigris hospital boat *Aerial,* "The general has the reputation of being a pusher and an able man, though extremely selfish and indifferent about the wounded."[5] These shortcomings notwithstanding, Gorringe appeared to be a counterweight to the meticulous commander of the relief force. In Money's opinion, Gorringe promised to "give Aylmer the driving power he seems to lack."[6]

By 4 February, Aylmer and his new chief of staff had devised a new plan to break through Ottoman defenses below Kut. After failing to overcome the enemy lines on the left bank of the Tigris at Hanna, Aylmer resolved to advance on the right bank, where the enemy presence was relatively sparse. While a small holding force pinned the Ottomans to the Hanna position, the bulk of the Tigris Corps would advance on the right bank to attack the enemy in the vicinity of Es Sinn. Depending on the outcome of the attack, the force would either continue across the Shatt-al-Hai and then across the Tigris to Kut, or simply facilitate the evacuation of 6 Indian Division from the town after Townshend made a sortie across to the right bank of the river. Increasingly aware that his relief was not a foregone conclusion, the commander of 6 Indian Division agreed to cooperate.[7]

Initially Aylmer and Gorringe had hoped to commence operations as soon as possible after 15 February. They faced opposition, however, from the commander in chief of the Indian Army, General Sir Beauchamp Duff, and the chief of the Imperial General Staff, General Sir William Robertson, the latter of whom had just assumed control over the campaign in Mesopotamia. Both Duff and Robertson favored delaying the advance until after 15 March, in order to await the arrival of two additional infantry divisions to strengthen the Tigris Corps. Aylmer and Lake countered that the arrival of additional Ottoman divisions and the expected onset of flooding in March threatened to undermine any offensive planned after the 15th. They also expressed doubts about the ability of the logistical system in Mesopotamia to support two additional divisions upriver from Amara. After considerable discussion by telegram, Aylmer resolved to advance in early March, by which point reinforcements as well as two additional infantry brigades were expected to have arrived.[8]

As relief efforts sputtered through January and subsided in February the soldiers of 6 Indian Division could do little but wait. The New Year had brought new hardships for the Kut garrison. While enemy shelling and sniping continued into January, the weather deteriorated significantly, forcing soldiers and sepoys to endure heavy rain and near-freezing temperatures clad only in their summer uniforms. Major E. G. Dunn, chief staff officer of the 18th Brigade, related in his diary on the 21st, "Troops here have no serge clothes, only the thin Indian khaki, with some warm underclothing, only what they stand up in."[9] Not surprisingly, the cold and wet conditions affected the health of the troops. According to Ronald Millar, thirty sepoys collapsed from exposure on 20 January alone.[10] Nonetheless, the collapse of morale that Charles Townshend feared did not ensue. Indeed, British units inside Kut remained relatively buoyant. Referring to his comrades in the Royal West Kents, Pte. H. J. Coombes recalled: "The worse conditions became, the louder they sang."[11]

The steadfastness of the troops more than a month into the siege stemmed in part from their faith in the Tigris Corps. At the beginning of January most soldiers expected relief "within a fortnight," after which they would return to Britain or India.[12] When Aylmer's force struggled to dislodge the Ottomans from their positions downriver, Townshend issued communiqués reassuring his subordinates that any delays in its progress were only temporary. In addition to remaining optimistic regarding their relief, the troops remained relatively well fed. Even in mid-January 1916, the British soldiers of 6 Indian Division received a full daily ration, comprising one pound of beef and one pound of bread, as well as allotments of jam, cheese, butter, sugar, tea, and dates. Sepoys' diets were less varied, but their daily ration still included one and a half pounds of flour for making chapattis, two ounces of sugar and of ghee, and four ounces of lentils, as well as twelve ounces of goat for those who ate meat.[13]

Aylmer's repulse at Hanna ushered in a period of growing hardship and uncertainty. As the relief force engaged the Ottomans on 21 January, the rising Tigris flooded British and Ottoman trenches running across the neck of the Kut peninsula, forcing both 6 Indian Division and the enemy forces opposing them to abandon their positions. The flooding compelled the soldiers of the Kut garrison to construct a series of bunds to prevent the inundation of additional trenches, but it also reduced the proximity of the two forces and the consequent threat of an Ottoman attack. While Townshend's troops retired to the "middle line" of their defensive system, 200 yards to the rear of their original position, the Ottomans fell back approximately 1,200 yards. According to Lieutenant D. A. Simmons, the floods made life "considerably easier" for units facing the enemy at the north end of the peninsula. Simmons related in his memoir of the siege, "The Turks were quite 1200 yards off and they had to cross all that distance of broken, swampy ground, so there wasn't much chance of us being surprised."[14]

The threat posed by an enemy attack, however, gave way to the more distant but equally ominous prospect of a prolonged siege that exhausted the resources of the Kut garrison. As Henry Rich of the 120th Rajputana Infantry remarked in his memoir, Aylmer's defeat at Hanna "was the first time some of us began to have doubts about an early relief."[15] The fact that the commander of 6 Indian Division shared these doubts is evident in his decision to reduce rations on 21 January.[16] Townshend had allotted full rations to his force for the first six weeks of the siege partly due to his confidence in an expeditious relief, but also due to his concerns regarding the reliability of his Indian subordinates. Given that his suspicions regarding Indian morale had not disappeared, Townshend's decision to reduce rations nonetheless is a clear indication of his reluctant acknowledgment of the possibility of a prolonged confinement inside Kut.

The reduction of rations had a significant impact on soldiers' lives. Initially, British soldiers saw little change in the amount of staples such as meat and bread that they received on a daily basis. Condiments and luxuries such as cheese, butter, jam, sugar, and tea, however, became increasingly scarce. Major Alexander Anderson, the commander of the Volunteer Artillery Battery, related regarding late January, "Now came the time for beginning to tighten belts. Luxuries had of course become scarce earlier and were only to be found in the hands of the very lucky few. Now it came to be the case of the gradual disappearance of the things that in ordinary times are looked upon as common necessities. As each gave out one came to realise what a long list such things make.

Instead of a variety of food, with pepper and mustard and similar helps, one came down to a monotonous repetition of the same dish without flavourings."[17]

Sepoys continued to receive one and a half pounds of flour or atta daily, as a result of the discovery of 927 tons of barley and 100 tons of wheat during the 21 January search of the town. Ghee also remained available, given that the search uncovered 19½ tons of it.[18] Nonetheless the Indian diet also grew increasingly tedious as sepoys' rations of lentils, dried fruits, and spices declined or disappeared. Just as significant as reductions were qualitative changes to soldiers' diets. The relative abundance of barley led to its increasing replacement of wheat as the basis for the bread issued to British soldiers. More significantly, the exhaustion of the garrison's supply of canned bully beef (corned beef) compelled Townshend's force to begin consuming its pack animals. Least objectionable and therefore first to be eaten were the oxen normally used to pull artillery pieces. By late January, however, these had been eaten and the garrison had begun slaughtering its horses and mules for food.

British soldiers adapted to these dietary adjustments without complaint. Captain J. S. S. Martin, a doctor attached to 6 Indian Division, declared in a letter intended for his mother that the addition of barley "makes the most delicious bread you have ever tasted; one knows it is made direct from the pure grain: nothing is wasted – it is dark brown & delightfully flavoured." Whether or not the other ranks agreed with this assessment, the inclusion of the whole grain in the flour used for their bread resulted in the decline of beriberi, an affliction of the nervous system caused by a lack of thiamin, or vitamin B1. According to Martin, its symptoms were "swelling of the legs, loss of power in the leg & sometimes other muscles, increasing weakness of the heart lungs & digestion till death very commonly comes from heart failure." By late February, he related, "the admission rate to hospitals here for this disease has fallen to nil."[19]

Although the transition from beef to horse and mule represented a more dramatic culinary adjustment, British soldiers made it with little difficulty. Horse meat exceeded soldiers' expectations. As H. J. Coombes recalled, the soldiers of the West Kents were "agreeably surprised" after receiving their first ration in late January. Anderson pronounced it "not nearly so unpleasant as one expected."[20] Soldiers quickly devised numerous methods of serving the meat. Martin related, "We have him in (horse) steak and kidney pie, horse olives, horse mince, horse rissoles, potted horse, horse soup, stuffed horse heart, horse liver, etc." Officers even reconciled themselves to consuming their own mounts. According to W. C. Spackman, the medical officer attached to the 48th Pioneers, "when an officer's charger became the victim, the mess in question had the melancholy privilege of claiming the tongue and heart, by far the most acceptable items for the table."[21] Mule proved even more popular. Captain W. M. A. Phillips of the 24th Punjabis commented in his diary on 3 February, "We all prefer mule to horse flesh – it is more tender although mule soup is pretty strong."[22]

Whatever their opinion of horse and mule, British soldiers proved resourceful in supplementing the bread and meat that comprised the staples of their diet. Officers' messes were particularly fortunate as many retained a variety of canned goods that relieved the increasing monotony of the rations. Henry Rich related in his memoir of the siege, "Our mess president was an astute fellow. He had a small amount of mess stores that had arrived in Kut just before the advance to Ctesiphon. He allowed us one item a day, maybe a tin of sardines or a pot of jam, between the seven of us."[23] Similarly, W. C. Spackman recalled that "for many weeks I was able to supplement mess rations with extra items from our stock or barter with other messes; tinned bacon against whisky or jam for biscuits."[24] Officers also augmented their rations at the bazaar inside the town of Kut. According to Ernest Walker, a doctor attached to the 120th Rajputana Infantry, which held the village of Yakusub, the officers of the battalion regularly sent their Arab interpreter across the Tigris to procure condensed milk, Arab cigarettes, and occasionally "a little jam or odds and ends."[25]

The continued availability of food in the bazaar may seem surprising after Townshend's initiation of a thorough search of the town on 21 January. To seize all available foodstuffs hidden inside of Kut, however, would likely have required repeated searches and the assignment of soldiers to patrol the bazaar for an extended period. Moreover, the food sold there provided a relief from the growing tedium of bread and horse meat. To eliminate this illicit source of sustenance might have damaged the morale of soldiers, sepoys, and civilians. Given that the 21 January search had uncovered enough food to sustain the garrison for several months, Townshend likely concluded that the costs of closing down the bazaar exceeded its potential benefits in terms of increasing his ability to hold out inside of Kut. Thus, ordinary soldiers frequented the bazaar throughout the month of February. The Reverend Harold Spooner recorded in his diary that "hundreds of hungry Tommies are to be seen crowding the bazaar (native) buying Arab food . . . to keep themselves going."[26] According to Alexander Anderson: "The principal item, which came very much into fashion, was 'kabobs,' made of a paste of atta and water fried in ghi. If you were lucky enough to have jam to eat with them they were excellent, but they were almost as good with a little salt."[27]

While the countryside around Kut did not abound with wildlife, soldiers also augmented their rations by fishing and shooting. According to Ernest Walker, "Everyone fished. We made bullet-proof ways down to the water & fished from them and really did well, nearly every day we had fish."[28] The catch was not particularly appetizing. Rich characterized it as "a loathsome kind of mud fish that lived in the river just below the water line. In normal times, it would make you sick even to look at it." Nonetheless, he continued, "We ate it with relish whenever we had a chance to catch one."[29] More palatable than the unnamed fish were the songbirds that roosted around Kut. Referring to February 1916 in his memoirs, the medical officer Charles Barber recalled that "a new sport arose about this time – shooting starlings and sparrows for the 'pot.' Of these species there seemed to be unlimited numbers. Every evening at sunset they came home to roost in clumps of palms, making the while a terrible clatter. Someone discovered how good 'starling pie' was, and it soon became a popular dish so long as atta or potato meal could be obtained. It was at any rate a notable addition to our menu, and a very welcome change from the eternal horse-meat."[30]

Although none of these methods provided sufficient food to replace bread and horse or mule meat as the staples of British soldiers' diet, officers and other ranks alike clearly found a variety of ways to supplement their diminishing and increasingly monotonous rations. The sepoys who comprised the majority of the Kut garrison, however, faced two additional challenges. First, Indians had struggled to obtain fruit and vegetables since arriving in Mesopotamia, and they were likely deficient in ascorbic acid at the outset of the siege.[31] Once Townshend's force became trapped inside Kut, any supplies of fresh produce quickly disappeared. While British soldiers continued to receive a minimal amount of fruit in the form of jam, Indians had no access to fruit or vegetables. Thus, by late January sepoys began to develop symptoms of scurvy. Soldiers found an antidote in the form of boiled herbs and grasses picked from inside the defensive perimeter.[32] This prevented the disease from reaching epidemic proportions, but scurvy continued to plague the garrison throughout the siege. Ernest Walker first noted its appearance in late January. Two months later the hospital in Kut held more than 500 sepoys afflicted with scurvy.[33]

The second and even more serious threat to the survival of the garrison was the depletion of sepoys' accustomed sources of protein. Traditionally, Indians who ate meat received goat, which offended neither Hindu nor Muslim sensibilities. Those who did not consume meat received milk.[34] When supplies of both of these items were exhausted by the end of January, however, the vast majority of sepoys declined to follow their British counterparts in transitioning to horse and mule. This had several negative consequences. First, refusing fresh meat likely increased sepoys' susceptibility to scurvy. It also left them without an adequate source of protein. Moreover, the Indians' eschewal of horse and mule intensified the growing food shortage inside Kut. In comparison to the available supply of grain, there was a relative abundance of transport animals in the town. The reluctance of Indians to eat them compelled British officers to augment Indian rations with additional grain, limiting the amount available to feed animals. As a result, horses and mules had to be killed faster than they could be eaten because there was not sufficient grain to keep them alive. The chief supply officer of 6 Indian Division reflected in April, "If the Indians had eaten meat in January there would have been no need to kill off animals and by shortening the Indian grain ration our grain would have lasted longer."[35]

British officers recognized the dangerous effects of this mass abstention, interpreting it as an expression of Indian religious beliefs. Given their post-1857 sensitivity to and support of such beliefs, they were reluctant simply to order sepoys and followers to supplement their rations with horse or mule. Instead, Charles Townshend took a more circum-spect approach. In early February he requested that British authorities in India obtain statements from Indian religious leaders sanctioning the consumption of horseflesh during the siege. By the middle of the month, Townshend received word that from Indian Army headquarters that the Imam Jumma Musjid and a "leading Pandit," both of Delhi, had no objections to the addition of horse meat to the diet of Muslims and Hindus respectively. The chief of the Indian General Staff promised to obtain similar blessing from "leading Granthis," authorizing Sikhs to eat horse. British officers then posted copies of these messages around Kut in hopes of swaying the Indians.[36]

These proclamations, however, had little impact. For Indians in Mes-opotamia, the consumption of horse meat was objectionable not simply because they believed it ran counter to religious orthodoxy, but also because it differed from the norms in their own communities. Captain W. A. Phillips of the 24th Punjabis commented in his account of the siege, "There is no doubt that all casts were very greatly prejudiced against eating horseflesh and that, not so much from religious motives as from the reason that it had never been done before."[37] By 1916 the original ranks of many Indian battalions had been depleted by casualties and diluted by reinforcements. Nonetheless, many men from the same communities still served together in the same units. Correspondence between soldiers and their relatives in India throughout the war was considerable.[38] Sepoys therefore had ample reason to fear that if they broke dietary taboos at the front without the complicity of their com-rades, news of their conduct would reach their home communities and they would be ostracized upon their return. H. C. W. Bishop, a lieuten-ant attached to the 66th Punjabis, recalled in his memoir of the siege, "They declared that every village pundit would be against them on their return and that, in consequence, no one would give them their daughters to marry."[39] Thus, the blessings of religious figures remote to the daily lives of most Indian soldiers were hardly sufficient to allay their fears. The lone battalion of Gurkhas in Townshend's force took to horse meat fairly readily, perhaps as a result of British efforts since 1857 to modify Gurkha dietary practices that undermined military efficiency.[40] The vast majority of Indians in Kut, however, continued to abstain.

As a result, the health of Indian troops deteriorated significantly during February 1916. In addition to succumbing to scurvy, sepoys' refusal to consume horse or mule left them more susceptible than their British counterparts to diseases such as jaundice and pneumonia.[41] Moreover, as malnutrition set in, Indians became weaker and increasingly unable to recuperate from wounds. The doctor Charles Barber described this phenomenon in his account of the siege:

> Thanks to the scurvy and the diminishing ration, the surgeon's hand often had to be held when in normal circumstances it would have healed with certainty. One of the hardest things the doctor had to bear was the sight sometimes of battered humanity beyond the reach of his art, because he could no longer expect Dame Nature to do her part. Large wounds would sometimes begin by showing promise of healing for a few days, but would then stop and progress no further; would bleed when touched, and by their presence react on the enfeebled body that had no energy to deal with them.[42]

Thus, while the British members of the Kut garrison devised a variety of methods to cope with the progressive disappearance of their regular rations as February progressed, their Indian counterparts proved understandably reluctant to abandon rules and practices that had long governed their military service to the Raj while ensuring their status in their home communities. This reluctance contributed to the deterioration of Indian health and morale as the siege continued through February.

RESUMPTION OF RELIEF OPERATIONS AND THE BATTLE FOR DUJAILA REDOUBT

By mid-February Charles Townshend's limited reserve of patience had dissipated. In addition to affecting sepoys' health, the replacement of regular rations with horse and mule was beginning to hurt Indian morale. Around the 7th Townshend discovered that Afridi Pathans of the 24th Punjabis were discouraging other Muslims from eating horse meat. He recalled in his memoir, "How much worry did I suffer on account of these – in my opinion – greatly overrated troops!"[43] To make matters worse, intelligence reports suggested the arrival of two more Ottoman divisions along with thirty-six guns by the end of February. Thus, on 13 February Townshend wired Aylmer describing himself as "very anxious" that the Tigris Corps commander resume offensive operations as soon as possible.[44]

Eight days later Aylmer seemingly obliged. On the morning of 22 February Gorringe led a column comprising 3 Indian Division, the 36th Infantry Brigade, and two artillery batteries up the right bank of the Tigris past Hanna. The guns bombarded the Ottoman camp behind the Hanna position on the opposite bank, surprising the enemy. Meanwhile, part of the column continued up the right bank to Sannaiyat.[45] Gorringe later contended that "*had we been in possession of a pontoon train,* it would have been practicable to have crossed the Tigris, thrown a bridge across it, and to have shut in the Turkish garrison in their Hanna position."[46] In his recent history of the Mesopotamia campaign, the historian Charles Townshend has apparently accepted this argument, characterizing this initiative as "a real missed opportunity for a decisive stroke."[47]

On 22 February, however, the commander of the Tigris Corps had neither the intention nor the capabilities to trap the Ottomans in the Hanna position or to evict them from it. As the *Official History* explains, this would have required Gorringe's force to cross the Tigris in sufficient strength to engage the enemy in both directions, attacking Ottoman units at Hanna while repelling additional forces coming down the left bank of the river to their aid. The only possible means of achieving this was by constructing a boat bridge extending 300 yards across the river, but to do so would have required Aylmer to dismantle his only existing bridge, near his camp at the Wadi, and then move the boats upriver in view of the Ottomans, who could bring artillery fire to bear "on almost any crossing place" once they discovered the operation in progress.[48] Thus, unless Gorringe's appearance upriver from Hanna was sufficient to provoke the enemy units on the other side of the river into retiring, his initiative stood little chance of achieving significant results. Given the limited Ottoman presence on the right bank, however, Aylmer had little to lose by allowing Gorringe to attempt it. Even if it did not bear fruit, such a feint would serve to placate Townshend and reassure the soldiers inside Kut that they had not been forgotten. Townshend indeed instructed his troops to prepare to make a sortie on the 22nd if the opportunity arose. Although it did not, Ernest Walker noted in his diary that the sound of artillery fire downriver "cheered us up very much."[49]

According to Moberly, "General Aylmer's real motive for this movement along the right bank was to reduce the distance his force would have to march to the attack of the Es Sinn position."[50] The failed operations of the relief force in January had convinced the Tigris Corps commander of the importance of careful preparations in order to concentrate as much force as possible at a vulnerable point in the Ottoman defenses without the enemy becoming aware of the impending operation. Thus, Aylmer initiated a variety of deception operations as he prepared to resume the offensive. In conjunction with Gorringe's advance up the right bank on 22 February, he directed a brigade to move through the Suwaikiya marsh in an attempt to threaten the left of the Ottoman line at Hanna. During the last week of February he also initiated repeated bombardments of the Hanna position and assembled materials indicating the impending construction of a bridge upriver from Hanna.[51] Meanwhile, he made preparations for his advance on the right bank. On 5 March the arrival of the 37th Brigade from India brought the strength of the Tigris Corps to about 24,000 infantry, 1,400 cavalry, and ninety-two guns. This enabled Aylmer to leave approximately 5,000 troops and twenty-four guns to hold the enemy to the Hanna position while he sent nearly 19,000 infantry, 1,200 cavalry, and sixty-eight guns up the right bank toward the Es Sinn position. Combined with the approximately 10,000 members of the Kut garrison under Townshend, who promised to cooperate with the attack, this force had a significant advantage over the 10,000–11,000 Ottoman soldiers that Aylmer believed to be holding the enemy line on the right bank. This position extended south from the Tigris to the Dujaila Redoubt, one of a series of mounds that rose approximately twenty feet above the otherwise flat terrain.[52]

Thus, on 6 March, Aylmer issued orders for an attack against the Es Sinn line. This operation exceeded his previous efforts significantly in terms of its scale and complexity. The force was to concentrate on the evening of 7 March on the right bank approximately 10.5 miles from Dujaila redoubt. Before beginning the march toward the enemy line to the west, it was to divide into three groups. The first, under Major-General Kemball, comprised the 9th, 28th, and 36th Infantry Brigades, along with supporting artillery batteries and sappers. The second consisted

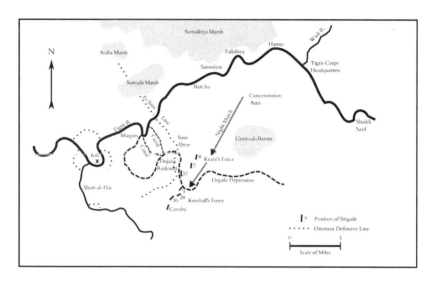

6.1. *The Attack on Dujaila Redoubt, 8 March 1916*

of the Cavalry Brigade under Brigadier-General R. C. Stephen, who had replaced Roberts in January. The third, commanded by Major-General Henry Keary, included the 7th, 8th, and most of the 37th Brigades, along with the bulk of the artillery. The 35th Brigade remained under Aylmer's control as a general reserve. After marching approximately six miles in the direction of the enemy line, the force was to diverge, with the first two groups moving southwest to a point about two miles south of the Dujaila Redoubt in the Dujaila depression, a shallow riverbed that provided limited cover from enemy observation and fire. Upon reaching this point at 6:15 AM on the 8th the cavalry would move west to provide cover while Kemball's group assaulted the redoubt from the south. Meanwhile, Keary's group was to continue advancing westward to positions approximately two miles east of Dujaila Redoubt and Sinn Abtar Redoubt to the north. At 6:15 AM, the artillery in Keary's force would come under Aylmer's command and begin shelling Dujaila Redoubt from these positions. The 37th Brigade, on the left of Keary's force, would support Kemball's attack to the south while the other infantry waited to assault the Sinn Abtar Redoubt and push north to the Tigris once the Dujaila position had fallen.[53]

Addressing the formation commanders involved in the attack on the afternoon of 7 March, Aylmer and Gorringe emphasized the importance of "vigour" and "dash" in its execution.[54] Yet the orders they issued discouraged these qualities. The attack required Aylmer's force to execute an extended march in darkness over unfamiliar terrain, followed by a complex combined-arms operation involving simultaneous complementary attacks, often without direct communication between adjacent units. While Keary and Kemball were able to communicate with Aylmer and with some of their subordinates by telephone, some brigade commanders proved difficult even to locate during the battle, and there does not appear to have been real-time communications between brigades.[55] Under these circumstances, the scope for miscues was considerable. Rather than allowing subordinate commanders to exercise their own initiative in responding to contingencies, however, Aylmer and Gorringe instead attempted to eliminate the fog of war by planning the operation in minute detail.[56] Thus, the operation order specified the marching formations for the units involved, the precise times and durations of halts to be made during the march to Dujaila Redoubt, and specific frontages and objectives for each brigade involved in Kemball's attack.[57] The meticulous nature of the plan undoubtedly reflected Aylmer's approach to command, which had been reinforced by his experiences in January, when, he believed, he had allowed too much initiative to his subordinates.[58] Nonetheless, it is significant that not only did Gorringe help plan the operation, but he would also have led it had he not suffered a minor but debilitating wound on 23 February. Given his predisposition to commanding in the field, it is likely that Gorringe was also reluctant to relinquish control of the operation. According to the postwar study of the campaign conducted at the Quetta Staff College, however, the detailed nature of the order "had a paralysing effect" on subordinate commanders.[59]

At least one of these subordinate commanders was sufficiently doubtful regarding the feasibility of the operation that he declined to play a leading role. According to the *Official History,* Aylmer intended that Keary's 3 Division would conduct the crucial assault on Dujaila Redoubt, but its commander "had other ideas of how success could best be attained."[60] While Keary's specific objections to the plan remain unclear, it is significant that he was one of the few formation commanders in the relief force in this period with extensive command experience on the Western Front. In 1914, Keary had accompanied the Indian Corps to France as a brigade commander. At fifty-six years of age, he was older than most of the officers who rose to command armies in the British Expeditionary Force. Keary nonetheless held high hopes for promotion, and in January 1915 he got his wish, as the commander of 3 Indian Division and two of its three brigade commanders were sacked. As the senior surviving officer in the formation, Keary was promoted to command the division.[61] This promotion simply whetted Keary's appetite. His letters to his brother in this period reveal a growing frustration as he failed to gain further recognition in the spring and summer of 1915 despite his apparent competence. Keary attributed his difficulties to a lack of contacts in the upper ranks of the British and Indian armies, which seemed to yield rewards for less capable officers. In June 1915 he commented sourly on the decoration of his predecessor in command of 3 Indian Division, H. B. B. Watkis, remarking, "I suppose they gave old Watkis his KCB as a sop, though why I don't know. He was a failure and has never done anything in the field at any time. But he is a Simla-ite in India and that may account for it." Keary also blamed the prejudices of senior officers in the British Army for his lack of progress. As he informed his brother, "The fact is that [Sir John] French and Douglas Haig hate the Indian Corps." He lamented having "the bad luck to be sent to France where we [Indian units] are in a minority rather than to Egypt or Dardanelles where we would be equal or in majority."[62]

In light of the disadvantages under which he apparently laboured in France, it might be expected that Keary would have welcomed the transfer of his division to Mesopotamia. On the contrary, the news sparked another bitter outburst to his brother. Keary complained, "I have been here a year and except for getting a Div[isio]n I have got nothing, and now to be kicked out of France where all our work will be forgotten at once to go and start afresh under a fresh commander who has his own troops who have been with him from the first, and of course will be employed and given any job of importance while we play second fiddle on the lines of communications, which is exactly what we are being sent over for. A squeezed orange sucked dry and chucked away."[63] Keary's cynicism and his apparent confidence in his own abilities suggest that he resented taking orders from commanders with less operational experience than himself. Moreover, despite the detailed nature of the plan to take Dujaila Redoubt, it likely appeared rather impetuous to Keary. In comparison with operations in which he had participated on the Western Front, the plan lacked artillery preparation and support, as well as definite information about the enemy's strength and location. While Keary's reluctance to participate may therefore be understandable, it further diminished the operation's chances of success by forcing Aylmer to delegate the crucial attack on Dujaila Redoubt to an ad hoc grouping of three brigades under Kemball, the commander of the 28th Brigade. The fact that the commanders and staffs of these formations had no previous experience working together compounded the difficulty of the operation.

Nonetheless, despite the combined challenges of distance, darkness, and unfamiliar terrain, the advance during the night of 7–8 March progressed reasonably smoothly. After several relatively minor delays, Kemball's force reached the Dujaila depression as dawn broke around 5:45 AM. Keary's force reached its assigned positions approximately forty-five minutes later. The Ottomans were completely unprepared for an attack on Dujaila Redoubt. Postwar correspondence with Turkish officers involved in the Mesopotamia campaign revealed that "the officer commanding on the right bank of the Tigris was at the start quite unaware of the surprise movement of the British." Thus, there were only about 2,000 Ottoman infantry holding the front line from the Tigris all the way to the redoubt on the morning of 8 March.[64] Kemball was not prepared, however, to take advantage of the surprise achieved by his force. Although the Cavalry Brigade to his left was ideally situated to threaten the Ottoman right flank and rear, Kemball could not direct it to advance because it remained under the control of Tigris Corps headquarters, which was not aware of the opportunity that had arisen. Thus, according to the Quetta Staff College study, "The Cavalry may be said to have exercised no effect on the battle. They hovered about in an ineffective way on the left, usually somewhat in rear of the infantry and always moving either with great deliberation or not at all."[65] Nor was Kemball willing to improvise with the force under his own control. When the commander of the 36th Brigade, Brigadier-General Christian, proposed abandoning Aylmer's plan and attacking the unprepared enemy, Kemball demurred, instead ordering all three brigades under his command to take cover in the Dujaila depression while he organized them to execute the plan detailed in Aylmer's operation order.[66]

This delayed the attack considerably. According to A. M. S. Elsmie, commanding the 28th Brigade on 8 March, "There was great confusion in the bed of the Dujailah. Men and animals mixed up anyhow and everywhere."[67] Kemball not only had to separate the brigades, but also to ensure that they deployed in the order and on the frontages specified in the directive issued by Aylmer and Gorringe. This entailed the movement of the 36th Brigade across the front of the 9th and 28th Brigades to its assigned position on the left flank.[68] As a result, Kemball's force did not begin advancing until after 9:30 AM, more than three hours behind schedule.[69] This delay had serious consequences for the success of the operation. After receiving a message from Kemball indicating that he was initiating his attack, Aylmer opened his artillery barrage against the Dujaila Redoubt at 7 AM. It was this that alerted the Ottomans to the impending attack and spurred the rapid transfer of reinforcements southward to positions around the embattled redoubt.[70] As a result, by the time Kemball's brigades finally began advancing they faced significant resistance from Ottoman forces south of the redoubt itself. To make matters worse, the 9th and 28th Brigades suffered considerable losses from machine-gun fire emanating from the 37th Brigade, which had been directed to support Kemball's advance on his right flank. Elsmie contended in a postwar letter to Moberly, "To the best of my belief the attack was held up by the fire of the brigade detailed to cover our advance." He elaborated in a subsequent letter: "No blame attaches to the brigade because it is impossible to guarantee that there will not be a mistake. Covering fire at long range especially is too dangerous." Nonetheless, he continued, "The O. C. Leicesters was shot at my side from this flank and several of my signallers were hit. The fire had also the disastrous effect of drawing off the 9th Brigade attack in its direction."[71]

This incident stemmed from the complexity of the operation, the speed with which it was initiated, and the rudimentary communications system available to facilitate its execution. The formations of the Tigris Corps began operations at daybreak on the 8th without conducting reconnaissance or even orienting themselves to their surroundings. Kemball reflected after the war, "Subordinate commanders must have started on the night march with only a hazy idea of the complicated manoeuvre about to take place." Moreover, he noted, "Troops in action in a country with a straight line for a horizon are apt to forget direction and shoot at anything they can see."[72] In addition, Kemball had no direct method of communicating with Brigadier-General F. J. Fowler, commanding the 37th Brigade, and each commander had only a vague idea of the other's location. As a result, it took over an hour for messages to travel between them on the morning of the 8th.[73] It was therefore difficult to determine the origin of friendly fire, and even harder to stop it in a timely manner.

The Ottomans took advantage of the delays and miscues plaguing Aylmer's attack, pushing increasing reinforcements into the front line around the Dujaila Redoubt. In essence, the Tigris Corps was attacking a rudimentary defense-in-depth. Rather than holding their front line in strength, the bulk of the Ottoman force was concentrated to the northwest, in a triangle formed by the Dujaila depression and two canals running south from the Tigris. From here they could move rapidly to the front using an "excellent system of communication trenches (from 2,000 to 4,000 yards long)."[74] By the afternoon, Ottoman troops from 51 Division were also being ferried across the Tigris to join the fight.[75] Faced with increasing resistance, Aylmer's artillery struggled to assist the infantry. Like the overall operation, the artillery program was carefully planned prior to the battle, and it proved difficult to abandon it in order to engage targets of opportunity and unexpected sources of enemy resistance. A shortage of forward observation officers exacerbated this problem. When the forward observation officer assigned to the 9th Brigade was killed on the morning of the 8th, for example, he was apparently not replaced. Even when observation officers were available, the rudimentary communications system rendered timely communication with the guns extremely difficult. As the 3 Indian Division war diary summarized the problem:

It is pointed out that it is very difficult for our infantry to get our guns onto
targets that are of importance. The guns have a detailed programme to adhere
to and if the trenches they are scheduled to bombard happen to be empty and
others, of which nothing was known previously, are inflicting heavy losses
on us and are manned it is difficult, even if the F.O.O. is up with the Inf[antry]
B[riga]de, to get the guns switched onto the new target. It is also stated that
during intensive bombardments when every battery had a fixed allotted task,
good targets of enemy moving across open to reinforce escaped without being
fired on.[76]

By mid-afternoon Aylmer realized that Kemball's force was unable to
take Dujaila Redoubt from the south. He therefore directed the 8th Brigade, part of Keary's force, to attack it from the east. This formation only
began to move forward at about 4 PM, by which point enemy defenses
had strengthened considerably. According to the Quetta Staff College
study, "The attack was delivered over 3,000 yards of perfectly flat open
ground with the sun low in the eyes of the attackers and behind the
backs of the defenders. It was delivered on the long face of the Redoubt,
where there were 3 to 4 lines of fire 200 yards in length, and had to cross
directly the Dujaila depression down which artillery and M.G. fire had
been well-organized by the Turks from the right (North) flank."[77] Despite the extent of enemy opposition, soldiers from the 1st Manchesters
and the 59th Rifles managed to enter the redoubt itself. This success
proved difficult to reinforce, however, as the artillery was unable to suppress Ottoman fire on the Dujaila depression. According to the 3 Indian
Division war diary, "The artillery appeared to be co-operating well onto
the DUJAILAH mound but apparently no fire was brought to bear on
the flank trenches NE and SE from which the heavy cross fire, that inflicted most casualties, came. The DUJAILAH depression was vigorously
enfiladed by MG from direction of SINN AFTAR and a very close and
accurate shrapnel fire from the same direction."[78]

Without additional troops and ammunition, the units that had
fought their way into the redoubt were unable to hold their positions
against enemy counterattacks, which forced them to retire around dusk.
Thus, the day ended with Dujaila Redoubt still in enemy hands. In the
evening it became clear to Aylmer that in addition to having incurred
thousands of casualties, his force faced a shortage of water. He therefore ordered subordinate commanders to prepare to withdraw the next

morning. After determining that enemy forces remained in the vicinity of the Es Sinn line early on the 9th, Aylmer ordered the Tigris Corps to make its way 18 miles back to the Wadi.

In the words of the official historian, the conduct of the Dujaila operation "has probably given rise to more comment and criticism than any other action in the campaign."[79] In addition to Aylmer, who devised the operation, George Kemball has been the recipient of much of this criticism. After the war, Ottoman officers disparaged Kemball's failure to capitalize on their ill-preparedness on the morning of 8 March, claiming that "it should have been possible to capture SAIS and to reach KUT-EL-AMARA with only a slight effort."[80] In his report on the operation, Gorringe also singled out Kemball for his lack of "energetic and bold action" in the initial stages of the battle.[81] While Kemball clearly missed an opportunity at the Dujaila Redoubt, it is difficult to fault him for drawing similar lessons to Aylmer from their previous experiences in 1916. Kemball was not a timid commander, but after taking heavy losses in hastily planned attacks in January he had learned to value careful planning and circumspection. After the war he maintained to Moberly that criticisms of his decisions "really rest on the assumption that I ought to have known that the Dujaila position was not held by 4,500 infantry with another 4,000 in reserve at Maqasis as we had been told." Moreover, he continued, "In practically every battle I had seen, it looked as if the Turks had gone, until they actually opened heavy fire."[82]

Nor was Kemball alone in his wariness. On the morning of the 8th Fowler's 37th Brigade was ordered to take up positions about 2,000 yards east of Dujaila Redoubt, from which it would support Kemball's attack. After discerning that the redoubt was only lightly defended, Fowler contacted Keary, his superior, asking permission "to push on and seize the Redoubt." Like Kemball, however, Keary proved unwilling to abandon Aylmer and Gorringe's plan without permission.[83] Overall, while the meticulous plan executed by Aylmer, Gorringe, and their subordinates had manifest shortcomings, it was an understandable response to the challenges they faced in Mesopotamia, and one that was broadly consistent with the ideas of British commanders on the Western Front in the same period.

More puzzling is the behavior of Charles Townshend on 8 March. Prior to the battle, Townshend had indicated that he would support the attack on the Es Sinn position by sending two full brigades across the Tigris to attack the enemy as soon as he observed Aylmer's force rounding the Dujaila Redoubt and beginning to roll up the enemy line at Es Sinn. He certainly prepared his force for this possibility. According to W. M. A. Phillips the 30th Brigade was "held in readiness to cross the river should the attack be successful."[84] Halil Bey was concerned about the possibility of a sortie from Kut, as he did not believe Ottoman forces on the right bank could withstand concurrent attacks from two directions. As the Ottomans observed in postwar correspondence, however, when the battle actually occurred, "General Townshend remained in complete inactivity as a spectator, and made no attempt to cooperate with Aylmer."[85] In his memoir Townshend attributed his inactivity primarily to Aylmer's lack of progress, but he was also clearly concerned about the possibility of an enemy attack on Kut itself. Three nights before the attack, several members of the boat crews that Townshend planned to use to get his force across the Tigris on the 8th escaped from Kut and apparently informed the Ottomans about his preparations for a sortie. As a result, he explained, "it was quite possible that, when the direction of [Aylmer's] attack was discovered, an attack would be made by the investing force at Kut on the north-west or north-east front of my defences in order to contain me in the town."[86]

Given the widespread expectation that seasonal flooding would soon impede further relief efforts, as well as the fact that the Kut garrison had repelled previous Ottoman attacks against the northern part of its defensive perimeter, initiating a sortie to assist Aylmer's potentially decisive operation might seem like an acceptable risk for Townshend to have taken. The commander of the Kut garrison believed, however, that such an initiative would require him to send his most reliable troops across the Tigris, leaving Kut itself in the hands of soldiers he did not trust. While Townshend's fears regarding his Indian subordinates in December had not been realized, the deterioration of their health and morale due to their abstention from horse and mule meat throughout February had raised his concerns again. As he noted in his memoir, desertion "became prevalent among the Indian troops" toward the end of February.[87] In light of his concerns, Townshend elected not to take action until he observed Aylmer's force rounding Dujaila Redoubt and beginning to roll up the Es Sinn line.

In light of the difficulties encountered by the Tigris Corps on the morning of 8 March, however, Townshend's intervention was required much earlier in the battle in order to deter the enemy from sending reinforcements to the vicinity of Dujaila Redoubt. In the view of the Quetta Staff College survey, waiting for Aylmer's force to take the redoubt "was tantamount to not cooperating at all" during the decisive phase of the battle. While there is limited benefit to speculating as to what might have happened had he actually conducted a sortie, the survey did so nonetheless, arguing that "the scales were held so evenly that a very little more weight on our side would have tipped them in our favour. This weight could have been provided by General Townshend crossing or even attempting to cross to the right bank."[88]

DETERIORATION OF THE KUT GARRISON

Aylmer's failure at Dujaila Redoubt caused considerable frustration inside Kut. Ernest Walker recorded in his diary, "We were absolutely on the tip-toe of expectation expecting any minute to see masses of the enemy retiring on our own bank & to get the order to burst out & take them in the flank." When the order never came, he continued, "we felt very down on our luck."[89] Other British officers recorded similar sentiments. W. C. Spackman recalled being "bitter and disconsolate" after the battle, while H. J. Coombes noted his "intense disappointment."[90] The flooding of the Tigris on 14 March compounded soldiers' dismay as it dashed any remaining hopes of an imminent end to their captivity. It also led to an increasing scarcity of food. In an effort to prolong the siege until another relief operation could be organized, Townshend ordered the slaughter of 1,100 pack animals in order to preserve grain for his Indian subordinates. He also shut down the food vendors in the Kut bazaar and reduced rations yet again. British soldiers now faced an unvarying daily allotment of 8 ounces of bread and 1¼ pounds of horse meat. Indians were allowed 12 ounces of horse and 10 ounces of atta, as well as 4 ounces of "parched barley," but the vast majority continued to refuse the meat.[91]

While British soldiers continued to look forward to relief, their prolonged captivity had clearly lowered their morale. J. S. Barker, an engineer inside Kut, characterized them as "apathetic" in the wake of the
Dujaila battle. Many had also become increasingly resentful of the Indians. As Barker himself commented in his diary: "The Indian troops'
feelings I know nothing about & care less. As regards modern war the
Indian soldier is as extinct as the dodo – so I heard a big soldier say a few
days ago – & it is absolutely true."[92] This resentment resulted in large part
from the Indians' abstention from horse and the consequent need to give
them extra grain rations. According to Walker, this "caused a lot of bad
feeling between British & Indian troops, even British officers of Indian
battalions lost touch with their men & spoke very bitterly about their
limitations." Walker spent the siege with two Indian battalions in the
village of Yakusub, across the Tigris from Kut. As he related: "We felt the
presence of a company of Norfolks a great comfort at this stage, as after
all in the two regiments we were only 13 white men leading 700 Asiatics
against 15,000 other Asiatics, from whom we were separated by a flimsy
barbed wire fence & a few hundred yards of mud."[93]

Indian opinions of their British counterparts are more difficult to
determine. It is clear, however, that Indian morale had deteriorated well
beyond apathy and resentment by mid-March. In Walker's words, the Indian ration of atta and barley "was just enough to keep the garrison alive
but not sufficient to enable men to do strenuous work."[94] The flooding
of the Tigris, however, forced sepoys to spend nights repairing trenches
inundated with water. As a result of malnourishment and overwork they
became increasingly susceptible to disease. The deteriorating conditions
inside Kut combined with the diminishing prospect of relief also led
to an increase in the incidence of desertion. British officers created a
strong deterrent by shooting any soldiers caught absconding from Kut.
They also posted notices warning that deserters would be proclaimed
outlaws in their home districts and have their property confiscated.[95]
Nevertheless, both British and Turkish accounts suggest that the rate
of desertion increased in March 1916, particularly in Muslim units. On
the 14th Townshend complained to Lake: "I have had five more Indian
Mehamadans desert last night, one of them a Havildar of the 103rd, 3
from the 67th Punjabis, and one of the 22nd Punjabis."[96]

A total of 147 soldiers successfully deserted to the enemy during the siege. A smaller number were shot while attempting to do so. There were also at least a few sepoys who left their units on the defensive perimeter and attempted to evade detection in the town of Kut.[97] Clearly this represents only a small proportion of the Indians in Townshend's force. According to E. G. Dunn, the chief of staff of the 18th Brigade, "The few desertions we have had have been from the Punjabi Regiments chiefly and mostly since the second failure to relieve us. Almost without exception they are young soldiers of from 14 to 16 months service only."[98] Given the penalties facing both successful and unsuccessful deserters, however, as well as the declining physical capabilities of the Indians, the growing incidence of desertion in March suggests mounting disaffection, or desperation among those trapped inside Kut.

Even more indicative of desperation is the incidence of suicide in this period. While it is doubtful that this was a widespread phenomenon, the bleak choice between starvation and breaking dietary taboos apparently compelled some sepoys to take their own lives. The medical officer W. C. Spackman recalled attending to "a young sepoy who had put the muzzle of his loaded rifle against his stomach and discharged it with his toe." Others chose less direct means. According to another officer, "Although the garrison was being issued with horsemeat, many of the Indian troops refused to eat it. Gen. Townshend obtained permission for them to do so, from their leaders in India, but some of them, rather than break their caste, preferred to commit suicide. To do this, they would walk to the river bank, stand with folded arms, and wait for an enemy sniper to shoot them."[99]

Townshend went to considerable lengths to maintain Indian morale in this period. On 16 March Lieutenant G. N. Rogers recorded in his diary that "Gen Townshend sent for four senior IOs and told them that all would be over by the end of this month & we would be relieved. Also that Gen Aylmah [*sic*] had been sent back owing to grave mistakes in his last attack which were the cause of the failure to relieve us & that Gen Gorringe was now commanding and that he assured them again that this month would see the end of all of our troubles."[100] Such promises, however, were counterproductive, for two reasons. First, the expectation of an imminent end to the siege encouraged Indians to continue their abstention from horse meat based on the expectation that they would soon have access to regular rations.[101] Consequently, their health continued to deteriorate. In addition, when March ended without further relief attempts, Townshend's credibility diminished even further in the eyes of his Indian subordinates.

By early April the Kut garrison faced a serious crisis. According to Townshend, his British subordinates remained "as tenacious and brave as ever." Their more numerous Indian counterparts, however, were increasingly "dejected and weak."[102] By this point sepoys were largely incapable of sustained physical exertion. The war diary of the 104th Rifles commented on 1 April that its soldiers were "not strong enough to work more than one hour a day."[103] In light of the deteriorating morale and physical condition of the majority of his force, Townshend admitted to Percy Lake in Basra that he was no longer capable of cooperating with any relief efforts. Thus, as his food and supplies grew increasingly scarce, the commander of the Kut garrison was increasingly incapable of influencing the outcome of the siege.

CONCLUSION

The relief of Kut depended on both the ability of the Tigris Corps to break through Ottoman positions below the town as well as Charles Townshend's ability to maintain the health and morale of his force. In February and March of 1916 neither Townshend nor his counterparts in the relief force were particularly successful in their respective tasks. Aylmer and Gorringe faced an extremely difficult challenge in moving 20,000 troops up the right bank of the Tigris without enemy detection and then conducting a combined-arms operation against the Es Sinn line. On the morning of 8 March they came remarkably close to success. Ultimately, however, the careful orchestration necessary to achieve the concentration of the relief force at a vulnerable point in the Ottoman defensive line deterred commanders such as Kemball and Keary from seizing the initiative when unforeseen opportunities appeared. Charles Townshend also contributed to the failure of the Dujaila operation by standing pat throughout. As he had done since the Battle of Ctesiphon, Townshend continued to tread carefully around his Indian subordinates in an effort to minimize disaffection. His inability to convince them to eat horse or mule, however, left sepoys increasingly malnourished and discontented by early March. Distrustful of the majority of his force, Townshend declined to make a potentially decisive intervention in the battle on 8 March. In turn, the failure of the relief force at Dujaila Redoubt exacerbated discontent inside Kut and left Townshend unable to contribute to his own relief. By adhering to the long-standing British policy of respect for the religious scruples and traditional practices of his subordinates, Townshend instead contributed to the demise of his force.

SEVEN

INNOVATION, STARVATION, AND SURRENDER

APRIL 1916

A SENSE OF FUTILITY PERVADES MOST ACCOUNTS OF THE FINAL weeks of the siege. Downriver from Kut the relief force threw itself repeatedly against formidable Ottoman defenses in a vain attempt to reach the embattled 6 Indian Division before its food supply was finally exhausted. Meanwhile, inside the town, Townshend progressively reduced his subordinates to a starvation diet in order to prolong his resistance.[1] In general terms these characterizations are accurate, but they do not tell the whole story. As Andrew Syk has argued, senior British commanders in Mesopotamia adopted a more methodical approach to operations in this period, emphasizing careful planning and close cooperation between infantry and artillery.[2] Townshend also changed tactics in an attempt to convince his Indian subordinates to abandon their aversion to horse meat.[3] New methods achieved unprecedented success both inside and outside of Kut in April 1916. Ultimately, however, they were introduced too late to avert the capitulation and captivity of Townshend's force as well as the demise of many of its members.

OPERATIONS OF THE RELIEF FORCE, 9 MARCH–10 APRIL

On 11 March Percy Lake replaced Fenton Aylmer, giving command of the Tigris Corps to Aylmer's chief of staff, George Gorringe. The change elicited few protests from members of the relief force. Recording Aylmer's departure in his diary, T. A. Chalmers acknowledged that "everyone is sorry to see him go as he was a thorough gentleman." Nonetheless, he continued, "As a general he was a complete failure, having through years of office work completely lost the personal touch so necessary if a man aspires to be a real leader of his fellows."[4] Aylmer's successor, however, generated little enthusiasm. After praising the Tigris Corps chief of staff effusively in late January, A. W. Money conceded to his wife on 11 March, "Gorringe is a very fine fellow, but I'm not sure he's really fit enough to take up the command." Chalmers suggested that Gorringe was largely responsible for the failure at Dujaila Redoubt, contending that he "was really running the last show with Aylmer as figure head."[5]

Notwithstanding the low expectations that accompanied his appointment, Gorringe benefited from an operational pause that enabled him to bolster the relief force with additional troops, artillery, equipment, and tactical expertise. By Charles Townshend's calculations, the drastic measures he implemented following the Dujaila operation enabled the survival of the Kut garrison until 15 April.[6] This gave Gorringe several weeks to plan and resume offensive operations. The flooding of the Tigris in mid-March hindered his preparations, inundating the road from Shaikh Saad to Tigris Corps headquarters at the Wadi, thus delaying the arrival of reinforcements and artillery pieces. It also kept troops busy repairing bunds rather than sapping toward Ottoman positions on both banks of the river.[7] Nevertheless, by the beginning of April the Tigris Corps had grown to an unprecedented size of approximately 30,000 infantry and 127 guns. The air component supporting Gorringe's operations had grown to eight planes, with aircraft devoted specifically to the task of artillery observation for the first time since relief operations began. Gorringe also had four gunboats at his disposal as well as pontoons and other bridging equipment that had not been available previously.[8]

These resources enabled the new commander of the Tigris Corps to develop a comprehensive plan to free Townshend's force by mid-April. The first phase involved dislodging the Ottomans from their positions in and across the river from the defile between the Tigris and the Suwaikiya marsh. Gorringe proposed to begin by capturing the Ottoman lines at Hanna. This would compel enemy forces on the left bank to retire to a second line at Sannaiyat, at the west end of the defile. This effected, Gorringe intended to use pontoon and boat bridges to transfer a full division across the river to attack the Ottoman positions at Abu Roman

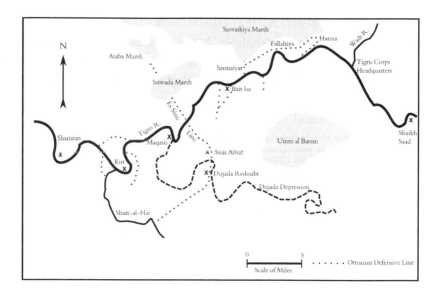

7.1. *Tigris Corps Area of Operations, April 1916*

and Bait Isa, from which he believed that the enemy could inundate the approaches to the Es Sinn line by opening bunds along the right bank of the Tigris. He would then return forces to the left bank to pry the enemy out of the defile once and for all. The capture of Sannaiyat would allow British units there to fire on other Ottoman positions along the right bank, presumably compelling their abandonment. By 8 April, Gorringe hoped to force the Ottomans back to an attenuated front extending from the western end of the Suwaikiya marsh southward through the Suwada marsh, across the river along the Es Sinn line to Dujaila Redoubt and then southwest all the way to the Shatt-al-Hai. Free to concentrate his force at a point of his choosing along this line, Gorringe believed he could break through and reach Kut before the 15th.[9] Delays in the arrival of aircraft as well as stormy weather at the end of March forced him to postpone his offensive from 1 until 5 April, but the Tigris Corps commander still believed that he could execute his plan successfully before Townshend's garrison succumbed to hunger.

Spearheading the initial stage of Gorringe's offensive was Major-General Stanley Maude's 13 Division, the first wholly British formation to fight in Mesopotamia. According to Maude's biographer, Charles Callwell, "The arrival of an entirely British Division at the front had given great encouragement to the Tigris Army Corps, and officers and men belonging to it could not but feel that the force which was trying to relieve Kut was looking to them for a lead."[10] It would prove difficult for 13 Division to live up to these expectations. Part of Kitchener's New Army, the division had first seen action at the Dardanelles in 1915, suffering heavy casualties that had only recently been replaced with "raw recruits" when it arrived in Mesopotamia.[11] Thus, in addition to being entirely unfamiliar with the terrain and weather in Mesopotamia, most officers and other ranks of the division had considerably less military experience than those of 3 and 7 Indian Divisions. As was the case inside Kut, however, the reputation of Indian, or "native," soldiers had diminished considerably in the eyes of their British counterparts in the relief force by the spring of 1916. As the cavalry officer J. E. Bridges commented in a February letter to his father: "I do hope we get more guns and British Infantry. The native production is now totally and absolutely discredited here, just as he has been in Europe and in every other theatre of war in which he has appeared. He is now admitted by everyone from General downwards to be more a real danger than a help."[12] Given the prevalence of attitudes such as this, 13 Division was viewed as an inherently superior formation regardless of its actual experience or effectiveness. Gorringe assumed that the Ottomans shared this opinion, as he attempted to conceal the arrival of a British division at Hanna in early April by retaining Indian troops in his front lines opposite the enemy.[13]

The credentials of 13 Division may have been debatable, but those of its commander were not. While Stanley Maude would ultimately be credited with reversing British fortunes in Mesopotamia and capturing Baghdad in 1917, he initially distinguished himself as commander of the 14th Brigade on the Western Front in 1914 and early 1915. Sir Horace Smith-Dorrien, commander of the British 2nd Army in 1915, described him as "one of my best brigadiers."[14] In the summer of 1915 Maude was promoted to major-general and sent to the Dardanelles to lead 13 Division. Over the first year of the war, he earned a reputation as meticulous and demanding, yet sympathetic toward his subordinates. As one of his staff officers described him: "To commence with . . . General Maude was a difficult man to work under – as his desire for, and knowledge of, detail was almost uncanny. But gradually and kindly he instilled his methods into his staff, and was not satisfied until he had done so."[15]

In a recent analysis of command in the Mesopotamia campaign, Andrew Syk has highlighted the emergence of a "managerial" command style in April 1916, characterized by detailed orders featuring "prescriptive timetables" and careful coordination between infantry and artillery, as commanders and staff officers "sought to trade in flexibility for greater certainty."[16] This approach was evident in Maude's initial attack on the Ottoman position at Hanna. By early April this position consisted of "five entrenched lines one behind the other covering a depth of about one and a half miles, with a number of guns positioned behind the third line."[17] Preparations to overwhelm it began in late March, as units of 7 Division dug saps progressively closer to the enemy's front line, British aircraft took photographs of the Ottoman trenches, and British officers determined the exact moment at which to initiate attacks so as to "get full advantage of the half-light."[18] On the 30th the artillery initiated the largest and most sophisticated bombardment that had been executed to that point in the Mesopotamia campaign. More than 120 guns, supplemented by those on the four gunboats on the Tigris, were assigned specific tasks including counterbattery fire, breaching of enemy defenses, and support of the advancing infantry on the day of the attack. By the morning of 5 April the guns had succeeded in destroying most of the wire in front of the enemy's first line and inflicting significant damage on Ottoman trenches and supply lines. According to the Ottoman staff officer Muhammad Amin, "This bombardment was particularly severe from the 30th March to the 4th April. Our powers of resistance were quite overwhelmed by the enemy's superior artillery, and our organization of supplies was destroyed."[19]

On the morning of the 5th, the emphasis of the artillery switched from destructive to suppressive fire. No bombardment preceded the attack by 13 Division. Instead, three minutes after the infantry began advancing, the guns opened on the third of the five Ottoman lines at Hanna and the trenches behind it. Once the infantry captured the first line, the guns initiated a rudimentary creeping barrage intended to move forward in advance of the troops on the ground.[20] To ensure coordination between artillery and infantry once the battle began, telephone lines linked artillery commanders with infantry brigade commanders, and forward observation officers accompanied every infantry battalion.[21] These new methods may have emanated from Gorringe's headquarters. It is more likely, however, that Maude and his staff developed them based on their experiences in Europe and at the Dardanelles.

Maude and his staff planned the infantry advance in even greater detail. At 4:55 AM on 5 April all three brigades advanced in unison, the soldiers in the outer brigades divided into eight lines and those in the center brigade, which comprised only three battalions, divided into six. The first battalion in each brigade was directed to capture and consolidate the first enemy line, while the second battalion proceeded to the second line, and the third battalion in each brigade assisted by the fourth battalion in the outer two brigades proceeded to the third enemy line. Orders issued prior to the attack included a map showing the objective of each battalion, and officers and NCOs were assigned specifically to the task of ensuring that no unit lost direction during the advance. Soldiers carried 220 rounds of ammunition, six sandbags, a day's ration as well as an iron ration, and a full water bottle. The infantry carried Mills grenades forward with them in canvas buckets, and even took measures to ensure that bayonet scabbards and entrenching tools did not "rattle together" as soldiers moved forward.[22]

Given the scale and duration of these preparations, however, it is not surprising that the Ottomans expected an assault at Hanna in early April. While German commanders on the Western Front in 1914 and 1915 as well as their Ottoman counterparts at the Dardanelles would likely have held their positions nonetheless, senior officers in the Ottoman 6th Army were not so inclined. By the end of March, von der Goltz's 6th Army headquarters in Baghdad was increasingly concerned about the arrival of enemy reinforcements, fearing "that the balance was turning in favour of the British." This belief influenced the decisions of subordinate commanders closer to the front. Surmising correctly that the artillery bombardment signalled the beginning of another offensive operation, Halil Bey conceded the Hanna position to the British, withdrawing Ottoman forces on the left bank to prepared positions at Sannaiyat, about six miles to the west. In order to buy time to "put the new line in a complete state of defence," Halil left a single regiment in a makeshift position at Falahiya, about halfway between Hanna and Sannaiyat.[23]

Thus, when 13 Division began advancing at 4:55 AM on 5 April, its infantry encountered little resistance. The divisional war diary commented laconically that "Turks were found to be holding the position lightly." T. A. Chalmers summarized the situation more colorfully and perhaps more accurately, commenting in his diary, "The Turks in fact sold us another pup and withdrew all their men and guns before the fight, as they knew they could not hold it without heavy loss through being unable to get away."[24] As a result, when the infantry reached the Ottoman position they found only "a few rifles and machine guns and a large notice on which was written 'Au revoir à la prochaine bataille.'"[25] By 5:40 AM the first and second Ottoman lines were in British hands. Units only began suffering significant casualties when they ran into their supporting artillery barrage, which had lingered just beyond the second enemy line based on the expectation that resistance would be greater. Once the barrage moved on, however, the infantry resumed the advance, capturing the third line before 6 AM.[26] As the morning progressed, units encountered increasing enemy fire, possibly from Ottoman positions at Fallahiya. By 11 AM 13 Division had suffered approximately 500 casualties. Therefore, rather than continuing to press forward, Gorringe directed 13 Division to halt at 12:20 PM, with the intent of resuming the advance at nightfall.[27]

The postwar study conducted by the Quetta Staff College argued that this delay "proved fatal to our success at Sannaiyat."[28] Clearly, rapid progress was essential if the Tigris Corps was to free the Kut garrison by 15 April. Nonetheless, given the strength of the enemy position at Sannaiyat, it is doubtful that 13 Division could quickly have overwhelmed it without preparations similar to those that enabled the capture of the Hanna position. Moreover, even to reach Sannaiyat on the afternoon of 5 April would have required a frontal attack across open ground in order to dislodge Ottoman troops from the Fallahiya position to the east.[29] Impromptu operations that traded human lives for speed were not in the tactical repertoire of the 13 Division commander. Nor, after witnessing the losses incurred during extemporized advances at Dujaila Redoubt, is it likely that Gorringe favored another such attack. Thus, 13 Division operations came to a halt until 7:15PM, when the artillery began bombarding the Fallahiya position. Fifteen minutes later Maude's infantry attacked it. Even though it was launched under the cover of darkness with artillery support, the attack still proved costly. The small Ottoman force assigned to hold the position fled to avoid capture, but not before inflicting "severe casualties" on the advancing force.[30] In his diary, Maude declared that "everything went splendidly. There were the usual lot of panic messages which came in and spoke of everything having failed and everyone being killed, but nothing could be better than the work of the Division and indeed throughout the day."[31] Nonetheless, by 9:30 PM when Maude's force secured the position, 13 Division had sustained 1,868 casualties since the beginning of the day.[32]

With the enemy apparently in retreat, Gorringe resolved to maintain the initiative and continue attacking on the left bank in an effort to drive the Ottomans out of the defile as quickly as possible. He thus ordered 7 Division to advance against Sannaiyat on the morning of the 6th. Unfortunately for Younghusband's force, it would enjoy none of the benefits that careful planning had accrued to 13 Division the previous day. Friction delayed the progress of 7 Division from the outset, as retiring troops from Maude's force disrupted its assembly behind the Fallahiya position. Beyond Fallahiya, units encountered a variety of unforeseen obstacles as they moved forward in darkness over unfamiliar territory. According to the divisional war diary: "A network of Turkish trenches had to be crossed and as these could not be reconnoitred beforehand they caused much difficulty. Some of these trenches were impassable, being 7' deep, and in such cases a way round had to be discovered. These entailed countermarches and changes of formation." Thus, as dawn broke, 7 Division found itself well short of Sannaiyat, and without even accurate maps of the terrain in front of it.[33]

At this point Younghusband conferred with George Kemball, whose 28th Brigade was leading the advance. Estimating that 7 Division remained a mile from Sannaiyat, Kemball advised entrenching before the onset of full daylight. Younghusband, however, believed that his force was much closer to the enemy position and therefore ordered it to deploy in line and attack as quickly as possible.[34] Thus, at 5:10 AM the 19th and 28th Brigades resumed advancing, with the 21st Brigade remaining in

reserve at Fallahiya. This was only fifteen minutes later than Maude had
initiated his attack the previous day, but while 13 Division had started
from positions as close as 150 yards to the Ottoman line at Hanna, 7
Division had to cover an expanse more than ten times as wide, as even
Kemball had underestimated the distance to Sannaiyat. Moreover, the
19th and 28th Brigades advanced without a clear grasp of the obstacles
that lay ahead of them, or the strength of the enemy opposition at
Sannaiyat.[35]

This opposition soon materialized. Rifle fire began at 5:35 AM, rapidly
increasing in intensity. By 5:40 Ottoman artillery had also opened on the
advancing troops. Gorringe had apparently made hurried arrangements
for the 9th Brigade R.F.A. to support 7 Division's attack from positions
near Fallahiya, but the trenches that had delayed the infantry proved
an even greater impediment to the guns, and they were unable to reach
their positions before the Ottomans opened fire. The war diary of the
28th Battery described the situation as its guns finally came into action:
"It was a terrible sight that met our eyes when we put up our observation
ladders and opened fire: for the 28th Infy Bde leading the advance of the
7th Div had been caught in column of fours by the MGs of the enemy
and the 43rd Lt Infty were lying in rows just as though the battalion had
been ordered to lie down when marching along a road. The attack had
failed before a gun had got into action."[36] Kemball's brigade managed to
advance to within 600 yards of the Ottoman position before enemy fire
forced it to stop and take cover. By 6 AM, however, the attack had ground
to a halt and the leading troops began to retire, eventually entrenching
just over half a mile from Sannaiyat. Younghusband's Division had suffered nearly 1,200 casualties on 6 April, most of them in the first hour of
daylight.[37]

Gorringe initially intended to resume the attack at 3 AM the next
morning. On the afternoon of the 6th, however, he postponed the operation for twenty-four hours due to flooding of positions adjacent to
the Suwaikiya marsh, which narrowed the front on which 7 Division
could attack. On the morning of 7 April, when units of the division came
under heavy fire as they attempted to move forward in preparation for
their advance, Younghusband requested another twenty-four-hour post-
ponement. While this delay resulted in part from the intensity of enemy
opposition at Sannaiyat, it also stemmed from the weakened state of

7 Division. As Maude observed in his diary, "7th Division do not appear fit to attack as their moral is bad."[38]

At this point Gorringe apparently concluded that capturing the Sannaiyat position would require additional reconnaissance, careful planning, and a stronger force. Thus, he ordered 13 Division to take over Younghusband's positions on the night of 8–9 April, and to attack Sannaiyat the following morning with 7 Division providing support.[39] Maude and his staff immediately began reconnoitring the enemy position. The artillery spent 8 April engaged in registration and shelling the wire in front of the Ottoman first line at Sannaiyat. On the evening of the 8th, staff officers laid down markers to indicate the position of each battalion involved in the advance. At 4:20 AM on 9 April, the 38th and 40th Brigades were to attack on a frontage of 600 yards, with the 39th Brigade following. Guided by sketch maps showing the objective of each unit, the infantry of the leading brigades were to advance in four long lines in single rank, each line 50 yards apart. The first two lines were to capture the first line of enemy trenches, which was approximately 650 yards distant. The third and fourth lines would then move on to the second enemy position, while the 39th Brigade, advancing in two long lines 100 yards behind the leading force, would capture the third enemy position. The artillery was to fire on enemy trenches on either side of 13 Division's attack as well as shelling rear areas to prevent reinforcements from reaching Sannaiyat. Once 13 Division had reached its objectives, 7 Division would continue the advance.[40]

While Maude's preparations featured the same attention to detail as his plans to capture the Hanna position, they did not include the lengthy preliminary artillery bombardment that apparently induced Halil to retire to Sannaiyat. Moreover, 13 Division had incurred significant losses since 5 April, with 40 percent of its officers becoming casualties at Hanna and Fallahiya.[41] Thus, Maude's force was ill-prepared for the opposition it faced on the 9th. While the attack began according to schedule, the advancing infantry faced fierce resistance as soon as the enemy detected their approach. As Gorringe related in his summary of the operation, "Some nine minutes after they had moved forward, and when they were within some 300 yards of the enemy's front line the enemy discovered the movement. Very lights were sent up, flares were lighted and a heavy musketry and shrapnel fire was opened." The first line of attackers pressed forward, entering the enemy's front trenches, but the second line "lost direction, wavered and fell back" on the remainder of the troops who had yet to begin advancing.[42] Despite the best efforts of their officers, the third and fourth lines "hung fire" and refused to advance.[43] This enabled the Ottomans to counterattack and drive the British infantry out of their first line trenches. Artillery officer Captain H. B. Latham recalled:

> The infantry of the 7th Divn were not to advance until the 13th Divn had swept all before it. But this latter Divn had deteriorated more rapidly than could be imagined and when the signal to advance was given the first line went forward and took the Turks' first line and the remainder didn't budge! It was a terrible sight from the Battery ladder to watch, the front line first of all being thrown out of the Turks' first line and then followed up, bayoneted and slain as they re- treated, without the rest of the Divn making any efforts to come to their help.[44]

Later in the day, Maude's troops managed to entrench themselves approximately 400 yards from the Sannaiyat position. Since the 5th, however, the division had suffered more than 3,500 casualties.[45] Accord- ing to Latham, "This was the end of the 13th Divn as a fighting unit & they were afterward only a rabble until reorganized later in the year."[46] Given the condition of Maude's division and the intensity of enemy op- position, Gorringe concluded that another attack on Sannaiyat would not be feasible for several days. His plan to relieve Townshend's garrison by 15 April had failed.

DRASTIC MEASURES – APRIL INSIDE KUT

The day after 13 Division's failed attack on Sannaiyat, Sir Percy Lake in- formed Townshend that it was "distinctly doubtful" that the relief force would reach Kut by the 15th, and requested that he take all possible mea- sures to prolong his resistance. With the prospect of surrender looming ever larger, the commander of 6 Indian Division immediately cut all soldiers' and followers' daily allotment of flour to only five ounces.[47] This meager ration would enable the survival of the garrison until 21 April. British soldiers had seen their daily ration of flour, which they received in the form of bread, diminish progressively from eight ounces in mid-March to six ounces at the beginning of April.[48] Consequently, yet another reduction did not have a catastrophic impact, particularly since each soldier continued to receive a pound of horse meat each day.[49] After weeks of inadequate rations, however, the novelty of whole-grain bread and horse meat had long since been overcome by pangs of hunger. According to the medical officer W. C. Spackman, "Bread was now issued in the form of little 10 oz loaves, one for every two individuals, and its exact division becomes the object of jealous scrutiny."[50] On 13 April the Reverend Harold Spooner noted the increasingly emaciated appearance of the soldiers in his diary, commenting, "The shortening of rations has told terribly on the Troops the last 3 days and everyone is looking pinched & white & weak."[51]

Notwithstanding the growing suffering of British soldiers inside Kut, the latest reduction of rations was particularly harmful to the Indians. Since January Townshend had allowed sepoys and followers additional rations of atta or grain in order to compensate for the absence of meat in their diet. Thus, at the beginning of April Indians still received ten ounces of atta every day.[52] Townshend explained in a 10 April communiqué to the garrison, however, "I am sorry that I can no longer favour the Indian soldiers in the matter of meal, but there is no possibility of doing so now."[53] Without any other source of nutrition available, five ounces of atta was clearly insufficient to sustain those who continued to refuse horse. In this context many sepoys and followers abandoned their objections to consuming the meat. According to Townshend, on 11 April more than 5,000 Indians accepted a twelve-ounce ration of horse. Even so, more than half of the 11,000 sepoys and followers remaining in Kut still continued to refuse horse meat in the face of starvation.[54] As Lieutenant G. N. Rogers of the 76th Punjabis complained in his diary: "Men are most obstinate about the meat question. The Sikhs have taken to it but the Jhats & Mohadins absolutely refuse to have anything to do with it."[55]

In desperation, Townshend finally attempted to compel the Indians to eat it. Rather than simply ordering them to do so, however, on 12 April he threatened "to replace all non-meat eaters who become too feeble to do their work efficiently as officers and NCOs by other men who *do* eat meat and remain strong."[56] Under normal circumstances, Indian soldiers were promoted on the basis of seniority. Thus, sepoys often served for decades before being promoted. The prospect of losing rank was thus a powerful incentive for officers and NCOs to abandon their reservations regarding the consumption of horse meat. In the process, they set an example for the rank and file as well as followers, the majority of whom proved willing to supplement their meager rations with horse once the taboo had been broken by their superiors, who were often respected senior members of their home communities. According to Rogers, the Indian officers of the 76th Punjabis "ate horse in front of their men who now appear to be willing to eat it. Several took little pieces & ate it & have asked for a ration tomorrow so I think it will be all right now."[57] While the decision often required considerable deliberation, by 14 April the vast majority of Indians had abandoned their earlier objections and nearly 10,000 were eating meat.[58]

Given the harmful impact of the Indians' eschewal of horse meat, and the fact that most incorporated it into their diets quickly when faced with coercive measures, it is puzzling that Townshend did not compel them to begin eating horse earlier in the siege. Certainly, this possibility occurred to British officers at the time. Two of Townshend's brigade commanders, Charles Melliss and Walter Delamain, favored ordering the Indians to supplement their rations with horse meat. Officers in closer contact with sepoys shared this view. Henry Rich claimed in a postwar interview that Indians "would have welcomed the order to do it."[59] This opinion, however, was not universally held. Indeed, many officers apparently believed that the risks associated with such an order outweighed its potential benefits. According to the official historian of the Mesopotamia campaign:

> It was a common impression among British officers of Indian units before the war that, if it was absolutely essential, their men would generally be prepared to accept a definite order that they were to eat what was necessary, and that they would be absolved by their religious authorities of any religious misdemeanour entailed by their action on the justification of emergency.... Anyone, however, with experience of the power and influence which caste, religion and tradition exercise in India will understand the difficulties and dangers in issuing such an order, especially if there is any chance of it not being universally obeyed.[60]

The perceived danger of sparking dissent or even mutiny in the ranks evidently deterred Townshend from ordering the Indians to eat horse meat, despite their deteriorating condition, and the fact that allowing them to consume extra flour instead of meat constituted an inefficient use of the garrison's food supply. Nor did officers in the vast majority of Indian units independently direct their troops to augment their rations with horse. Only in two battalions, the 2/7th Gurkhas and the 103rd Indian Infantry, was the consumption of horse made compulsory.[61] On the whole, British officers proved reluctant to force the matter, even after they had gone to the trouble of obtaining the blessing of Indian religious leaders. Townshend and his subordinates may have underestimated Indians' willingness to break dietary taboos if compelled to do so, but their wariness is understandable. Given that some sepoys ostensibly disapproved of the entire Mesopotamia campaign on religious grounds, British officers did not want to exert excessive pressure on the Indians over another issue perceived to be of religious significance. This cautious approach was consistent with the post-1857 British policy of respecting Indian religious grievances.[62] As Townshend himself admitted, however, it "weakened my power of resistance by one month."[63]

Moreover, by mid-April many sepoys were so sick and malnourished that they did not benefit from the new addition to their diet. Captain A. J. Shakeshaft of the 2/Norfolks observed a decline in the incidence of scurvy among Indians, which he attributed to their consumption of horse.[64] Nonetheless, malnutrition had already weakened sepoys and followers considerably, leaving them vulnerable to a wide range of afflictions. As Colonel Patrick Hehir, the chief medical officer inside Kut, recorded: "The present condition of nutrition and health of the average man of the garrison is physiologically highly unsatisfactory. His stamina is greatly lowered, his resistance to disease-causes considerably reduced, and should he suffer from any disease, such as pneumonia or bronchitis, fever from any cause, dysentery, or severe diarrhoea, it will greatly tax his vital powers."[65] Thus, April 1916 saw an increase in fatalities due to seemingly minor afflictions exacerbated by malnutrition. Observers often attributed these deaths to dysentery or a similar condition they termed "enteritis" or "gastro-enteritis," but these were likely symptoms of viral or bacterial infections that soldiers were increasingly unable to resist.[66] According to Hehir, "On an average fifteen men are dying daily: of these, five a day are dying of chronic starvation, and ten with chronic starvation with diarrhoea, bronchitis or some other simple malady supervening."[67] British soldiers succumbed in this period, the most prominent being F. A. Hoghton, commander of the 17th Brigade, who died on 12 April, apparently after consuming poisonous vegetation.[68] Given the deficiencies of Indian rations throughout the siege, however, it is not surprising that malnutrition took a much heavier toll on sepoys and followers. Although it is difficult to determine precisely how many members of the Kut garrison perished due to any specific cause, one study indicates that the number of Indians who died from disease and starvation inside Kut exceeded the number of British personnel by ten times.[69]

Despite their deteriorating condition and the continued struggles of the relief force, many soldiers inside Kut clung to the increasingly faint hope of relief. According to Spooner, "We get cheered when we hear the guns below tho' we have heard them for three months now. They'll come in time – but only just in time I think."[70] Those who had lost confidence in the Tigris Corps still entertained the possibility of "marching out with all the honours of war" and "going to India on parole."[71] For a growing number of soldiers, sepoys, and followers, however, any of these outcomes would arrive too late.

EXHAUSTION OF THE RELIEF FORCE, 11–22 APRIL

Even after the costly failure of the attacks on the left bank from 5–9 April, Gorringe remained convinced that Sannaiyat remained "the key to our further operations." On the afternoon of the 9th, however, Lake interceded, directing him to advance on the right bank against the Sinn Abtar Redoubt.[72] A successful attack on this position required control of Ottoman positions along the Tigris at Abu Roman and Bait Isa. While Keary's 3 Division had occupied Abu Roman earlier in the month, approximately one mile to the west the Ottomans remained in control of the Bait Isa position, from which they could flood the territory to the south. Gorringe therefore directed Keary to begin moving toward Bait Isa on 12 April, but flooding delayed the advance. So too did Keary's methodical approach to operations. With 3 Division making little headway by the 13th, Gorringe ordered it to reconnoitre the trenches in the direction of Bait Isa that night, capturing the position if possible "so as to make up for the time which had been lost."[73] When the 7th Brigade reported its objective to be held in strength, however, Keary declined to order an attack. According to J. W. Barnett, a medical officer in 3 Division, Keary "refused to attack unless [he] had free hand & good reconnaissance."[74]

Stormy weather on subsequent days delayed the operation further, as aircraft were unable to assist with artillery registration.[75] Thus, it was only on 17 April, over a week since the last major operation against Sannaiyat, that 3 Division attacked Bait Isa. Like Maude's 5 April assault on the Hanna position, Keary's attack relied on suppressive fire. At 6:45 A M the infantry of the 7th and 9th Brigades advanced under a simultaneous artillery barrage, reaching the enemy trenches and bayonetting enemy soldiers "whom they found sitting under the parapet of their front trenches, before the barrage lifted."[76] While this degree of coordination between infantry and artillery was an impressive achievement, particularly in Mesopotamia in 1916, its effect was only temporary. After capturing Bait Isa, killing approximately 300 enemy soldiers and capturing another 150, the two brigades consolidated their positions and prepared to hand them over that evening to 13 Division before moving on toward the Es Sinn line. Around 6 PM, however, Ottoman forces launched a series of counterattacks, forcing the 7th and 9th Brigades into a disorderly retirement, with the 7th Brigade abandoning multiple machine guns. Maude recorded that "the 3rd Division, and especially the native troops ran like hares."[77]According to T. A. Chalmers, "One of our officers is reported to have shot four or five men for running away."[78] The fleeing infantry fell back on the 8th Brigade, which was in reserve to the rear. This brigade held fast, along with a remnant of the 7th Brigade led personally by its commander Major-General Egerton. According to Gorringe, Egerton's force "held its ground in the face of heavy odds, the brigade commander and his staff more than holding their own with bombs."[79] Chalmers related in his diary, "The Turks came on again and again but we held firm and when morning came hundreds of them were shot down within 50 yds of us."[80]

According to Muhammad Amin, the Ottoman XIII Corps suffered 3,541 casualties in the counterattack. The postwar study by the Quetta

Staff College attributed its ferocity to the fact that "Khalil realized that the battle had reached a critical stage, and that our possession of Bait Isa gave us freedom of manoeuvre on the right bank."[81] Amin's account, however, suggests that the XIII Corps commander, Ali Ihsan, was "by no means perturbed" by Keary's capture of Bait Isa.[82] In addition to the formidable Sannaiyat position, Ottoman forces continued to occupy the Es Sinn line several miles upriver on the right bank. Furthermore, unlike in early March, the approaches to this line were obstructed by flooding. Thus, the capture of Bait Isa did not bring the Tigris Corps significantly closer to freeing the Kut garrison. Moreover, Ottoman commanders understood that the situation inside of Kut was deteriorating rapidly. In addition to Indian deserters, a growing stream of Arabs began trying to escape the town in April, despite the longstanding Ottoman practice of shooting civilians as they attempted to do so. According to Amin, "Between 14 and 26 April we know that 1615 left the town. Subsequent observation showed me that double that number had come through the lines." The fact that British sources do not refer to a significant decline in the local population suggests that these numbers may be exaggerated. Nonetheless, April saw the increasing flight of civilians from Kut on a scale so large that Ottoman commanders deemed it inhumane or impractical to kill them all. The size of the exodus, along with information provided by those the Ottomans apparently captured, indicated clearly that Townshend's force was nearing the end of its endurance.[83] Thus, rather than resulting from concern over Keary's progress, the counterattack on Bait Isa reflected a growing confidence among senior Ottoman commanders that victory at Kut was within their grasp.

The loss of Bait Isa was a significant setback for the Tigris Corps. While it had incurred only about 300 casualties in capturing the position on the morning of 17 April, 3 Division had suffered another 1,200 by the next morning. According to Gorringe, Keary's formation was "much shaken" by the counterattack and was subsequently placed in reserve. The Tigris Corps commander persisted for another day in his efforts to advance on the right bank, ordering 13 Division to recapture Bait Isa. When its 39th Brigade advanced on the morning of the 19th, however, it made little headway. Flooding inhibited the force's progress, with some soldiers drowning as they attempted to advance. Others were hit by fire from the artillery supporting the advance.[84] While these mishaps were symptoms of a hastily planned operation, Maude also attributed the failure to a "want of officers."[85] More generally, 13 Division suffered from a want of able soldiers. According to the artillery officer H. B. Latham, "The 13th Divn was finished. The men could not stand the increasing heat and were going sick in droves."[86] Having lost over a third of its strength since the beginning of the month, Maude's force was no more effective than 3 Indian Division.

According to the *Official History*, on the evening of 19 April Lake and Gorringe determined that the enemy had withdrawn troops from the Sannaiyat position and therefore "decided to seize the opportunity and attack it."[87] It is difficult to avoid the conclusion, however, that with no realistic options remaining on the right bank, the two commanders were grasping at their only remaining hope of relieving the Kut garrison before its food supply ran out. Beginning on the 15th, Gorringe had begun dropping staples such as flour and sugar into Kut from the air. Townshend acknowledged in his memoir that this was the first attempt in history to supply a besieged force using aircraft, but he characterized the initiative as a "complete failure."[88] Over the first two days, pilots managed to drop inside the Kut perimeter less than half of the daily allotment of 5,000 pounds that Townshend had deemed necessary to prolong the siege. Thus, on 17 April he reduced rations yet again to only four ounces of flour and eight ounces of horse, which would enable the two staples to last until 24 and 29 April respectively.[89] With the garrison reduced to a diet that the medical officer Ernest Walker characterized as "starvation pure & simple," it was increasingly clear that the siege would be over, one way or another, by the end of the month.[90]

Holding positions 400–600 yards from the Ottoman line at Sannaiyat, 7 Division remained relatively robust in comparison to the beleaguered 3 and 13 Divisions. Attacking the formidable enemy position in the second half of April, however, was an even more daunting task than that which had frustrated Younghusband and Maude earlier in the month. Flooding had reduced the front on which 7 Division could advance from the full 800-yard width of the defile at Sannaiyat to only 600 yards.[91] Even that portion of the front deemed to be usable was so wet and muddy that artillery officers calculated the rate of the barrage preceding the infantry attack based on the assumption that soldiers would have to negotiate knee-deep water.[92] Younghusband planned to attack on the morning of the 22nd, with the artillery opening a forty-minute slow bombardment at 6:20 AM. This was to be followed by nine-minute "intense bombardment" under which the infantry of the 19th and 21st Brigades would attack, each formation on a 300-yard front.

Given the condition of the battlefield, however, the prospects for the success of Younghusband's plan were so unpromising that one of his brigade commanders opted out minutes before the operation began. At 6:05 AM, Brigadier-General Charles Norie, commanding the 21st Brigade, informed Younghusband by telephone that his advance was "not feasible on account of the water."[93] The Quetta Staff College study deemed Norie's decision "inexplicable." As the divisional war diary took pains to note, "There had been practically no alteration in the water on this front during the preceding 24 hours, and the report received during the night had given no grounds to lead the GOC to imagine that the difficulties in front of the 21st Brigade had increased."[94] Perhaps because of his experiences on the Western Front in 1914 and 1915, however, Norie came to a different conclusion. As he explained in correspondence with the historian W. D. Bird after the war, the ground in front of the 21st Brigade "was covered with water & pitted with shell holes & with barbed wire on it. The enemy's trenches which were in front of us were (we had every reason to believe) empty of defenders but full of water & too deep with water & mud to be held. I did enquire what on earth was to be gained by the proposed attack as you suggest."[95]

Norie's decision forced the attack to proceed on a 300-yard front, further diminishing its chances of success. Nonetheless, he was ultimately correct in his assessment of the viability of the operation. Now attacking on its own, the 19th Brigade proceeded without difficulty to the first Ottoman line, delayed only by the artillery barrage, which had assumed a slower advance.[96] Once the soldiers reached the first line, however, they found it unoccupied and full of water. The ground between it and the equally uninhabited second Ottoman line proved to be "a bog," with men becoming stuck "up to their armpits."[97] As the infantry negotiated this morass they faced increasing fire from enemy troops holding positions approximately 200 yards behind the Ottoman third line. A small number of soldiers made their way to the third line, but they found that most of their rifles had become clogged with mud. So helpless were they that according to the war diary, "the Turks were able to stand up and to come out of their trenches to fire with safety." Increasing enemy counterattacks soon forced the infantry to withdraw, and by 8:20 AM all of the attacking troops had returned to their original positions. By late morning, under a flag of truce both armies began collecting casualties left on the battlefield.[98]

In Norie's opinion, "the order to attack over open ground such as we had in front of us on 21st/22nd April was absurd & murderous & all to no purpose."[99] Younghusband's division suffered 1,300 casualties, a significant number considering a single brigade led the attack. In its aftermath Gorringe concluded that his force was spent. He related in his final report on the April relief operations:

> Our losses had exceeded 33 per cent of our strength, and this was considerably exceeded in the case of British officers and especially was this the case in the 13th Division, on whom the effect of the recent operations was most marked. The time had come when the limit of endurance had been reached, and I asked reluctantly for an interview with the Army commander and informed him that to call on the men or further efforts, within the time limit imposed by the food supply of Kut, could no longer give any prospect of success, and that it was necessary to face the situation and give up on any further attempts to relieve Kut.[100]

THE END OF THE SIEGE

Despite Gorringe's admission of failure, Sir Percy Lake was not yet willing to admit defeat. In an effort to prolong the resistance of the Kut garrison until the Tigris Corps was able to resume operations, he initiated a final effort to resupply Townshend's force via the Tigris. On the evening of 24 April, the riverboat *Julnar,* fortified with steel plates around its bridge and engine and laden with 270 tons of supplies, embarked from Fallahiya. Although British observers believed that Arab spies had informed the enemy of the impending operation, the appearance of the ship at Sannaiyat apparently caught Ottoman forces by surprise.[101] The *Julnar* bypassed the Sannaiyat position, but a strong current inhibited its forward progress as enemy fire intensified, with a shell striking its bridge as it approached Maqasis. Shortly afterward the ship became grounded, apparently after striking a cable running across the river. Its captain, Lieutenant H. O. B. Firman, R.N., was killed by enemy fire, while its second-in-command, Lieutenant-Commander C. H. Cowley, of the Royal Naval Volunteer Reserve, was apparently wounded and taken prisoner but later died under mysterious circumstances. Muhammad Amin alleged that Cowley was shot while trying to escape, but British officers believed that the Ottomans executed him as a traitor due to his Armenian ancestry.[102] In any case, the capture of the *Julnar* forced even Lake to admit defeat. At 3:30 AM on 26 April he directed Townshend to open negotiations with Halil Bey, who had taken command of the Ottoman 6th Army following von der Goltz's passing a week earlier.[103] In his diary, Ernest Walker described the unfamiliar quiet that ensued as talks commenced: "All our men & the Turks also came out & sat on parapets of trenches & looked at each other, a queer sight. What struck us all at once, was the extraordinary crushing, overpowering *silence*. After 5 months when not for a minute night or day did one cease to hear the crack of rifles, rattle of machine guns & explosions of guns, shells & Bombs, this silence was almost uncanny."[104]

While his subordinates marveled at the sudden calm, Townshend was busy trying to extract his force from Kut through negotiations. With Lake's approval he offered the Ottomans a million pounds sterling and forty guns in exchange for the release of his force. While Halil passed this offer on to the Ottoman minister of war, Enver Pasha, neither was particularly interested in bargaining with the British. In response to Townshend's proposal, Enver countered that the commander of 6 Indian Division might go free, but only if he left his garrison and all of weapons and equipment to the Ottomans.[105] Townshend did not feel bound by honor to surrender with his force if a face-saving alternative could be found. Ten days earlier he had proposed unsuccessfully to Lake that he might lead a handpicked force in an attempt to break out of Kut so that he "might be of further use to the state."[106] Even Townshend recognized, however, that to walk free in exchange for a ransom of guns and ammunition while his long-suffering subordinates went into captivity was unconscionable. While Lake sought permission from London to double the money on offer in hopes of freeing the entire garrison, the depletion of food supplies inside Kut quickly brought these ineffectual negotiations, and the siege itself, to an end. Townshend commented in his memoir, "[I] had not a biscuit up my sleeve to argue with. . . . I had to get food at once or all my men would lay down and die."[107] W. C. Spackman provided a graphic description of the situation in Kut in late April. As he related, "Dysentery, fever, anaemia and t.b. were carrying off twenty men a day, men already weakened by starvation, malaria, scurvy and beri-beri, their gums oozing pus, their cheeks sunken, with every rib outlined and their legs and feet misshaped with dropsy, and without even the spirit to beat off the flies that swarmed upon them."[108] Thus, as his subordinates consumed their last rations on the 28th, Townshend ordered them to destroy all weapons, ammunition, and other equipment of military value in preparation for surrender.

Even as his negotiating position eroded, Townshend continued to issue reassuring communiqués to his force. On the 28th he announced, "Negotiations are still in progress, but I hope to be able to announce your departure for India on parole." On the 29th, as he prepared to hand Kut over to Halil, he declared, "There are strong grounds for hoping that the Turks will eventually agree to all being exchanged."[109] Townshend's use of communiqués to sustain the morale of his troops earlier in the siege is understandable, but given that he was about to surrender to an opponent who showed little interest in bargaining, these messages appear overly optimistic at best, and deliberately misleading at worst. It must be acknowledged, however, that Townshend had spent the previous six months attempting to sustain the apparently tenuous loyalty of Indian soldiers whose motivations he never fully comprehended. Old habits died hard as he continued in his attempts to placate his subordinates even as the force prepared to surrender and enter Ottoman captivity.

As a result of Townshend's efforts, members of 6 Indian Division continued to hope that they would be exchanged for Ottoman prisoners even after the conclusion of the siege.[110] Few, however, would be so fortunate. On the morning of 29 April soldiers and sepoys hurriedly destroyed their weapons and equipment in preparation for the enemy's arrival. Spackman related, "Everywhere you looked you saw columns of smoke rising into the clear sky as piles of saddles, broken mule carts and every variety of equipment of potential use to the enemy burnt away briskly, the flames fed with matting, fodder, empty boxes and surplus fire-

wood. Rifle bolts were dumped into the river, rifles smashed except for a
few kept as protection against possible Arab miscreants in the town."[111]
Early in the afternoon an Ottoman force entered the town to accept
the surrender of Townshend's force. Claiming sickness, the commander
of the Kut garrison left this unpleasant duty to W. S. Delamain.[112]

Although Ottoman commanders were irritated by the destruction
of the weapons and equipment inside Kut, their subordinates treated British and Indians alike with respect. They were less courteous,
however, toward the inhabitants of the town. According to Spackman,
"Whilst none of us at this time suffered any ill-treatment and very few
were robbed, it was a very different fate that was reserved for the local
inhabitants. All their goods and personal possessions were confiscated and looted, and a terrible revenge was taken against all those who
had, or were suspected of helping us."[113] Muhammad Amin maintained that Ottoman forces targeted only a small minority of the local
population, executing only fourteen. Ernest Walker described harsher
and more widespread reprisals. He related, "They shot & hanged 42
of the chief Arabs of Kut including the sheikh. His son had both hands
chopped off at the wrists. Sassoon the Jew contractor who sold us a lot
of stuff was so horribly tortured on the roof of a house that he tried to
commit suicide by jumping off it. He succeeded in breaking both his
thighs & in this condition was dragged off to the nearest palm tree &
hanged. The Arab women suffered also as one would expect."[114]

While the members of Townshend's force escaped the brutal punishment inflicted on the local inhabitants, their suffering did not diminish following their surrender. The Ottomans lacked shelters, food, and
medical supplies to care for their new prisoners. Consequently, when a
medical mission visited Halil on 30 April and asked permission to send
two ships full of rations to Kut and to exchange Ottoman prisoners for
sick and wounded soldiers and sepoys, the Ottoman commander readily agreed. A total of 1,136 of the "worst cases" were immediately sent
downriver, followed by another 345 in the summer of 1916. Nearly 12,000
soldiers, sepoys, and followers, however, went into captivity.[115] The first
to do so was their commander, who embarked on a ship for Baghdad, en
route to Constantinople, on 3 April. Muhammad Amin described the
rousing farewell provided by the soldiers, many of whom still revered

Townshend despite the outcome of the siege. In his words, "I witnessed the prisoners' last respects to General Townshend as he passed up the river. The sight must have cheered the General and was a sure sign of the happy relations between the leader and his men in such unhappy circumstances."[116] Townshend would spend the rest of the conflict near the Ottoman capital in the comfortable surroundings afforded a captive senior officer, oblivious to the fate of his subordinates as he campaigned unsuccessfully for promotion to lieutenant-general.

The following day, British and Indian officers began to board ships for Baghdad. It was not until the 6th that the rank and file embarked on foot, destined for what Patrick Crowley has characterized as "two years of horror," beginning with forced marches to Baghdad, Mosul, and then westward into Syria and southern Anatolia. Compelled initially to subsist on minimal rations and water, many collapsed while marching and were killed by their captors or left to die by the roadside. Although a few managed to escape, most of those who survived the initial marches spent the rest of the war performing forced labor, often constructing Ottoman railways. Of 10,486 Indians who went into Ottoman captivity, 3,063 did not survive. British personnel suffered even more acutely, with 1,755 of 2,592 dying before the end of the conflict.[117]

CONCLUSION

By early April 1916 the days of the Kut garrison were numbered. Recognizing the gravity of the situation, both George Gorringe and Charles Townshend embraced new methods in an attempt to avert defeat. Notwithstanding the reputation for aggressiveness he had earned prior to 1916, Gorringe had become increasingly circumspect by April. After presiding over the defeat at Dujaila Redoubt in March, the commander of the Tigris Corps increasingly delegated the planning and conduct of operations to subordinates with experience at the Dardanelles and on the Western Front. As a result, the operations of the relief force in April placed increased emphasis on carefully planned artillery bombardments as well as close cooperation between infantry and artillery. These new tactics were certainly not perfect. As was the case on the Western Front in 1916, soldiers advancing in line across the battlefield were extremely vulnerable to entrenched enemy defenders. Nonetheless, given time to plan operations carefully, commanders such as Maude and Keary achieved significant success against Ottoman positions much stronger than those the Tigris Corps faced in January and March.

Nevertheless, in order to break through Ottoman defenses or compel Halil to withdraw his forces below Kut, Gorringe and his subordinates needed time to plan and execute a sequence of operations similar to that against Hanna and Fallahiya on 5 April. Although the Tigris Corps had soldiers, guns, and expertise in unprecedented quantities, the one commodity of which they had less was time. This was due in part to the shortcomings of the logistical system in Mesopotamia that had hindered relief operations since January. Even more so, however, it was due to the depletion of food supplies inside Kut. Charles Townshend took what he perceived to be significant risks in order to compel his Indian subordinates to eat horse meat by mid-April. These tactics quickly proved successful, but by the time Townshend implemented them, his supplies of horse, grain, and flour were nearly gone due to the practice of killing animals in order to enable Indians to consume larger rations of grain and atta. Moreover, many of his subordinates were so weakened by malnutrition that they did not benefit from the consumption of horse. While both Gorringe and Townshend embraced innovative methods in the face of defeat, they did so too late to save the vast majority of the members of the Kut garrison.

CONCLUSION

IN RETROSPECT, THE SIEGE OF KUT-AL-AMARA APPEARS TO FIT neatly into a narrative of hubris, comeuppance, and redemption. After easily securing its strategic objective at the head of the Persian Gulf, Britain initiated a reckless offensive to seize the prestigious but unnecessary prize of Baghdad from an adversary its leaders dismissed due to their own prejudices and preconceptions. Predictably, the offensive ended in Townshend's humiliating surrender at Kut-al-Amara, but out of defeat arose a new commitment to the campaign that resulted in the capture of Baghdad less than a year later. To the soldiers and sepoys in Mesopotamia in 1915 and 1916, however, neither the siege nor its bitter conclusion appeared to be predetermined. On 24 November 1915 the outcome of the Battle of Ctesiphon, and perhaps the entire campaign, hung in the balance, dependent at least partially on which commander regained his composure first. After withdrawing from Ctesiphon, Townshend only resolved to halt at Kut during the darkest hours of his hurried retreat from Umm-at-Tubul. He regretted his decision almost as soon as he made it.

Townshend's decisions are fully comprehensible only in the context of his relationship with the sepoys and followers who comprised the majority of his force. Signs of wavering Indian morale during and after the battle at Ctesiphon left Townshend increasingly fearful of a collapse of discipline if he did not allow his troops to rest and recuperate, preferably out of contact with the enemy. The onset of the siege did nothing to ease his anxiety. While 6 Indian Division repelled Ottoman attacks on Kut with relative ease, mounting evidence of disaffection within Indian units as December progressed led him repeatedly to emphasize to Sir John Nixon the necessity of rapid relief. These requests had serious consequences, as they contributed significantly to Nixon's decision to initiate relief operations in early January 1916, before the arrival of essential supplies and staff, and before the inexperienced commanders of the relief force had the opportunity to become familiar with the enemy and the environment in which they were operating. Despite these handicaps, the relief force came close to succeeding at Shaikh Saad and the Wadi, but Fenton Aylmer and his subordinates understandably struggled to master combined arms tactics in the limited time at their disposal. Hampered by limited intelligence and a lack of real-time communications, they were unable to coordinate artillery fire and the movements of separate infantry formations with sufficient precision to dislodge the Ottomans. As a result, Nixon effectively squandered the relief force's best opportunity to reach Kut before the enemy established formidable defenses in the defile between the Tigris and the Suwaikiya marsh.

By the time the arrival of reinforcements and good weather enabled the resumption of attacks in early March, the strengthening of Ottoman defenses on the left bank of the Tigris compelled Aylmer and Gorringe to devise a very complicated operation to attack more distant enemy positions on the right bank. In addition, the losses incurred in January, perhaps combined with the increasing influence of commanders schooled on the Western Front, led to the emergence of an increasingly methodical approach to operations intended to facilitate coordination between formations. This was a logical response to the difficulties encountered at Shaikh Saad, the Wadi, and Hanna. Nonetheless, it discouraged improvisation in response to unexpected opportunities that still existed due to the relative scarcity of Ottoman forces on the right bank of the Tigris. So too did the inability of senior commanders to integrate cavalry into combined operations, a problem that Townshend also experienced at Ctesiphon. Despite the drawbacks of the plan to assault Dujaila Redoubt, however, it is impossible to understand the outcome of the resulting battle without reference to Townshend's failure to launch a sortie from Kut as he had promised to do. While the threat of Indian desertion or uprising no longer preoccupied him to the same extent as in December, Townshend continued to tread carefully around his Indian subordinates. Fearing their reaction in the event of an Ottoman attack on Kut, he declined to take advantage of an opportunity that even the enemy commander recognized at the time.

By April both Townshend and his counterparts in the relief force acknowledged the necessity of new methods. Downriver from Kut this resulted in the adoption of tactics imported from other theaters, including the use of suppressive fire to cover the advance of the infantry. While these tactics showed flashes of potential, they required increasingly detailed preparations that slowed the pace of relief operations just as time was becoming precious. Attempts to expedite them resulted in heavy losses to units already weakened severely by earlier attacks. Inside of Kut, Townshend finally overcame his Indian subordinates' longstanding aversion to horse meat, but like the tactics employed by the relief force, his measures were introduced too late to prolong significantly the resistance of his garrison.

In assessing responsibility for the disaster at Kut it is important to acknowledge that both Townshend's initial advance and the subsequent relief operations, conducted against stubborn and capable Ottoman defenders, were hindered considerably by a lack of resources. Nonetheless, the actions of 6 Indian Division and the relief force had a significant and perhaps decisive impact on the outcome of the siege. It is difficult to attach too much blame to the commanders of the relief force. Even in comparison to their counterparts on the Western Front, Aylmer, Gorringe, and their subordinates experienced an exceedingly sharp learning curve under severe resource and time constraints. The fact that their tactics evolved so dramatically between January and April 1916 raises questions about the dissemination of information throughout the British and Indian armies during the preceding year, but it also indicates the adaptability of commanders faced with the formidable task of overcoming Ottoman defenses below Kut.

Some British soldiers inside Kut blamed the outcome of the siege on the sepoys of 6 Indian Division. Like soldiers throughout history, however, Townshend's Indian subordinates served with the expectation that the command structure above them would provide a range of benefits in return. In the Indian Army these included effective leadership, adequate rations, and medical care, as well as support for the beliefs and practices specific to their home communities. For sepoys of 6 Indian Division as well as the relief force, the conditions of the Mesopotamia campaign failed to meet their expectations in a variety of respects, and it is therefore not surprising that some resorted to self-inflicted wounds, desertion, and even suicide. Even if they questioned their commitment to service, however, the majority did not take measures to escape it. While there were cases of insubordination in the relief force, these were not confined to Indian personnel. Some sepoys proved reluctant to make frontal attacks against enemy positions in January, but so too did the soldiers of the British 13 Division in April. Indians inside Kut abstained from horse meat for weeks, but this was largely because Townshend did not compel them to do so until mid-April, at which point they submitted. Overall while a minority of sepoys, particularly trans-frontier Pathans, proved unwilling to serve under the conditions they faced in Mesopotamia, the response of the majority exceeded the expectations of many British commanders.

Among those commanders was Charles Townshend, who spent much of the period under examination awaiting a collapse of Indian morale and discipline. Ultimately, it is difficult to avoid the conclusion that the commander of 6 Indian Division bears significant responsibility for the demise of his garrison. Historians have attributed Townshend's acceptance of a siege at Kut as well as his subsequent demands for relief to his driving ambition to further his career and burnish his reputation, but these and other decisions were driven primarily by his ongoing concerns regarding the morale of his Indian subordinates. Townshend was not alone in his sensitivity to Indian attitudes, particularly regarding issues perceived to be of religious significance. Indeed, respect for the specific beliefs and practices of Indian personnel was perceived as integral to the cohesion of the post-1857 Indian Army. It is significant, however, that subordinate officers who had closer contact with sepoys inside Kut, such as Charles Melliss, W. S. Delamain, and Henry Rich, disagreed with Townshend's pessimistic assessments of their morale as well as his reluctance to compel the consumption of horse meat. While Townshend's decisions may have been consistent with normal practices in the Indian Army, his gnawing fear of insubordination left him unable to abandon those practices in circumstances in which the survival of his garrison was at stake. Townshend's paralysis in this regard resulted at least in part from the distant relationship he had maintained with Indian personnel throughout his career. Despite his long record of service in the Indian Army, Charles Townshend lacked the detailed knowledge and understanding of his Indian subordinates necessary to perceive differences of opinion between different ethnic and religious groups, and perhaps more importantly, to judge the extent to which he could infringe upon their specific beliefs and practices in circumstances of life and death. To return to J. A. Lovat-Fraser's letter to Lord Curzon, quoted in the first chapter of this study, Townshend did not "thoroughly understand Indian troops." This was a principal factor in the defeat of 6 Indian Division at Kut-al-Amara in 1916.

NOTES

PREFACE

1. A. J. Barker, *The Bastard War: The Mesopotamian Campaign of 1914–1918* (New York: Dial Press, 1967); Russell Braddon, *The Siege* (London: Jonathan Cape, 1969); Ronald Millar, *Kut: The Death of an Army* (London: Secker and Warburg, 1969). See also Paul K. Davis, *Ends and Means: The British Mesopotamian Campaign and Commission* (London: Associated University Presses, 1994).

2. Patrick Crowley, *Kut 1916: Courage and Failure in Iraq* (Stroud, UK: Spellmount, 2009).

3. Charles Townshend, *When God Made Hell: The British Invasion of Mesopotamia and the Creation of Iraq, 1914–1921* (London: Faber and Faber, 2010).

4. Andrew Syk, "Command in Indian Expeditionary Force D: Mesopotamia, 1915–1916," in *The Indian Army in the Two World Wars*, ed. Kaushik Roy (Leiden: Brill, 2011); Ross Anderson, "Logistics of the Indian Expeditionary Force D in Mesopotamia, 1914–1918," in ibid.; Kaushik Roy, "From Defeat to Victory: Logistics of the Campaign in Mesopotamia, 1914–1918," *First World War Studies* 1, no. 1 (March 2010): 35–55.

5. Edward J. Erickson. *Ottoman Military Effectiveness in the First World War: A Comparative Study* (London: Routledge, 2007).

6. See for example, Jeffrey Greenhut, "Sahib and Sepoy: An Inquiry into the Relationship between the British Officers and Native Soldiers of the British Indian Army" *Military Affairs* 48, no. 1 (January 1984): 15–18; Greenhut, "The Imperial Reserve: The Indian Corps on the Western Front, 1914–1915" *Journal of Imperial and Commonwealth History* 12, no. 1 (October 1988): 54–73; David Omissi, *The Sepoy and the Raj: The Indian Army, 1860–1940* (London: Macmillan, 1994), and *Indian Voices of the Great War: Soldiers' Letters, 1914–1918* (London: Macmillan, 1999); G. M. Jack, "The Indian Army on the Western Front, 1914–1915: A Portrait of Collaboration," *War in History* 13, no. 3 (July 2006): 329–362; Claude Markovits, "Indian Soldiers' Experiences in France during World War I: Seeing Europe from the Rear of the Front," in *The World in World Wars: Experiences, Perceptions and Perspectives from Africa and Asia*, ed. Heike Liebau et al. (Leiden: Brill, 2010), 29–54; Radhika Singha, "Front Lines and Status Lines: Sepoy and 'Menial' in the Great War, 1916–1920," in ibid., 55–106; Ravi Ahuja, "The Corrosiveness of Comparison: Reverberations of Indian

Wartime Experiences in German Prison Camps (1915–1919)," in ibid., 29–54, 55–106; 131–166.

1. CHARLES TOWNSHEND AND HIS ARMY

1. F. J. Moberly, *The Campaign in Mesopotamia: 1914–1918* (London: His Majesty's Stationery Office, 1924), 1:484.

2. Crowley, *Kut,* 46.

3. Singha, "Front Lines and Status Lines," 60.

4. Markovits, "Indian Soldiers' Experiences," 37–39.

5. Omissi, *The Sepoy and the Raj,* 103–104.

6. Greenhut, "The Imperial Reserve," 54–73.

7. For examples of this approach, see Nikolas Gardner, "Sepoys and the Siege of Kut-al-Amara, December 1915–April 1916," *War in History* 11, no. 3 (July 2004): 307–326; Jack, "The Indian Army on the Western Front, " 329–362; Mark Harrison, "Medicine and the Management of Modern Warfare," *History of Science* 34, no. 106 (1999): 397–398.

8. Omissi, *The Sepoy and the Raj,* 10–11.

9. Ibid., 26–29. See also Greenhut, "Sahib and Sepoy," 15–18.

10. Kaushik Roy, "The Construction of Regiments in the Indian Army: 1859–1913," *War in History* 8, no. 2 (April 2001): 127–148.

11. Gordon Corrigan, *Sepoys in the Trenches: The Indian Corps on the Western Front, 1914–1915* (Staplehurst, UK: Spellmount, 1999), 129.

12. Townshend, *When God Made Hell,* 23.

13. H. H. Rich, "Background to Mesopotamia," H. H. Rich Papers, MES 086, Liddle Collection, Brotherton Library, University of Leeds, Leeds, UK. On the

similar origins of combatants and followers, see Singha, "Front Lines and Status Lines," 67–68.

14. Omissi, *Indian Voices of the Great War,* 12. See also Jack, "The Indian Army on the Western Front," 336.

15. Ravi Ahuja, "The Corrosiveness of Comparison," 136–137.

16. Jack, "The Indian Army on the Western Front," 335.

17. Tan Tai-Yong, "An Imperial Home Front: Punjab and the First World War," *Journal of Military History* 64, no. 2 (April 2000): 378.

18. Roy, "From Defeat to Victory," 41. See also Anderson, "Logistics of the Indian Expeditionary Force D," 112.

19. Syk, "Command in Indian Expeditionary Force D," 69.

20. Mark Harrison, "The Fight Against Disease in the Mesopotamia Campaign," in *Facing Armageddon: the First World War Experienced,* ed. Peter Liddle and Hugh Cecil (London: Leo Cooper, 1996), 485.

21. Ibid., 475, 477.

22. Mark Harrison, *The Medical War: British Military Medicine in the First World War* (New York: Oxford University Press, 2010), 210; Anderson, "Logistics of the Indian Expeditionary Force D," 114.

23. Harrison, *The Medical War,* 208; Anderson, "Logistics of the Indian Expeditionary Force D," 115.

24. Roy, "From Defeat to Victory," 41.

25. Sir Walter Lawrence to Lord Kitchener, 27 December 1915, Lawrence Papers, MSS Eur F143/65, India Office Records (IOR), British Library, London. See also Omissi, *The Sepoy and the Raj,* 118.

26. Corrigan, *Sepoys in the Trenches,* 12.

27. Charles V. F. Townshend, *My Campaign in Mesopotamia,* (London: Butterworth, 1920), 230.

28. Omissi, *The Sepoy and the Raj,* 106.

29. Rich, "Background to Mesopotamia."

30. "War Record of the 27ᵗʰ Punjabis, 1916," Lieutenant-Colonel H. S. Vernon Papers, MSS Eur D744, IOR.

31. Phillip Stigger, "How Far was the Loyalty of Muslim Soldiers in the Indian Army More in Doubt Than Usual throughout the First World War?" *Journal of the Society of Army Historical Research* 87 (2009): 227.

32. H. S. Vernon, "Lecture: Indian Reservists in France," Lieutenant-Colonel H. S. Vernon Papers, MSS Eur D744, IOR.

33. Omissi, *Indian Voices of the Great War,* 10.

34. A. J. Barker, *The Neglected War: Mesopotamia, 1914–1918* (London: Faber and Faber, 1967), 122.

35. Edwin Latter, "The Indian Army in Mesopotamia, 1914–1918, Part II," *Journal of the Society for Army Historical Research* 72, no. 291 (Autumn 1994): 168.

36. Lawrence to Kitchener, 15 June 1915, MSS Eur 143/65, IOR.

37. Omissi, *The Sepoy and the Raj,* 156.

38. "War Record of the 27th Punjabis, 1916," Lieutenant-Colonel H. S. Vernon Papers, MSS Eur D744, IOR.

39. Jaqual Singh to *Akhbar-I-Jang,* 10 August 1015, MSS Eur F143/75, IOR. See also Jehan Khan to Gholem Mohamed Khan, 23 February 1916, MSS F143/91, IOR.

40. Jack, "The Indian Army on the Western Front," 359; Omissi, *Indian Voices of the Great War,* 17.

41. Lawrence to Kitchener, 15 June 1915, MSS Eur 143/65, IOR.

42. Markovits, "Indian Soldiers' Experiences in France during World War I," 34.

43. Latter, "The Indian Army in Mesopotamia, 1914–1918, Part II," 167.

44. Markovits, "Indian Soldiers' Experiences in France during World War I," 34.

45. Omissi, *Indian Voices of the Great War,* 14–15; Omissi, *The Sepoy and the Raj,* 121, 140; Arnold Wilson, *Loyalties: Mesopotamia, 1914–1917: A Personal and Historical Record* (London: Humphrey Milford, 1930), 84n2;

46. "Report of the Sedition Committee, 1918," Papers of 1st Viscount Chelmsford, MSS Eur E264/43, IOR.

47. "Telegram from Viceroy, 3 February 1915," Edmund Barrow Papers, MSS Eur E420/10, IOR.

48. Omissi, *Indian Voices of the Great War,* 14–15.

49. "Report of the Sedition Committee, 1918," Papers of 1st Viscount Chelmsford, MSS Eur E264/43, IOR.

50. Edmund Candler, *The Sepoy,* (London: John Murray, 1919), 70–71. See also Latter, "The Indian Army in Mesopotamia, 1914–1918, Part II," 167.

51. Omissi, *The Sepoy and the Raj,* 121.

52. Ibid., 120.

53. "Telegram from Viceroy, dated 11 March 1915"; "Telegram from Viceroy, dated 3 March 1915," Edmund Barrow Papers, MSS Eur E420/10, IOR.

54. Sowar Jivan Mal, 28th Cavalry, Persian Gulf, to Lance Daffadar Ganda Singh, 28th Cavalry (attached 2nd Lancers) France, 17 November 1915, MSS Eur F143/88, IOR.

55. John Terraine, *Mons: The Retreat to Victory* (London: Leo Cooper, 1991), 22–23.

56. Peter Liddle interview with Major G. L. Heawood, MES 044, Liddle Collection. See also Sir John Mellor to H. H. Rich, 5 November 1970, Rich Papers, MES 086, Liddle Collection.

57. Peter Liddle interview with Major-General H. H. Rich, June 1973, Tape 56, MES 086, Liddle Collection.

58. Nadia Atia, "War in the Cradle of Civilization: British Perceptions of Meso-

potamia 1907–1921" (unpublished doctoral thesis, Queen Mary, University of London, 2010), 79–81.

59. Peter Liddle interview with Major G. L. Heawood, MES 044, Liddle Collection.

60. E. O. Mousley, *Secrets of a Kuttite: An Authentic Story of Kut, Adventures in Captivity and Stamboul Intrigue* (New York: John Lane, 1921), 10–11.

61. Townshend, *My Campaign in Mesopotamia*, 320.

62. Erroll Sherston, *Townshend of Chitral and Kut* (London: Heinemann, 1928), 169–170.

63. Townshend, *When God Made Hell*, 95.

64. Peter Liddle interview with Sir John Mellor, January 1971, MES 067, Liddle Collection.

65. Ibid.

66. Millar, *Kut*, 21.

67. Sherston, *Townshend of Chitral and Kut*, 175.

68. Ibid., 184–210.

69. Ibid., 216.

70. Ibid., 236.

71. Townshend to Lord Curzon, 4 September 1915, Curzon Papers, MSS Eur F112.163, IOR.

72. Townshend, *When God Made Hell*, 72–73; Sherston, *Townshend of Chitral and Kut*, 238–247.

73. Barker, *The Bastard War*, 67–68.

74. Townshend, *My Campaign in Mesopotamia*, 77.

75. Townshend to Curzon, 7 November 1915, Curzon Papers, MSS Eur F112.163, IOR.

76. Sherston, *Townshend of Chitral and Kut*, 267.

77. Townshend, *My Campaign in Mesopotamia*, 86.

78. A. G. Kingsmill to H. H. Rich, 16 November 1970; H. G. Thomson to Rich,

27 November 1970. See also, J. J. Bouch to Rich, n.d.; T. R. Wells to Rich, 7 November 1970; Mellor to Rich, 5 November 1970, H. H. Rich Papers, MES 086, Liddle Collection.

79. Sherston, *Townshend of Chitral and Kut*, 104.

80. Rich, "Answers to the Townshend Questionnaire," Rich Papers, MES 086, Liddle Collection.

81. Omissi, *The Sepoy and the Raj*, 137–148.

82. Lovat-Fraser to Curzon, 10 August 1916, Curzon Papers, MSS Eur F112.163, IOR.

2. TOWNSHEND'S ADVANCE ON BAGHDAD

1. Barker, *The Bastard War*, 105.

2. Braddon, *The Siege*, 87.

3. Millar, *Kut*, 43.

4. David French, *British Strategy and War Aims, 1914–1916* (London: Allen and Unwin, 1986), 144–146; French, "The Dardanelles, Mecca and Kut: Prestige as a Factor in British Eastern Strategy, 1914–1916," *War and Society* 5, no. 1 (May 1987): 45–61.

5. Davis, *Ends and Means*, 138.

6. Richard Popplewell, "British Intelligence in Mesopotamia, 1914–1916," in *Intelligence and Military Operations*, ed. Michael Handel (London: Frank Cass, 1990), 162.

7. Latter, "The Indian Army in Mesopotamia," 160–179.

8. Kaushik Roy, "The Army in India in Mesopotamia from 1916 to 1918," in *1917: Beyond the Western Front*, ed. Ian F. W. Beckett (Leiden: Brill, 2009), 131–158.

9. Erickson, *Ottoman Military Effectiveness in the First World War*, ch.3.

10. Townshend, *My Campaign in Mesopotamia*, 161.

11. See, for example, Davis, *Ends and Means*, 116; Millar, *Kut*, 11; Crowley, *Kut 1916*, 32.

12. Townshend, *My Campaign in Mesopotamia*, 86..

13. Townshend to Lord Curzon, 4 September 1915, Curzon Papers, MSS Eur F112/163, India Office Records (IOR), British Library. Emphasis in original.

14. H. A. Holdich to Moberly, 7 October 1922, CAB 45/91, the National Archives (TNA), Kew.

15. B. T. Reynolds, "The First Battle of Kut," *Military Engineer* 29, no. 166 (July–August 1937), 236.

16. Kemball to Moberly, 10 April 1922, CAB 45/91, TNA; Reynolds, "The First Battle of Kut," 237–240.

17. Reynolds, "The First Battle of Kut," 240.

18. Townshend, *My Campaign in Mesopotamia*, 121.

19. Reynolds, "The First Battle of Kut," 235–238.

20. Barker, *The Bastard War*, 86–87.

21. A. J. Barker to H. H. Rich, 3 April 1966, Major General Sir Charles Townshend Papers, Liddell Hart Centre for Military Archives (LHCMA), King's College, London.

22. Holdich to Moberly, 16 October 1922, CAB 45/91, TNA.

23. Townshend, *My Campaign in Mesopotamia*, 119.

24. Barker, *The Bastard War*, 94–95.

25. "Extract from Private Letter Written on 30th September," CAB 45/91, TNA.

26. Holdich to Moberly, 16 October 1922, CAB 45/91. See also Delamain to Moberly, 17 September 1922, CAB 45/91, TNA.

27. Holdich to Moberly, 16 October 1922, CAB 45/91.

28. Mesopotamia Commission, *Report of the Commission Appointed by Act of Parliament to Enquire into the Operations of War in Mesopotamia, Together with a Separate Report by Commander J. Wedgwood, DSO, MO, and Appendices* (London: HMSO, 1917), 27. WO 106/911, TNA.

29. Townshend, *My Campaign in Mesopotamia,*, 130.

30. Austen Chamberlain to Lord Curzon, 15 May 1916, Curzon Papers, MSS Eur F112/163, IOR.

31. Townshend to Lord Curzon, 7 November 1915, Curzon Papers, MSS Eur F112/163, IOR.

32. Erickson, *Ottoman Military Effectiveness*, 73.

33. "Battle of Ctesiphon (Suliman Pak) 1915 Nov.–Dec.," by Staff Bimbashi Muhammed Amin, 17, CAB 44/33, TNA.

34. W. D. Bird, *A Chapter of Misfortunes: The Battles of Ctesiphon and of the Dujailah in Mesopotamia, with a Summary of the Events That Preceded Them* (London: Forster Groom, 1923), 50–51.

35. Townshend, *My Campaign in Mesopotamia*, 165.

36. Ibid., 167.

37. A. H. C. Kearsey, *A Study of the Strategy and Tactics of the Mesopotamia Campaign, 1914–1917* (Aldershot, UK: Gale and Polden, 1934), 51.

38. Barker, *The Bastard War*, 105.

39. Townshend, *My Campaign in Mesopotamia*, 119, 147.

40. J. E. Bridges to his father, 16 January 1916, Papers of Major J. E. Bridges, NAM 2007–03–57, National Army Museum (NAM), London.

41. Transcript of Rich interview with Peter Liddle, June 1973, MES 086, Liddle Collection, Brotherton Library, University of Leeds, Leeds UK.

42. Reynolds, "The First Battle of Kut," 238.

43. *Critical Study of the Campaign in Mesopotamia up to April 1917: Compiled*

by Officers of the Staff College, Quetta, October-November 1923, Part 1 (Calcutta: Government of India Press, 1925), 64–65.

44. On the tendency of British officers to visit the front in 1914, and the tendency of anxiety to skew decisions made in close proximity to battle, see Nikolas Gardner, *Trial by Fire: Command and the British Expeditionary Force in 1914* (Westport, Conn.: Praeger, 2003).

45. H. C. W. Bishop, *A Kut Prisoner* (London: John Lane, 1920), 5.

46. F. J. Moberly, *The Campaign in Mesopotamia* (London: HMSO, 1924), 2:74–76; Bird, *A Chapter of Misfortunes,* 61–63.

47. B. T. Reynolds, "The Battle of Ctesiphon and the Retreat to Kut," *Military Engineer* 30, no. 169 (January–February 1938): 37.

48. Bird, *A Chapter of Misfortunes,* 65–66.

49. Kemball to Moberly, 10 April 1922, CAB 45/91. See also Holdich to Moberly, 7 October 1922, CAB 45/91. According to Holdich, Hoghton "was not a thruster in any sense."

50. Colonel W. C. Spackman, "Besieged in Kut and What Happened After," MES 100, Liddle Collection.

51. Reynolds, "The Battle of Ctesiphon and the Retreat to Kut," 38.

52. Moberly to Kemball, August 1922, CAB 45/91, TNA.

53. Amin, "Battle of Ctesiphon (Suliman Pak) 1915 Nov.–Dec.," 73. CAB 44/33, TNA.

54. For reference to V.P. as the strongest point in the Ottoman position, see Peter Liddle interview with H. Rich, June 1971, MES 086, Liddle Collection.

55. Amin, "Battle of Ctesiphon (Suliman Pak) 1915 Nov.–Dec.," 68. CAB 44/33, TNA.

56. Ibid., 69.

57. Reynolds, "The Battle of Ctesiphon and the Retreat to Kut," 39.

58. Townshend, *My Campaign in Mesopotamia,* 176. For a similar explanation see Bird, *A Chapter of Misfortunes,* 71.

59. Townshend, *My Campaign in Mesopotamia,* 179.

60. Reynolds, "The Battle of Ctesiphon and the Retreat to Kut," 39.

61. Ibid.

62. Spackman, "Besieged in Kut and What Happened After," MES 100, Liddle Collection.

63. Amin, "Battle of Ctesiphon (Suliman Pak) 1915 Nov.–Dec.," 92–93. CAB 44/33, TNA.

64. B. T. Reynolds, "The Battle of Ctesiphon and the Retreat to Kut, Part 2," *Military Engineer* 30, no. 170 (March–April 1938): 127.

65. Amin, "Battle of Ctesiphon (Suliman Pak) 1915 Nov.–Dec.," 111. CAB 44/33, TNA.

66. Ibid., 105.

67. On the limitations of effects based operations, see Justin Kelly and David Kilcullen, "Chaos versus Predictability: A Critique of Effects-Based Operations," *Security Challenges* 2, no. 1 (2006): 63–73.

68. Moberly, *The Campaign in Mesopotamia,* 2:66; see also Bird, *A Chapter of Misfortunes,* 49n.

3. RETREAT FROM CTESIPHON

1. Barker, *The Bastard War.* 115.

2. Braddon, *The Siege,* 105.

3. Charles Townshend, *When God Made Hell,* 167.

4. Charles V. F. Townshend, *My Campaign in Mesopotamia,* 184.

5. Ibid., 185–186.

6. Moberly, *The Campaign in Mesopotamia,* 2:109; Bird, *A Chapter of Misfortunes,* 88.

7. Reynolds, "The Battle of Ctesiphon and the Retreat to Kut," 127.

8. Moberly, *The Campaign in Mesopotamia*, 2:110.

9. Townshend, *My Campaign in Mesopotamia*, 188.

10. Moberly, *The Campaign in Mesopotamia*, 2:111.

11. Townshend, *My Campaign in Mesopotamia*, 190.

12. Chalmers Diary, 28 November 1915, Private Papers of T. A. Chalmers, Imperial War Museum, London, UK.

13. Moberly, *The Campaign in Mesopotamia*, 2:112–113.

14. Townshend, *My Campaign in Mesopotamia*, 189–190.

15. Moberly, *The Campaign in Mesopotamia*, 2:116.

16. Ibid., 112–113; "From Nixon, 29 November 1915," Papers of Lord Curzon, MSS Eur, F112/163, British Library, London.

17. Townshend, *My Campaign in Mesopotamia*, 190–191.

18. Barker, *The Bastard War*, 116; Moberly, *The Campaign in Mesopotamia*, 2:115n.

19. Bird, *A Chapter of Misfortunes*, 91; Moberly, *The Campaign in Mesopotamia*, 2:125. Moberly suggests that Townshend's force may have been even weaker, with an effective strength of only 6,500 "rifles and sabres."

20. Moberly, *The Campaign in Mesopotamia*, 2:108, 486–487. Townshend's force suffered 4,593 casualties at Ctesiphon.

21. Amin, "Battle of Ctesiphon (Suliman Pak) 1915 Nov.–Dec.," 147. CAB 44/33, TNA.

22. Moberly, *The Campaign in Mesopotamia*, 2:113.

23. Ibid., 2:114–115.

24. Amin, "Battle of Ctesiphon (Suliman Pak) 1915 Nov.–Dec.," 153. CAB 44/33, TNA.

25. Ibid., 154.

26. Moberly, *The Campaign in Mesopotamia*, 2:110.

27. Amin, "Battle of Ctesiphon (Suliman Pak) 1915 Nov.–Dec.," 184. CAB 44/33, TNA. See also Reynolds, "The Battle of Ctesiphon and the Retreat to Kut," 129.

28. Amin, "Battle of Ctesiphon (Suliman Pak) 1915 Nov.–Dec.," 156–159; Reynolds, "The Battle of Ctesiphon and the Retreat to Kut," 129.

29. Amin, "Battle of Ctesiphon (Suliman Pak) 1915 Nov.–Dec.," 163–165; Moberly, *The Campaign in Mesopotamia*, 2:117–118.

30. Townshend, *My Campaign in Mesopotamia*, 192.

31. Peter Liddle interview with Major General H. H. Rich, June 1973, Tape 56, MES 086, Liddle Collection.

32. Moberly, *The Campaign in Mesopotamia*, 2:118.

33. W. C. Spackman, "Besieged in Kut and What Happened After: A Doctor in Battle and Captivity," W. C. Spackman Papers, MES 100, Liddle Collection, University of Leeds, Leeds, UK. See also Mousley, *The Secrets of a Kuttite*, 14; Spink Diary, 1 December 1915, Lieutenant H. Spink Papers, MSS Eur F188, British Library, London.

34. Moberly, *The Campaign in Mesopotamia*, 2:120.

35. Amin, "Battle of Ctesiphon (Suliman Pak) 1915 Nov.–Dec.," 180–183; Moberly, *The Campaign in Mesopotamia*, 2:120.

36. Amin, "Battle of Ctesiphon (Suliman Pak) 1915 Nov.–Dec.," 183.

37. Mousley, *The Secrets of a Kuttite*, 15.

38. G. W. R. Bishop to A. J. Barker, 1 June 1965, Charles Townshend Papers, Liddell Hart Centre for Military Archives,

King's College, London; Bishop to H. W. Rich, n.d., H. H. Rich Papers, MES 086, Liddle Collection.

39. Moberly, *The Campaign in Mesopotamia*, 2:120–122.

40. Reynolds, "The Battle of Ctesiphon and the Retreat to Kut," 129.

41. Moberly, *The Campaign in Mesopotamia*, 2:120.

42. Moberly to W. D. Bird, 29 August 1921, CAB 45/90, TNA.

43. Townshend, *My Campaign in Mesopotamia*, 193.

44. Amin, "Battle of Ctesiphon (Suliman Pak) 1915 Nov.–Dec.," 168, 174; Moberly, *The Campaign in Mesopotamia*, 2:121.

45. Mousley, *The Secrets of a Kuttite*, 16. See also G. L. Heawood to H. H. Rich, n.d., MES 086, Liddle Collection.

46. Townshend, *My Campaign in Mesopotamia*, 196–197. Emphasis in original.

47. "Narrative from Memory Written by Lt. Colonel S. De V. Julius of Events at the End of November 1915 at Kut in Mesopotamia," CAB 45/91, TNA.

48. J. C. Rimington, "Kut-al-Amarah," *Army Quarterly* 6, no. 1 (April 1923): 21–26.

49. "Narrative from Memory Written by Lt. Colonel S. De V. Julius," CAB 45/91, TNA.

50. Townshend, *My Campaign in Mesopotamia*, 209.

51. Ibid., 211.

52. Ibid., 198.

53. Ibid., 212.

54. Moberly, *The Campaign in Mesopotamia*, 2:122.

55. H. G. Thomson to H. H. Rich 27 November 1970, H. H. Rich Papers, MES 086, Liddle Collection.

56. E. W. C. Sandes to H. H. Rich, 3 November 1970, H. H. Rich Papers, MES 086, Liddle Collection. Emphasis in original. See also Callaway to Rich, n.d.; Ken

Crawford to Rich, 16 March 1971, Rich Papers, MES 086, Liddle Collection; Spink Diary, 2 December 1915, Lieutenant H. Spink Papers, MSS Eur F188, IOR.

57. Barker, *The Bastard War*, 124.

58. Townshend, *When God Made Hell*, 175.

59. H. S. Soden to Rich, 29 November 1970, MES 086, Rich Papers, Liddle Collection.

60. Wells to Rich, 7 November 1970, MES 086, Liddle Collection.

61. J. J. Bouch to H. H. Rich, n.d., MES 086, Liddle Collection.

62. John Mellor to Rich, 5 November 1970, MES 086, Liddle Collection. See also, D. Miles to Rich, 12 December 1970; Rich, "Answers to the Townshend Questionnaire," MES 086, Liddle Collection.

63. Moberly, *The Campaign in Mesopotamia*, 2:160.

64. R. V. Martin to H. H. Rich, 13 June 1971, Rich Papers, MES 086, Liddle Collection.

65. H. H. Rich interview with Peter Liddle, June 1973, Rich Papers, MES 086, Liddle Collection.

66. Moberly, *The Campaign in Mesopotamia*, 2:125.

67. W. C. Spackman to Rich, n.d., Rich Papers, MES 086, Liddle Collection.

68. G. L. Heawood to Rich, 11 November 1970, Rich Papers, MES 086, Liddle Collection.

69. Townshend, *When God Made Hell*, 175.

70. F. E. G. Talbot, "The Siege of Kut al Amara from the Turkish Point of View," 2, CAB 44/34, TNA.

71. Moberly, *The Campaign in Mesopotamia*, 2:139; Edward J. Erickson, *Ottoman Army Effectiveness in World War I: A Comparative Study* (Abingdon: Routledge, 2007), 80; Talbot, "The Siege of Kut al Amara from the Turkish Point of View,"

2, CAB 44/34, TNA. Talbot's account suggests that the Ottomans closed the neck of the peninsula on the night of 6 December, but the *Official History* and Erickson date this and other events in this period one day later. The inconsistency appears to arise from difficulty in converting the dates used by the Ottomans in 1915 to those used in the West.

72. Talbot, "The Siege of Kut al Amara from the Turkish Point of View," 4, CAB 44/34, TNA.

73. Erickson, *Ottoman Army Effectiveness*, 84.

74. Rimington, "Kut-al-Amarah," 25.

75. Moberly, *The Campaign in Mesopotamia*, 2:111.

76. Ibid., 136; Townshend, *My Campaign in Mesopotamia*, 216.

77. Moberly, *The Campaign in Mesopotamia*, 2:135–138.

78. Ibid., 139; Townshend, *My Campaign in Mesopotamia*, 220.

4. OUTSET OF THE SIEGE

1. *Report of the Commission Appointed by Act of Parliament to Enquire into the Operations of War in Mesopotamia* (London: His Majesty's Stationery Office, 1917), 31. See also Barker, *The Bastard War*, 126.

2. Barker, *The Bastard War*, 129.

3. Charles Townshend, *When God Made Hell*, 181.

4. Braddon, *The Siege*, 122–123.

5. Charles V. F. Townshend, *My Campaign in Mesopotamia*, 219.

6. Moberly, *The Campaign in Mesopotamia*, 2:193.

7. Townshend, *My Campaign in Mesopotamia*, 220.

8. Moberly, *The Campaign in Mesopotamia*, 2:153–54.

9. Townshend, *When God Made Hell*, 185.

10. Millar, *Kut*, 56.

11. H. J. Coombes, "The Batch," H. J. Coombes Papers, MES 025, Liddle Collection, Brotherton Library, University of Leeds, Leeds, UK.

12. Moberly, *The Campaign in Mesopotamia*, 2:157.

13. Ibid., 158. See also Millar, *Kut*, 57; Bird, *A Chapter of Misfortunes*, 93–94.

14. Millar, *Kut*, 57; Townshend, *When God Made Hell*, 185; Crowley, *Kut 1916*, 39.

15. Townshend, *My Campaign in Mesopotamia*, 215, 253.

16. H. H. Rich, "Personal Account of the Defence of WOOLPRESS during the Siege of Kut-al-Amara," Major-General H. H. Rich Papers, MES 086, Liddle Collection.

17. Wilson, *Loyalties*, 91.

18. "Extracts from Private Diary of Siege of Kut Belonging to Colonel H. Maule," CAB 45/91, the National Archives (TNA), Kew, London, UK.

19. A. J. Anderson Diary, 18 February 1916, Major Sir Alexander Anderson Papers, Imperial War Museum, London, UK (IWM).

20. Townshend, *My Campaign in Mesopotamia*, 253.

21. Ibid., 227–228. See also Wilson, *Loyalties*, 91–92.

22. Townshend, *My Campaign in Mesopotamia*, 211.

23. Moberly, *The Campaign in Mesopotamia*, 2:159.

24. E. W. C. Sandes, *In Kut and Captivity with the Sixth Indian Division* (London: John Murray, 1919), 121.

25. D. A. Simmons, "Story of My Experiences in the Early Stages of the Campaign in Mesopotamia," D. A. Simmons Papers, MES 096, Liddle Collection.

26. Millar, *Kut*, 66–67; Moberly, *The Campaign in Mesopotamia*, 2:161–162.

27. W. C. Spackman, "Besieged in Kut and What Happened After: A Doctor

in Battle and Captivity," Colonel W. C. Spackman Papers, MES 100, Liddle Collection; H. H. Rich, "Personal Account of the Defence of WOOLPRESS during the Siege of Kut-al-Amara," Major-General H. H. Rich Papers, MES 086, Liddle Collection.

28. Millar, *Kut*, 67.

29. Moberly, *The Campaign in Mesopotamia*, 2:162.

30. Walker typescript diary, 4 December 1915, Major-General Sir George Walker Papers, IWM.

31. G. L Heawood to H. H. Rich, 11 November 1970, H. H. Rich Papers, MES 086, Liddle Collection. See also transcript of Peter Liddle interview with G.L. Heawood, October 1976, G. L. Heawood Papers, MES 044, Liddle Collection.

32. Moberly, *The Campaign in Mesopotamia*, 2:168.

33. Simmons, "Story of My Experiences in the Early Stages of the Campaign in Mesopotamia," D. A. Simmons Papers, MES 096, Liddle Collection.

34. Townshend, *My Campaign in Mesopotamia*, 222.

35. "The Siege of Kut-al-Amara by Muhammad Amin Bey (Translated by Lt.-Col. G. O. de R. Channer) with a Summary by Colonel F. E. G. Talbot," 8, CAB 44/34, TNA.

36. Erickson, *Ottoman Military Effectiveness in World War I*, 84.

37. "The Siege of Kut-al-Amara by Muhammad Amin Bey," 9, CAB 44/34, TNA.

38. Moberly, *The Campaign in Mesopotamia*, 2:170.

39. "Extract from Regimental History," 111, H. H. Rich Papers, MES 086, Liddle Collection; "The Siege of Kut-al-Amara by Muhammad Amin Bey," 15–16, CAB 44/34, TNA.

40. According to Muhammad Amin's account, Nurettin's force suffered 1,138 casualties up to 13 December. According

to the British *Official History*, 6 Indian Division suffered 618 casualties from 9 to 12 December. Moberly's account does not list casualties for 13 December, but in his memoir, Townshend claimed that his division suffered 133 casualties that day. See "The Siege of Kut-al-Amara by Muhammad Amin Bey," 16, CAB 44/34, TNA; Moberly, *The Campaign in Mesopotamia*, 2:171–173; Townshend, *My Campaign in Mesopotamia*, 226.

41. Moberly, *The Campaign in Mesopotamia*, 2:134.

42. Ibid., 173.

43. Moberly, *The Campaign in Mesopotamia*, 2:174–175; "The Siege of Kut-al-Amara by Muhammad Amin Bey," 17–18, CAB 44/34, TNA.

44. "The Siege of Kut-al-Amara by Muhammad Amin Bey," 17–18, CAB 44/34, TNA.

45. Moberly, *The Campaign in Mesopotamia*, 2:176–178; "The Siege of Kut-al-Amara by Muhammad Amin Bey," 27–28, CAB 44/34, TNA; H. J. Coombes, "The Batch," Coombes Papers, MES 024, Liddle Collection.

46. "The Siege of Kut-al-Amara by Muhammad Amin Bey," 29, CAB 44/34, TNA.

47. Moberly, *The Campaign in Mesopotamia*, 2:180.

48. Ibid.; "The Siege of Kut-al-Amara by Muhammad Amin Bey," 30, CAB 44/34, TNA.

49. "The Siege of Kut-al-Amara by Muhammad Amin Bey," 32, CAB 44/34, TNA.

50. Bird, *A Chapter of Misfortunes*, 114–115.

51. Moberly, *The Campaign in Mesopotamia*, 2:198; Bird, *A Chapter of Misfortunes*, 115.

52. Spackman, "Besieged in Kut and What Happened After," MES 100, Liddle Collection; Moberly, *The Campaign in Mesopotamia*, 2:178.

53. Townshend, *When God Made Hell*, 191.

54. Lieut. H. S. D. McNeal, RFA, "Report on the Siege of Kut-al-Amara, 5 December 1915 to 29th April 1916," Curzon Papers, MSS Eur F112/163, British Library (BL), London, UK.

55. Townshend, *My Campaign in Mesopotamia*, 225.

56. Ibid., 228.

57. Moberly, *The Campaign in Mesopotamia*, 2:177–180. The 22nd Punjabis were the only battalion of 17th Brigade that did not participate in the Christmas Eve battle at the fort. Hoghton requested 150 British soldiers from the Norfolk Regiment, which were in reserve in the town of Kut, but these did not arrive at the fort until 3 AM on 25 December.

58. Wilson, *Loyalties*, 86.

59. Diary of Reverend H. Spooner, 26 December 1915, Harold Spooner Papers, IWM.

60. A. C. Lock Memoir, A. C. Lock Papers, IWM.

61. Townshend to GOC, IEFD, 10 March 1916, WO 106/697, TNA; "Intelligence Summary," 14 January 1916, WO 157/783, TNA. See also Spooner Diary, 24 January 1916, Spooner Papers, IWM.

62. Sandes, *In Kut and Captivity*, 155.

63. Townshend to GOC, IEFD, 10 March 1916, WO 106/697; Townshend, *My Campaign*, 233–237.

64. Townshend, *My Campaign in Mesopotamia*, 236.

65. Major J. B. K. Davie to GOCS 16, 17, 18, 30 Bdes, 29 December 1915, "Insubordination among Trans-Frontier Pathans," India Office Records (IOR) L/MIL/7/18848, BL.

66. "Telegram from Viceroy, dated 11th March 1915," Edmund Barrow Papers, MSS EUR 420/10, India Office Records, British Library.

67. Wilson, *Loyalties*, 54. For other examples of British military opinion regarding Arab atrocities, see Lieutenant H. Spink, Diary, 28 November 1915, Spink Papers, MSS Eur F188, India Office Records, British Library; Captain J. W. Barnett Diary, 8 February 1916, J. W. Barnett Papers, IWM.

68. Wilson, *Loyalties*, 92.

69. Townshend, *My Campaign in Mesopotamia*, 227.

70. Wilson, *Loyalties*, 92.

71. Townshend, *When God Made Hell*, 184; Millar, *Kut*, 70.

72. Peter Liddle Interview with Sir John Mellor, January 1971, Sir John Mellor Papers, MES 067, Liddle Collection.

73. Walker Diary, 29 April 1916, General Sir Ernest Walker Papers, IWM; H. Spooner Diary, 15 January 1916, Reverend H. Spooner Papers, Liddle Collection, Brotherton Library, University of Leeds; A. J. Anderson Papers, IWM, London.

74. Townshend, *My Campaign in Mesopotamia*, 227.

75. Millar, *Kut*, 90.

76. Townshend, *My Campaign in Mesopotamia*, 229.

77. Ibid., 222.

78. D. A. Simmons, "Story of My Experiences in the Early Stages of the Campaign in Mesopotamia," D. A. Simmons Papers, MES 096, Liddle Collection. See also, "Extracts from the Diary of Lieut. W. W. A. Phillips, 24th Punjabis," W. W. A. Phillips Papers, MES 082, Liddle Collection; J. J. Bouch to Rich, n.d., MES 086, Liddle Collection; Millar, *Kut*, 101.

79. Rich, "Personal Account of the Defence of WOOLPRESS during the Siege of Kut-al-Amara," Major-General H. H. Rich Papers, MES 086, Liddle Collection. See also Warren Sandes to Rich, 3 November

1970, W. C. Spackman, "Questionnaire re
the Townshend Myths," M ES 086, Liddle
Collection.

80. R. V. Martin to Rich, 13 January
1971, Rich Papers, M ES 086, Liddle Collection; Spackman, "Besieged in Kut," M ES
100, Liddle Collection.

81. "Extracts from Private Diary of
Siege of Kut Belonging to Colonel H.
Maule," CAB 45/91, TNA.

82. Bird, *A Chapter of Misfortunes.*

83. Lieut. H. S. D. McNeal, RFA,
"Report on the Siege of Kut-al-Amara, 5
December 1915 to 29th April 1916," Curzon
Papers, MSS EUR F112/163, BL; Walker Di-
ary, 22–31 January 1916, Major General Sir
Ernest Walker Papers, IWM.

84. Transcript of Peter Liddle interview with Sir John Mellor, Tape 138, January 1971, Sir John Mellor Papers, M ES 067,
Liddle Collection.

85. J. J. Bouch to H. H. Rich, Rich Papers, M ES 086, Liddle Collection.

86. Peter Liddle interview with Major-
General H. H. Rich, Tape 55, Rich Papers,
M ES 086, Liddle Collection. See also
Bishop, *A Kut Prisoner,* 16–17.

87. Millar, *Kut,* 68. See also Townshend, *My Campaign in Mesopotamia,* 227.

88. Moberly, *The Campaign in Mesopotamia,* 2:192–194.

89. Ibid., 198–199.

90. Ibid., 200; Townshend, *My Campaign in Mesopotamia,* 236.

91. Moberly, *The Campaign in Mesopotamia,* 2:207.

5. OPERATIONS OF THE
RELIEF FORCE

1. Barker, *The Neglected War,* 183; *Re-
port of the Commission Appointed by Act of
Parliament to Enquire into the Operations of
War in Mesopotamia,* 31.

2. Moberly, *The Campaign in Mesopotamia,* 2:192.

3. Ibid., 203

4. Ibid., 193–194.

5. J. W. B. Merewhether and Sir Frederick Smith, *The Indian Corps in France,*
(New York: Dutton, 1918), 185–192, 233–
254, 344–353, 377, 405–423.

6. Moberly, *The Campaign in Mesopotamia,* 2:490. On 3 January 1916, 7 Indian
Division comprised the 28th Brigade,
which had been in Egypt, the 35th Brigade, which consisted of units from India
and elsewhere in the Middle East, and the
19th Brigade, which had been a component of 7 Indian Division in France. The
19th contained two battalions – the 1st
Seaforth Highlanders and the 125th (Napier's) Rifles – which had fought in Europe,
but neither had been part of the brigade
when it left Europe. The only other battalion that had served in Europe was the 2/
Leicestershires, which had joined the 28th
Brigade prior to its departure from Egypt.

7. *Report of the Commission Appointed
by Act of Parliament to Enquire into the
Operations of War in Mesopotamia,* 31; Syk,
"Command in the Indian Expeditionary
Force D," 93; Anderson, "Logistics of the
Indian Expeditionary Force D in Meso-
potamia: 1914–1918," 119; Barker, *The Ne-
glected War,* 183; George Younghusband,
Forty Years a Soldier (London: Herbert
Jenkins, 1923), 287.

8. Moberly, *The Campaign in Mesopotamia,* 2:206–207.

9. Ibid., 203.

10. 7 Division General Staff War Diary,
January 1916, WO 95/5127, the National
Archives (TNA), Kew, London.

11. Younghusband, *Forty Years a Soldier,* 287.

12. Moberly, *The Campaign in Mesopotamia,* 2:212–213.

13. Elsmie to Moberly, 29 April 1923,
CAB 45/91, TNA; Younghusband, "Report
of Operations of the 7th Division from Jan

1st to the Capture of Sheikh Saad on Jan 8th," WO 95/5127, TNA.

14. Moberly, *The Campaign in Mesopotamia*, 2:214–215.

15. Ibid., 216.

16. Moberly, *The Campaign in Mesopotamia*, 2:216; Elsmie to Moberly, 29 April 1923, CAB 45/91, TNA.

17. *Report of the Commission Appointed by Act of Parliament to Enquire into the Operations of War in Mesopotamia*, 32.

18. Elsmie to Moberly, 29 April 1923, CAB 45/91, TNA.

19. "The Siege of Kut al Amara, by Muhammad Amin Bey (translated by Lt.-Col. G.O. de R. Channer) with a summary by Colonel F. E. G. Talbot," 41–42, CAB 44/34, TNA; "Short Comments on the Battles of Sheikh Saad (5th–7th January, 1916), the WADI (13th Jan) and SAIS, or DUJAILA Redoubt (8th March)," CAB 45/88, TNA.

20. "Short Comments on the Battles of Sheikh Saad (5th–7th January, 1916), the WADI (13th Jan) and SAIS, or DUJAILA Redoubt (8th March)," CAB 45/88, TNA.

21. "The Siege of Kut al Amara," 42, CAB 44/34, TNA; "Short Comments on the Battles of Sheikh Saad (5th–7th January, 1916), the WADI (13th Jan) and SAIS, or DUJAILA Redoubt (8th March)," CAB 45/88, TNA; 7 Division General Staff War Diary, 3 January 1916, WO 95/5127, TNA; Moberly, *The Campaign in Mesopotamia*, 2:490; David Kenyon, "Indian Cavalry Divisions in Somme: 1916," in Roy, ed., *The Indian Army in the Two World Wars*, 37. Amin's account suggests that the Ottoman force opposing Kemball on 6 January "probably" comprised "at least 2,000" troops. It seems unlikely that the force exceeded this number significantly, however, given that it consisted primarily of a regiment that had already suffered heavy casualties in recent months. More-

over, another Ottoman officer contended that the strength of the entire Ottoman force on both sides of the river consisted of only 3,400 troops. The 7 Division War Diary lists the strength of Younghusband's force as 13,345 on 3 January, which suggests that each of the four brigades of the division were at or near their full strength of approximately 3,250 personnel and the 6th Cavalry Brigade, which contained fourteen squadrons as well as an artillery battery, ammunition column, and signal troops, included at least 1,400 personnel.

22. Moberly, *The Campaign in Mesopotamia*, 2:218.

23. Elsmie to Moberly, 29 April 1923, CAB 45/91, TNA.

24. Moberly, *The Campaign in Mesopotamia*, 2:222–223.

25. Elsmie to Moberly, 29 April 1923, CAB 45/91, TNA; Younghusband, "Report of Operations of the 7th Division from Jan 1st to the Capture of Sheikh Saad on Jan 8th," WO 95/5127, TNA.

26. 7 Division General Staff War Diary, 7 January 1916, WO 95/5127, TNA.

27. "The Siege of Kut al Amara," 41, CAB 44/34, TNA

28. Elsmie to Moberly, 29 April 1923, CAB 45/91, TNA.

29. Younghusband, "Report of Operations of the 7th Division from Jan 1st to the Capture of Sheikh Saad on Jan 8th," WO 95/5127, TNA.

30. 7 Division General Staff War Diary, 7 January 1916, WO 95/5127, TNA.

31. Elsmie to Moberly, 29 April 1923, CAB 45/91, TNA.

32. 7 Indian Division General Staff War Diary, 8 January 1916, WO 95/5127, TNA.

33. Moberly, *The Campaign in Mesopotamia*, 2:235.

34. Ibid., 2:234.

35. 7 Indian Division General Staff War Diary, 8 January 1916, WO 95/5127, TNA.

36. "The Siege of Kut al Amara," 43, CAB 44/34, TNA.

37. Ibid., 44.

38. Moberly, *The Campaign in Mesopotamia*, 2:237.

39. A. W. Money to Moberly, 7 February 1923, CAB 45/91, TNA.

40. 7 Indian Division General Staff War Diary, 10–11 January 1916, WO 95/5127, TNA.

41. Younghusband, *Forty Years a Soldier*, 282.

42. Moberly, *The Campaign in Mesopotamia*, 2:204.

43. Bowker to his wife, 11 January 1916, Private Papers of F. I. Bowker, Imperial War Museum (IWM), London.

44. Merewhether and Smith, *The Indian Corps in France*, 458.

45. Edmund Candler, *The Long Road to Baghdad*, vol. 1 (New York: Houghton Mifflin, 1919), 28.

46. Lawrence to Kitchener, 15 December 1915, Papers of Sir Walter Lawrence, MSS EUR F143/65, India Office Records (IOR), British Library (BL), London.

47. Moberly, *The Campaign in Mesopotamia*, 2:204.

48. From _____, Force "D," Mesopotamia, to _____, France, 5 February 1916, MSS Eur F143/92, IOR. Letters are included in a published censor's report and do not include soldiers' names.

49. From _____, Force "D," Mesopotamia, to _____, France, 7 February 1916, MSS Eur F143/92, IOR.

50. From _____, Mesopotamia, to Sowar _____, France, 11 March 1916, MSS Eur F143/92, IOR.

51. Barker, *The Bastard War*, 165.

52. Harrison, *The Medical War*, 214.

53. Bridges to his father, 16 January 1916, Papers of Major J. E. Bridges, NAM 2007–03–57, National Army Museum (NAM), London.

54. Crowley, *Kut 1916*, 75; Moberly, *The Campaign in Mesopotamia*, 2:241.

55. Chalmers diary, 11 January 1916, Papers of T. A. Chalmers, IWM.

56. Moberly, *The Campaign in Mesopotamia*, 2:239–241.

57. Ibid., 243.

58. Aylmer to GHQ Basrah, 13 January 1916, 2:15 AM, WO 158/664, TNA.

59. Moberly, *The Campaign in Mesopotamia*, 2:245.

60. 7 Indian Division War Diary, 12 January 1916, WO 95/5127, TNA; Moberly, *The Campaign in Mesopotamia*, 2:245.

61. Aylmer to GHQ Basrah, 14 January 1916, 11.35 AM, WO 158/664, TNA; 7 Indian Division War Diary, 13 January 1916, WO 95/5127, TNA.

62. "Short Comments on the Battles of Sheikh Saad (5th–7th January, 1916), the WADI (13th Jan) and SAIS, or DUJAILA Redoubt (8th March)," CAB 45/88, TNA.

63. Moberly, *The Campaign in Mesopotamia*, 2:251.

64. Elsmie to Moberly, 9 July 1923, CAB 45/91, TNA.

65. Chalmers Diary, 13 January 1916, Papers of T. A. Chalmers, IWM.

66. Moberly, *The Campaign in Mesopotamia*, 2:251.

67. Elsmie to Moberly, 9 July 1923, CAB 45/91, TNA.

68. Moberly, *The Campaign in Mesopotamia*, 2:257–59.

69. 7 Indian Division War Diary, 15 January 1916, WO 95/5127, TNA.

70. Moberly, *The Campaign in Mesopotamia*, 2:266.

71. Ibid., 2:260.

72. Ibid., 2:258.

73. Corps to GHQ, 17 January 1916, 1:15 AM, Corps to GHQ, 16 January 1916, received 1:36 AM, WO 158/664, TNA.

74. GHQ to Corps, 17 January 1916, 7:10 AM, WO 158/664, TNA.

75. Corps to GHQ, 17 January 1916, 9:35 PM, WO 158/664, TNA.

76. Moberly, *The Campaign in Mesopotamia,* 2:259.

77. Corps to GHQ, 17 January 1916, 9:35 PM; Corps to GHQ, 18 January 1916, 12:50 PM; Corps to GHQ, 18 January 1916, 10:50 PM; Corps to GHQ, 20 January 1916, 3:50 PM, WO 158/664, TNA.

78. Moberly, *The Campaign in Mesopotamia,* 2:260.

79. Younghusband, *Forty Years a Soldier,* 291; Moberly, *The Campaign in Mesopotamia,* 2:266.

80. Moberly, *The Campaign in Mesopotamia,* 2:260–268.

81. 7 Indian Division War Diary, 20 January 1916, WO 95/5127, TNA; see also Chalmers Diary, 21 January 1916, Papers of T. A. Chalmers, IWM.

82. Moberly, *The Campaign in Mesopotamia,* 2:267–269.

83. Corps to GHQ, 21 January 1916, WO 158/664; 7 Indian Division War Diary, 19 January 1916, WO 95/5127, TNA.

84. Chalmers Diary, 21 January 1916, Papers of T. A. Chalmers, IWM.

85. 7 Indian Division War Diary, 21 January 1916, WO 95/5127, TNA.

86. Ibid.

87. Corps to GHQ, 22 January 1916, 1:15 AM, WO 158/664; 7 Indian Division War Diary, 21 January 1916, WO 95/5127, TNA.

88. Moberly, *The Campaign in Mesopotamia,* 2:275, 493.

89. 7 Indian Division War Diary, 21 January 1916, WO 95/5127, TNA.

90. Chalmers Diary, 21 January 1916, Papers of T. A. Chalmers, IWM.

91. Corps to GHQ, 24 January 1916, WO 158/665, TNA. Catty quoted in Harrison, *The Medical War,* 215.

92. Corps to GHQ, 24 January 1916, WO 158/665, TNA.

93. Charles V. F. Townshend, *My Campaign in Mesopotamia,* 253.

94. Ibid., 259.

95. Corps to GHQ and 6 Division, 26 January 1916, WO 158/665, TNA.

96. Younghusband, *Forty Years a Soldier,* 285.

6. DEPRIVATION AND DEFEAT

1. Moberly, *The Campaign in Mesopotamia,* 2:283, 506.

2. 3 Indian Division War Diary, 27 January 1916, WO 95/5094, the National Archives (TNA), Kew, London.

3. A. W. Money to Mrs. Money, 24 January 1916, Papers of Major-General Sir A. W. Money, 1992-11-19, National Army Museum (NAM), London.

4. A. W. Money to Mrs. Money, 27 January 1916, 1992-11-19, NAM.

5. T. A. Chalmers Diary, 24 February 1916, Papers of T. A. Chalmers, Imperial War Museum (IWM), London.

6. Money to Mrs. Money, 28 January 1916, 1992-11-19, NAM.

7. Moberly, *The Campaign in Mesopotamia,* 2:294–296, 504.

8. Ibid., 2:297–300.

9. E. G. Dunn Diary, 21 January 1916, CAB 45/94, TNA.

10. Millar, *Kut,* 157.

11. H. J. Coombes, "The Baton," 83, H. J. Coombes Papers, MES 025, Liddle Collection, Brotherton Library, University of Leeds, Leeds, UK.

12. Millar, *Kut,* 127.

13. H. H. Rich, "Personal Account of the Defence of WOOLPRESS Village during the Siege of Kut-al-Amara," Rich Papers, MES 086, Liddle Collection.

14. D. A. Simmons, "The Story of My Experiences in the Early Stages of the

Campaign in Mesopotamia," 124, MES 096, Liddle Collection.

15. Rich, "Personal Account of the Defence of WOOLPRESS Village," MES 086, Liddle Collection.

16. Moberly, *The Campaign in Mesopotamia*, 2:307.

17. Anderson Diary, 26 January 1916, Papers of A. J. Anderson, IWM.

18. Moberly, *The Campaign in Mesopotamia*, 2:307.

19. J. S. S. Martin to his mother, 29 February 1916, Papers of Major-General J. S. S. Martin, IWM.

20. Anderson Diary, 26 January 1916, A. J. Anderson Papers, IWM; Coombes manuscript diary, 30 January 1916, Coombes Papers, MES 025, Liddle Collection.

21. Spackman, "Besieged in Kut," Spackman Papers, MES 100, Liddle Collection.

22. W. M. A. Phillips Diary, 3 February 1916, CAB 45/93, TNA. See also H. J. Coombes manuscript diary, 30 January 1916, H. J. Coombes Papers, MES 025, Liddle Collection; W. C. Spackman, "Besieged in Kut and What Happened After: A Doctor in Battle and Captivity," W. C. Spackman Papers, MES 100, Liddle Collection.

23. Rich, "Personal Account of the Defence of WOOLPRESS Village," Rich Papers, MES 086, Liddle Collection.

24. Spackman, "Besieged in Kut and What Happened After," Spackman Papers, MES 100, Liddle Collection.

25. Walker typescript diary, 22–31 January 1916, Papers of Major-General Sir Ernest Walker, IWM.

26. Spooner Diary, 15 February 1916, Papers of Reverend Harold Spooner, IWM.

27. Anderson Diary, 18 February 1916, Papers of A. J. Anderson, IWM.

28. Walker typescript diary, 22–31 January 1916, Papers of Major-General Sir Ernest Walker, IWM.

29. Rich, "Personal Account of the Defence of WOOLPRESS Village," Rich Papers, MES 086, Liddle Collection.

30. Charles H. Barber, *Besieged in Kut and After* (London: Blackwood, 1917), 156–157.

31. Harrison, *The Medical War*, 268.

32. Spackman, "Besieged in Kut," Spackman Papers, MES 100, Liddle Collection.

33. Notes, 7 April, Private Diary of Colonel E. C. Dunn, CAB 45/94, TNA; Walker typescript diary, 22–31 January 1916, Papers of Major-General Sir Ernest Walker, IWM.

34. Spackman, "Besieged in Kut," Spackman Papers, MES 100, Liddle Collection; Peter Liddle interview with H. H. Rich, June 1973, Tape 055, MES 086, Liddle Collection.

35. "Notes on Rations etc.," CAB 45/92, TNA.

36. Millar, *Kut*, 190–191; Charles V. F. Townshend, *My Campaign in Mesopotamia*, 273, 278; Townshend to Head Quarters, 8 February 1916, Appendix Y, "Report from Lieutenant-General P. H. N. Lake on the Defence of Kut-al-Amara under Major-General C. V. F. Townshend," WO 106/907, TNA.

37. Captain W. A. Phillips, I.A.R.O., "Resumé of the Siege," CAB 45/93, TNA.

38. See Omissi, *Indian Voices of the Great War*.

39. Bishop, *A Kut Prisoner*, 23.

40. Roy, "The Construction of Regiments in the Indian Army," 136.

41. Walker typescript diary, 8–22 February 1916, Papers of Major-General Sir Ernest Walker, IWM; Anderson Memoirs, A. J. Anderson Papers, MES 003 Liddle Collection; "Extracts from Diary Kept

during Siege of Kut-al-Amara," Spackman
Papers, MES 100 Liddle Collection; "A Di-
ary of the Siege of Kut-al-Amara," W. M. A.
Phillips Papers, MES 082, Liddle Collec-
tion; Mousley, *The Secrets of a Kuttite;*
Sandes, *In Kut and Captivity,* 193.

42. Barber, *Besieged in Kut,* 190–191.

43. Townshend, *My Campaign in
Mesopotamia,* 273; Townshend to GHQ, 8
February 1916, WO 106/907, TNA.

44. Townshend, *My Campaign in
Mesopotamia,* 279.

45. Moberly, *The Campaign in Mesopotamia,* 2:303.

46. "Despatch by Lieutenant-General
Sir G. F. Gorringe, KCB, CMG, DSO, on
the Operations of the Tigris Column,
23rd January to 30th April 1916," L/
MIL/17/15/109, British Library (BL), London. Emphasis in original.

47. Charles Townshend, *When God
Made Hell,* 209.

48. Moberly, *The Campaign in Mesopotamia,* 2:303–304.

49. Walker typescript diary, 23–28 February 1916, Papers of Major-General Sir
Ernest Walker, IWM.

50. Moberly, *The Campaign in Mesopotamia,* 2:305.

51. Ibid., 2:303, 313.

52. Ibid., 2:312, 319.

53. Tigris Corps Order No. 26, 6
March 1916, Appendix XXIV, in Moberly,
The Campaign in Mesopotamia, 2:519–520.

54. Moberly, *The Campaign in Mesopotamia,* 2:318.

55. Syk, "Command in the Indian Expeditionary Force D," 96; Brian N. Hall,
"Technological Adaptation in a Global
Conflict: The British Army and Communications beyond the Western Front,
1914–1918," *Journal of Military History* 78
no. 1 (January 2014): 56.

56. *Critical Study of the Campaign in
Mesopotamia up to April 1917,* 180.

57. A. M. S. Elsmie to Moberly, 29 April
1923, CAB 45/91, TNA; Tigris Corps Order
No. 26, 6 March 1916, Appendix XXIV, in
Moberly, *The Campaign in Mesopotamia,*
2:519–520.

58. Moberly, *The Campaign in Mesopotamia,* 2:320.

59. *Critical Study of the Campaign in
Mesopotamia,* 180.

60. Moberly, *The Campaign in Mesopotamia,* 2:318.

61. Keary to Frank Keary, 4 January
1915, Papers of Sir Henry D'U. Keary Papers, IWM.

62. Keary to Frank Keary, 11 June 1915,
Keary Papers, IWM.

63. Keary to Frank Keary, 4 November
1915, Keary Papers, IWM.

64. "Answers to Questions asked
through BAQI BEY, the Chief of Staff at
the Constantinople Command," CAB
45/88, TNA.

65. *Critical Study of the Campaign in
Mesopotamia,* 184.

66. "General Kemball's Remarks on
Chapter V of Major-General Bird's Book,
'A Chapter of Misfortunes,'" CAB 45/91,
TNA; Moberly, *The Campaign in Mesopota-
mia,* 2:322–323.

67. Elsmie to Moberly, 29 April 1923,
CAB 45/91, TNA.

68. *Critical Study of the Campaign in
Mesopotamia,* 182.

69. Moberly, *The Campaign in Mesopotamia,* 2:325.

70. "Answers to Questions asked
through BAQI BEY, the Chief of Staff at
the Constantinople Command," CAB
45/88, TNA.

71. Elsmie to Moberly, 30 March 1923,
29 April 1923; Kemball to Moberly, 7 May
1923, CAB 45/91, TNA.

72. "General Kemball's Remarks on
Chapter V of Major-General Bird's Book, 'A
Chapter of Misfortunes,'" CAB 45/91, TNA.

73. Moberly, *The Campaign in Mesopotamia*, 2:330.

74. *Critical Study of the Campaign in Mesopotamia*, 192.

75. Moberly, *The Campaign in Mesopotamia*, 2:338–339.

76. 3 Indian Division War Diary, 8 March 1916, WO 95/5094, TNA.

77. *Critical Study of the Campaign in Mesopotamia*, 192.

78. 3 Indian Division War Diary, 8 March 1916, WO 95/5094, TNA.

79. Moberly, *The Campaign in Mesopotamia*, 2:349.

80. "Answers to Questions asked through BAQI BEY, the Chief of Staff at the Constantinople Command," CAB 45/88, TNA.

81. "Despatch by Lieutenant-General Sir G. F. Gorringe, KCB, CMG, DSO, on the Operations of the Tigris Column, 23rd January to 30th April 1916," L/MIL/17/15/109, BL.

82. "General Kemball's Remarks on Chapter V of Major-General Bird's Book, 'A Chapter of Misfortunes,'" CAB 45/91, TNA.

83. *Critical Study of the Campaign in Mesopotamia*, 192.

84. "Extracts from the Diary of W. M. A. Phillips, 24th Punjabis," W. M. A. Phillips Papers, MES 082, Liddle Collection.

85. "Answers to Questions asked through BAQI BEY, the Chief of Staff at the Constantinople Command," CAB 45/88; "The Siege of Kut al Amara, by Muhammad Amin Bey (translated by Lt.-Col. G. O. de R. Channer) with a summary by Colonel F. E. G. Talbot," 54, CAB 44/34, TNA.

86. Townshend, *My Campaign in Mesopotamia*, 288.

87. Ibid., 283.

88. *Critical Study of the Campaign in Mesopotamia*, 241.

89. Walker typescript diary, 8 March 1916, Papers of Major-General Sir Ernest Walker, IWM.

90. H. J. Coombes, "The Batch," 127, H. J. Coombes Papers, MES 025, Liddle Collection; "Extracts from the Diary of W. M. A. Phillips, 24th Punjabis," W. M. A. Phillips Papers, MES 082, Liddle Collection.

91. H. H. Rich, "Personal Account of the Defence of WOOLPRESS Village during the Siege of Kut-al-Amara," Rich Papers, MES 086, Liddle Collection; Anderson Diary, 8 March 1916, A. J. Anderson Papers, IWM.

92. J. S. Barker to Mrs. Barker, 11 March 1916, Papers of J. S. Barker, IWM.

93. Walker typescript diary, 9–31 March 1916, Papers of Major-General Sir Ernest Walker.

94. Ibid.

95. Millar, *Kut*, 181; Townshend, *My Campaign in Mesopotamia*, 237; Transcript of Peter Liddle interview with H. H. Rich, June 1973, MES 086, Liddle Collection; Spooner diary, 30 March 1916, Rev. H. Spooner Papers, IWM; Rogers Diary, 6 April 1916, G. N. Rogers Papers, IWM; "Resume of the Siege," W. M. A. Phillips Papers, CAB 45/93, TNA.

96. Townshend to GHQ, 14 March 1916, "Insubordination among Trans-Frontier Pathans," L/MIL/7/18848, IOR, BL.

97. G. N. Rogers Diary, 1 March 1916, G. N. Rogers Papers, IWM.

98. Dunn Diary, 17 March 1916, E. G. Dunn Papers, CAB 45/94, TNA.

99. Coombes, "The Baton," H. J. Coombes Papers, MES 025; "March and April in Kut," W. C. Spackman Papers, MES 100, Liddle Collection.

100. G. N. Rogers Diary, 16 March 1916, G. N. Rogers Papers, IWM.

101. Moberly, *The Campaign in Mesopotamia*, 2:444.

102. Townshend, *My Campaign in Mesopotamia*, 230.

103. "Diary of the Siege of Kut-al-Amarah," Bell-Syer Papers, MES 008, Liddle Collection.

7. INNOVATION, STARVATION, AND SURRENDER

1. See, for example, Barker, *The Bastard War*, 224–227; Braddon, *The Siege*, 226–250.

2. Syk, "Command in the Indian Expeditionary Force D," 98.

3. Gardner, "Sepoys and the Siege of Kut-al-Amara," 320–323.

4. Chalmers Diary, 13 March 1916, Private Papers of T. A. Chalmers, Imperial War Museum (IWM), London.

5. A. W. Money to Mrs. Money, 11 March 1916, Papers of Major-General Sir A. W. Money, 1992-11-19, National Army Museum (NAM), London; Chalmers Diary, 13 March 1916, Chalmers Papers, IWM.

6. Charles V. F. Townshend, *My Campaign in Mesopotamia*, 303.

7. Moberly, *The Campaign in Mesopotamia*, 2:366.

8. "Despatch by Lieutenant-General Sir G. F. Gorringe, KCB, CMG, DSO, on the Operations of the Tigris Column, 23rd January to 30th April 1916," 16, L/MIL/17/15/109, British Library (BL), London; Moberly, *The Campaign in Mesopotamia*, 2:365, 371.

9. Moberly, *The Campaign in Mesopotamia*, 2:365.

10. Charles Callwell, *The Life of Sir Stanley Maude: Lieutenant-General, KCB, CMG, DSO* (London: Constable, 1920), 206.

11. *Critical Study of the Campaign in Mesopotamia up to April 1917*, 199.

12. Bridges to his father, 7 February 1916, Papers of Major J. E. Bridges, NAM 2007-03-57, National Army Museum (NAM), London.

13. "Despatch by Lieutenant-General Sir G.F. Gorringe,"18, L/MIL/17/15/109, BL.

14. Callwell, *The Life of Sir Stanley Maude*, 151.

15. Ibid., 163.

16. Syk, "Command in the Indian Expeditionary Force D," 98.

17. Moberly, *The Campaign in Mesopotamia*, 2:373.

18. "Summary of Operations by 13th Division from 1st to 30th April, 1916," 13 Division War Diary, WO 95/5147, the National Archives (TNA), Kew, London; Moberly, *The Campaign in Mesopotamia*, 2:374–375.

19. "The Siege of Kut al Amara, by Muhammad Amin Bey (translated by Lt.-Col. G. O. de R. Channer) with a summary by Colonel F. E. G. Talbot," 57, CAB 44/34, TNA; "Despatch by Lieutenant-General Sir G. F. Gorringe," p. 17, L/MIL/17/15/109, BL.

20. Moberly, *The Campaign in Mesopotamia*, 2:374.

21. Syk, "Command in the Indian Expeditionary Force D," 99.

22. "Summary of Operations by 13th Division from 1st to 30th April, 1916," 13 Division War Diary, WO 95/5147.

23. "The Siege of Kut al Amara, by Muhammad Amin Bey," 57, CAB 44/34, TNA

24. Chalmers Diary, 5 April 1916, Private Papers of T. A. Chalmers, IWM; 13 Division War Diary, 5 April 1916, WO 95/5147, TNA.

25. *Critical Study of the Campaign in Mesopotamia*, 200. In English: "Good-bye until the next battle."

26. 13 Division War Diary, 5 April 1916, WO 95/5147, TNA.

27. "Summary of Operations by 13th Division from 1st to 30th April, 1916," 13 Division War Diary, WO 95/5147.

28. *Critical Study of the Campaign in Mesopotamia*, 201.

29. "Despatch by Lieutenant-General Sir G. F. Gorringe," 18, L/MIL/17/15/109, BL.

30. 13 Division War Diary, 5 April 1916, WO 95/5147, TNA.

31. Andrew Syk, ed., *The Military Papers of Lieutenant-General Sir Frederick Stanley Maude, 1914–1917* (Stroud, UK: History Press for the Army Records Society, 2012), 136–137.

32. "Despatch by Lieutenant-General Sir G. F. Gorringe," 19, L/MIL/17/15/109, BL.

33. 7 Indian Division War Diary, 6 April 1916, WO 95/5127, TNA.

34. Moberly, *The Campaign in Mesopotamia*, 2:381.

35. Ibid., 369; 7 Indian Division War Diary, 6 April 1916, WO 95/5127, TNA.

36. 28th Field Battery war diary, 19 April 1916, Papers of J. Coombey, IWM.

37. "Despatch by Lieutenant-General Sir G. F. Gorringe," 20, L/MIL/17/15/109, BL; 7 Indian Division War Diary, 6 April 1916, WO 95/5127, TNA.

38. Syk, *The Military Papers of Lieutenant-General Sir Frederick Stanley Maude*, 139.

39. Moberly, *The Campaign in Mesopotamia*, 2:386–389.

40. "Summary of Operations by 13th Division from 1st to 30th April, 1916," 13 Division War Diary, WO 95/5147; Moberly, *The Campaign in Mesopotamia*, 2:389–390; "Despatch by Lieutenant-General Sir G. F. Gorringe," 21, L/MIL/17/15/109, BL.

41. Moberly, *The Campaign in Mesopotamia*, 2:392.

42. "Despatch by Lieutenant-General Sir G. F. Gorringe," 21, L/MIL/17/15/109, BL.

43. 13 Division War Diary, 9 April 1916, WO 95/5127. See also Money to Mrs. Money, 11 April 1916, Papers of Major-General Sir A. W. Money, 1992-11-19, NAM; Chalmers Diary, 11, 13 April 1916, Papers of T. A. Chalmers, IWM.

44. Captain H. B. Latham, "Appendix III – First Attack on Sannaiyat," 28th Field Battery War Diary, Papers of J. Coombey, IWM.

45. Moberly, *The Campaign in Mesopotamia*, 2:392.

46. Latham, "Appendix III – First Attack on Sannaiyat," 28th Field Battery War Diary, Papers of J. Coombey, IWM.

47. Extracts from Private Diary of A. J. Shakeshaft, C Company 2/Norfolk Regiment, CAB 45/92; Private Diary of Captain W. A. Phillips, IARO, 10 April 1916, CAB 45/93, TNA; Moberly, *The Campaign in Mesopotamia*, 2:393.

48. D. A. Simmons, "The Story of My Experience in the Early Stages of the Campaign in Mesopotamia," 130, MES 096, Liddle Collection.

49. H. H. Rich, "Personal Account of the Defence of WOOLPRESS village during the siege of KUT_AL_AMARA," Rich Papers, MES 086, Liddle Collection.

50. W. C. Spackman, "Besieged in Kut and What Happened After: A Doctor in Battle and Captivity," W. C. Spackman Papers, MES 100, Liddle Collection.

51. Spooner Diary 13 April 1916, Papers of the Reverend Harold Spooner, IWM.

52. Townshend, *My Campaign in Mesopotamia*, 310

53. Ibid., 321.

54. Ibid., 322, 325.

55. Rogers Diary, 10 April 1916, Papers of G. N. Rogers, IWM.

56. "Communiqué to Indian Troops, 12 April 1916," CAB 45/92, TNA. Emphasis in original.

57. Rogers Diary, 11–12 April 1916, Papers of G. N. Rogers, IWM.

58. Townshend, *My Campaign in Mesopotamia*, 327.

59. Transcript of Peter Liddle interview with H. H. Rich, June 1973, H. H. Rich Papers, MES 086, Liddle Collection; Wilson, *Loyalties*, 95.

60. Moberly, *The Campaign in Mesopotamia*, 2:445.

61. Byron Farwell, *Armies of the Raj: From the Great Indian Mutiny to Independence, 1858–1947* (London: Norton, 1991), 260.

62. On this policy see Kaushik Roy, "Coercion through Leniency: British Manipulation of the Courts-Martial System in the Post-Mutiny Indian Army, 1859–1913," *Journal of Military History* 65, no. 4 (October 2001): 948.

63. "Communique to the Troops, 10 April 1916," CAB 45/92, TNA.

64. Shakeshaft Diary, 15 April 1916, CAB 45/92, TNA.

65. Frank D. Ashburn, ed., *The Ranks of Death: A Medical History of the Conquest of America* (New York: Coward-McCann, 1947), 60.

66. For examples of fatalities attributed to "enteritis," see Shakeshaft Diary, 19 April 1916, CAB 45/92, TNA; "Story of My Experiences in the Early Stages of the Campaign in Mesopotamia," D. A. Simmons Papers, MES 096, Liddle Collection.

67. Ashburn, *The Ranks of Death*, 60.

68. Townshend, *My Campaign in Mesopotamia*, 310.

69. C. T. Atkinson, "History of the Second Battalion, The Dorsetshire Regiment, 1914–1919," in Anon., *History of the Dorsetshire Regiment, 1914–1919* (Uckfield, UK: Naval and Military Press, 2010), 1:217.

70. Spooner Diary, 13 April 1916, Papers of the Reverend Harold Spooner, IWM.

71. Walker Diary, 16–21 April 1916, Papers of Major-General Sir Ernest Walker, IWM.

72. "Despatch by Lieutenant-General Sir G. F. Gorringe," 22, L/MIL/17/15/109, BL.

73. Moberly, *The Campaign in Mesopotamia*, 2:401.

74. Barnett Diary, 17 April 1916, Papers of J. W. Barnett, IWM; 3 Division War Diary, 13 April 1916, WO 95/5094, TNA.

75. "Despatch by Lieutenant-General Sir G. F. Gorringe," 24, L/MIL/17/15/109, BL; 3 Division War Diary, 14–15 April 1916, WO 95/5094, TNA.

76. *Critical Study of the Campaign in Mesopotamia*, 205.

77. Syk, *The Military Papers of Lieutenant-General Sir Frederick Stanley Maude*, 142.

78. Chalmers Diary, 18 April 1916, Papers of T. A. Chalmers, IWM; "Despatch by Lieutenant-General Sir G. F. Gorringe," 26, L/MIL/17/15/109, BL.

79. "Despatch by Lieutenant-General Sir G. F. Gorringe," 26, L/MIL/17/15/109, BL.

80. Chalmers Diary, 23 April 1916, Papers of T. A. Chalmers, IWM.

81. *Critical Study of the Campaign in Mesopotamia*, 205.

82. "The Siege of Kut al Amara, by Muhammad Amin Bey," 59, CAB 44/34, TNA.

83. Ibid., 63–64.

84. Moberly, *The Campaign in Mesopotamia*, 2:422.

85. Callwell, *The Life of Sir Stanley Maude*, 218.

86. Latham, "Appendix III – First Attack on Sannaiyat," 28th Field Battery War Diary, Papers of J. Coombey, IWM.

87. Moberly, *The Campaign in Mesopotamia*, 2:422.

88. Townshend, *My Campaign in Mesopotamia*, 325.

89. Ibid., 327–330.

90. Walker Diary, 16–21 April, Papers of Major-General Ernest Walker, IWM.

91. 7 Indian Division War Diary, 21 April 1916, WO 95/5127, TNA.

92. *Critical Study of the Campaign in Mesopotamia*, 208.

93. 7 Indian Division War Diary, 22 April 1916, WO 95/5127, TNA.

94. Ibid.; *Critical Study of the Campaign in Mesopotamia*, 208.

95. Norie to Bird, 4 September 1921, CAB 45/91, TNA.

96. *Critical Study of the Campaign in Mesopotamia*, 208.

97. 7 Indian Division War Diary, 22 April 1916, WO 95/5127, TNA.

98. Ibid.

99. Norie to Bird, 4 September 1921, CAB 45/91, TNA.

100. "Despatch by Lieutenant-General Sir G. F. Gorringe," 29, L/MIL/17/15/109, BL.

101. "The Siege of Kut al Amara, by Muhammad Amin Bey," 64, CAB 44/34, TNA; Spackman, "Besieged in Kut," MES 100, Liddle Collection; Moberly, *The Campaign in Mesopotamia*, 2:436.

102. Crowley, *Kut 1916*, 161; Spackman, "Besieged in Kut," MES 100, Liddle Collection; "The Siege of Kut al Amara, by Muhammad Amin Bey," 64, CAB 44/34, TNA.

103. Moberly, *The Campaign in Mesopotamia*, 2:436–437.

104. Walker Diary 27 April 1916, Papers of Major-General Ernest Walker, IWM.

105. "The Siege of Kut al Amara, by Muhammad Amin Bey," 64, CAB 44/34,

TNA; Moberly, *The Campaign in Mesopotamia*, 2:456.

106. Townshend, *My Campaign in Mesopotamia*, 329.

107. Ibid., 335.

108. Spackman, "Besieged in Kut," MES 100, Liddle Collection.

109. Crowley, *Kut 1916*, 164–165.

110. Walker Diary, 1 May 1916, Private Papers of Major-General Ernest Walker, IWM.

111. Spackman, "Besieged in Kut," MES 100, Liddle Collection.

112. Moberly, *The Campaign in Mesopotamia*, 2:461.

113. Spackman, "Besieged in Kut," MES 100, Liddle Collection.

114. Walker Diary, 29 April 1916, Private Papers of Major-General Ernest Walker, IWM.

115. Moberly, *The Campaign in Mesopotamia*, 2:461; "The Siege of Kut al Amara, by Muhammad Amin Bey," 69–70, CAB 44/34, TNA.

116. "The Siege of Kut al Amara, by Muhammad Amin Bey," 72, CAB 44/34, TNA.

117. Crowley, *Kut 1916*, 181, 253.

BIBLIOGRAPHY

PRIMARY DOCUMENTS

British Library, London

India Office Records

L/MIL/17/15/109, "Despatch by Lieutenant-General Sir G. F. Gorringe, KCB, CMG, DSO, on the Operations of the Tigris Column, 23rd January to 30th April 1916"
L/MIL/7/18848, "Insubordination among Trans-Frontier Pathans"
MSS EUR D744, Vernon Papers
MSS EUR E264/43, Chelmsford Papers
MSS EUR E420/10, Edmund Barrow Papers
MSS EUR F112/163, Curzon Papers
MSS EUR F143/65, Lawrence Papers
MSS EUR F143/75, Correspondence regarding Indian newspaper *Akbar-i-Jang*
MSS EUR F143/88, Extracts from censored Indian letters
MSS EUR F143/91, Extracts from censored Indian letters
MSS EUR F143/92, Extracts from censored Indian letters
MSS EUR F188, Spink Papers

Imperial War Museum, London

Papers of Major A. J. Anderson
Papers of J. W. Barnett
Papers of F. I. Bowker
Papers of T. A. Chalmers
Papers of J. Coombey
Papers of Sir Henry D'U. Keary
Papers of A. C. Lock
Papers of Major-General J. S. S. Martin
Papers of G. N. Rogers
Papers of the Reverend Harold Spooner
Papers of Major-General Sir Ernest Walker

Liddell Hart Centre for Military Archives, King's College, London

Sir Charles Townshend Papers

Liddle Collection, Brotherton Library, University of Leeds, Leeds UK

Papers of A. J. Anderson, MES 003
Papers of L. Bell-Syer, MES 008
Papers of H. J. Coombes, MES 025
Papers of G. L. Heawood, MES 044
Papers of Sir John Mellor, MES 067
Papers of W. M. A. Phillips, MES 082
Papers of H. H. Rich, MES 086
Papers of D. A. Simmons, MES 096
Papers of W. C. Spackman, MES 100

National Army Museum, London

Papers of Major J. E. Bridges, NAM 2007-03-57
Papers of Major-General Sir A. W. Money, NAM 1992-11-19

The National Archives, London

CAB 44/34, Translated histories by Ottoman staff officer Muhammad Amin
CAB 45/88, Comments and accounts of Battles of Shaikh Saad, the Wadi, and Dujaila Redoubt
CAB 45/90, Official historians' correspondence and papers
CAB 45/91, Official historians' correspondence and papers
CAB 45/92, Private diaries, Mesopotamia campaign
CAB 45/93, "The Siege of Kut-al-Amara," by Captain W. W. A. Phillips
CAB 45/94, Private diaries, Mesopotamia campaign
WO 95/5094, 3 Indian Division War Diary
WO 95/5127, 7 Indian Division War Diary
WO 95/5147, 13 Division War Diary
WO 106/907, "Defence of Kut-al-Amarah," Report by Lieutenant-General Sir P. H. N. Lake
WO 157/783, Intelligence summaries
WO 158/664, IEFD Headquarters, correspondence and papers
WO 158/665, IEFD Headquarters, correspondence and papers

PUBLISHED SOURCES

Ahuja, Ravi. "The Corrosiveness of Comparison: Reverberations of Indian Wartime Experiences in German Prison Camps (1915–1919)." In *The World in World Wars: Experiences, Perceptions and Perspectives from Africa and Asia,* ed. Heike Liebau et al., 131–166. Leiden: Brill, 2010.
Anderson, Ross. "Logistics of the Indian Expeditionary Force D in Mesopotamia, 1914–1918." In *The Indian Army in the Two World Wars,* ed. Kaushik Roy, 105–144. Leiden: Brill, 2011.
Ashburn, Frank D., ed. *The Ranks of Death: A Medical History of the Conquest of America.* New York: Coward-McCann, 1947.
Atia, Nadia. "War in the Cradle of Civilization: British Perceptions of Mesopotamia 1907–1921." Unpublished doctoral thesis, Queen Mary, University of London, 2010.
Barber, Charles H. *Besieged in Kut and After.* London: Blackwood, 1917.
Barker, A. J. *The Bastard War: The Mesopotamia Campaign of 1914–1918.* New York: Dial Press, 1967.
———. *The Neglected War: Mesopotamia, 1914–1918.* London: Faber and Faber, 1967.
Bird, W. D. *A Chapter of Misfortunes: The Battles of Ctesiphon and of the Dujailah in Mesopotamia, with a Summary of the Events That Preceded Them.* London: Forster Groom, 1923.
Bishop, H. C. W. *A Kut Prisoner,* London: John Lane, 1920.
Braddon, Russell. *The Siege.* London: Jonathan Cape, 1969.
Callwell, Charles. *The Life of Sir Stanley Maude: Lieutenant-General, KCB, CMG, DSO,* London: Constable, 1920.
Candler, Edmund. *The Long Road to Baghdad.* London: Cassell, 1919.
———. *The Sepoy.* London: John Murray, 1919.
Corrigan, Gordon. *Sepoys in the Trenches: The Indian Corps on the Western Front, 1914–1915.* Staplehurst, UK: Spellmount, 1999.

*Critical Study of the Campaign in Meso-
potamia up to April 1917: Compiled by
Officers of the Staff College, Quetta,
October-November 1923, Part 1 - Report.*
Calcutta: Government of India Press,
1925.

Crowley, Patrick. *Kut 1916: Courage and
Failure in Iraq.* Stroud, UK: Spellmount, 2009.

Davis, Paul K. *Ends and Means: The British
Mesopotamian Campaign and Commis-
sion.* London: Associated University
Presses, 1994.

Erickson, Edward J. *Ottoman Army Effectiveness in the First World War: A
Comparative Study.* London: Routledge,
2007.

Farwell, Byron. *Armies of the Raj: From the
Great Indian Mutiny to Independence,
1858-1947.* London: Norton, 1991.

French, David. *British Strategy and War
Aims, 1914-1916.* London: Allen and
Unwin, 1986.

———. "The Dardanelles, Mecca and
Kut: Prestige as a Factor in British
Eastern Strategy, 1914-1916." *War and
Society* 5, no. 1 (May 1987): 45-61.

Gardner, Nikolas. "Sepoys and the Siege
of Kut-al-Amara, December 1915–April
1916." *War in History* 11, no. 3 (July
2004): 307–326.

———. *Trial by Fire: Command and the
British Expeditionary Force in 1914.*
Westport, Conn.: Praeger, 2003.

Greenhut, Jeffrey. "The Imperial Reserve:
The Indian Corps on the Western
Front, 1914-1915." *Journal of Imperial
and Commonwealth History* 12, no. 1
(October 1988): 54-73.

———. "Sahib and Sepoy: An Inquiry
into the Relationship between the British Officers and Native Soldiers of the
British Indian Army." *Military Affairs,*
48, no. 1 (January 1984): 15-18.

Hall, Brian N, "Technological Adaptation in a Global Conflict: The British
Army and Communications beyond
the Western Front, 1914-1918." Journal
of Military History 78, no. 1 (January
2014): 37-71.

Harris, J. P. *Douglas Haig and the First
World War.* New York: Cambridge University Press, 2008.

Harrison, Mark. "The Fight against Dis-
ease in the Mesopotamia Campaign."
In *Facing Armageddon: the First World
War Experienced,* ed. Peter Liddle and
Hugh Cecil, 475–489. London: Leo
Cooper, 1996.

———. *The Medical War: British Military
Medicine in the First World War.* New
York: Oxford University Press, 2010.

———. "Medicine and the Management
of Modern Warfare." *History of Science*
34, no. 106 (1999): 397–410.

*History of the Dorsetshire Regiment, 1914–
1919.* Vol. 1. Uckfield, UK: Naval and
Military Press, 2010.

Jack, G. M. "The Indian Army on the
Western Front, 1914-1915: A Portrait
of Collaboration." *War in History* 13, no.
3 (July 2006): 329-362.

Kearsey, A. H. C. *A Study of the Strategy
and Tactics of the Mesopotamia Campaign, 1914-1917.* Aldershot, UK: Gale
and Polden, 1934.

Kelly, Justin, and David Kilcullen. "Chaos
versus Predictability: A Critique
of Effects-Based Operations." *Security
Challenges* 2, no. 1 (2006): 63–73.

Kenyon, David. "Indian Cavalry Divisions
in Somme, 1916." In *The Indian Army in
the Two World Wars,* ed. Kaushik Roy,
33–62. Leiden: Brill, 2011.

Latter, Edwin. "The Indian Army in Mesopotamia, 1914–1918, Part II." *Journal of
the Society for Army Historical Research,*
72, no. 291 (Autumn 1994): 160–179.

Markovits, Claude. "Indian Soldiers' Experiences in France during World War I: Seeing Europe from the Rear of the Front." In *The World in World Wars: Experiences, Perceptions and Perspectives from Africa and Asia,* ed. Heike Liebau et al., 29–54. Leiden: Brill, 2010.

Merewhether, J. B., and Sir Frederick Smith. *The Indian Corps in France.* New York: Dutton, 1918.

Millar, Ronald. *Kut: The Death of an Army.* London: Secker and Warburg, 1969.

Moberly, F. J. *The Campaign in Mesopotamia: 1914–1918.* 2 vols. London: His Majesty's Stationery Office, 1924.

Mousley, E. O. *Secrets of a Kuttite: An Authentic Story of Kut, Adventures in Captivity and Stamboul Intrigue.* New York: John Lane, 1921.

Omissi, David. *Indian Voices of the Great War: Soldiers' Letters, 1914–1918.* London: Macmillan, 1999.

———. *The Sepoy and the Raj: The Indian Army, 1860–1940.* London: Macmillan, 1994.

Popplewell, Richard. "British Intelligence in Mesopotamia, 1914–1916." In *Intelligence and Military Operations,* ed. Michael Handel, 139–172. London: Frank Cass, 1990.

Report of the Commission Appointed by Act of Parliament to Enquire into the Operations of War in Mesopotamia. London: His Majesty's Stationery Office, 1917.

Reynolds, B. T. "The Battle of Ctesiphon and the Retreat to Kut, Part 1." *Military Engineer* 30, no. 169 (January–February 1938): 34–39.

———. "The Battle of Ctesiphon and the Retreat to Kut, Part 2." *Military Engineer* 30, no. 170 (March–April 1938): 125–130.

———. "The First Battle of Kut." *Military Engineer* 29, no. 166 (July–August 1937): 235–240.

Rimington, J. C. "Kut-al-Amarah." *Army Quarterly* 6, no. 1 (April 1923): 21–26.

Roy, Kaushik. "The Army in India in Mesopotamia from 1916 to 1918." In *1917: Beyond the Western Front,* ed. Ian F. W. Beckett, 131–158. Leiden: Brill, 2009.

———. "Coercion through Leniency: British Manipulation of the Courts-Martial System in the Post-Mutiny Indian Army, 1859–1913." *Journal of Military History* 65, no. 4 (October 2001): 937–964.

———. "The Construction of Regiments in the Indian Army: 1859–1913." *War in History* 8, no. 2 (April 2001): 127–148.

———. "From Defeat to Victory: Logistics of the Campaign in Mesopotamia, 1914–1918." *First World War Studies* 1, no. 1 (March 2010): 35–55.

———, ed. *The Indian Army in the Two World Wars.* Leiden: Brill, 2011.

Sandes, E. W. C. *In Kut and Captivity with the Sixth Indian Division.* London: John Murray, 1919.

Sherston, Erroll. *Townshend of Chitral and Kut.* London: Heinemann, 1928. Singha, Radika. "Front Lines and Status Lines: Sepoy and 'Menial' in the Great War, 1916–1920." In *The World in World Wars: Experiences, Perceptions and Perspectives from Africa and Asia,* ed. Heike Liebau et al., 55–106. Leiden: Brill, 2010.

Stigger, Phillip. "How Far Was the Loyalty of Muslim Soldiers in the Indian Army More in Doubt Than Usual throughout the First World War?" *Journal of the Society of Army Historical Research* 87 (2009): 225–233.

Syk, Andrew. "Command in Indian Expeditionary Force D: Mesopotamia, 1915–1916." In *The Indian Army in the Two World Wars,* ed. Kaushik Roy, 63–104. Leiden: Brill, 2011.

———, ed. *The Military Papers of Lieutenant-General Sir Frederick Stanley Maude,*

1914–1917. Stroud, UK: History Press for the Army Records Society, 2012.

Tan Tai-Yong. "An Imperial Home Front: Punjab and the First World War." *Journal of Military History* 64, no. 2 (April 2000): 371–410.

Terraine, John. *Mons: The Retreat to Victory*. London: Leo Cooper, 1991.

Townshend, Charles. *When God Made Hell: The British Invasion of Mesopotamia and the Creation of Iraq, 1914–1921*. London: Faber and Faber, 2010.

Townshend, Charles V. F. *My Campaign in Mesopotamia*. London: Butterworth, 1920.

Wilson, Arnold. *Loyalties: Mesopotamia, 1914–1917: A Personal and Historical Record*. London: Humphrey Milford, 1930.

Younghusband, George. *Forty Years a Soldier*. London: Herbert Jenkins, 1923.

INDEX

NIKOLAS GARDNER is Associate Professor and Co-Chair of the War Studies Program at the Royal Military College of Canada in Kingston, Ontario. He is the author of *Trial by Fire: Command and the British Expeditionary Force in 1914* (2003), as well as numerous articles and book chapters on the history of the First World War, the British Empire, and strategic thought.

CPSIA information can be obtained at www.ICGtesting.com
Printed in the USA
LVOW01s1959161214

419129LV00018B/83/P